Complementation and Case Grammar

SUNY Series in Linguistics
Mark Aronoff, Editor

COMPLEMENTATION AND CASE GRAMMAR
A Syntactic and Semantic Study of Selected Patterns of Complementation in Present-Day English

Juhani Rudanko

State University of New York Press

Published by
State University of New York Press, Albany

© 1989 State University of New York

For information, address State University of New York
Press, State University Plaza, Albany, N.Y., 12246

Library of Congress Cataloging-in-Publication Data

Rudanko, Martti Juhani.
    Complementation and case grammar: a syntactic and semantic study
of selected patterns of complementation in present-day English /
Juhani Rudanko.
        p.   cm. — (SUNY series in linguistics)
    Bibliography: p.
    Includes index.
    ISBN 0-88706-931-2.   ISBN 0-88706-932-0 (pbk.)
    1. English language—Complement. 2. English language—Case.
3. English language—Syntax. 4. English language—Semantics.
I. Title. II. Series
PE1319.R84 1989
425—dc19   88-20983
                                                                            CIP

10   9   8   7   6   5   4   3   2   1

2/25/91

CONTENTS

ACKNOWLEDGEMENTS

It is my pleasure to thank SUNY Press for including the present book in its series.

Parts of three sections of the present book have appeared in article form. Parts of sections 2.1 through 2.4 appeared in *English Studies,* volume 66, no. 1 (February 1985), pp. 48–73, under the title "Classes of Verbs Governing Subject-Controlled Forward Equi in Present-Day English"; parts of sections 3.1 through 3.3 appeared in *English Studies,* volume 65, no. 2 (April 1984), pp. 141–161, under the title "On Some Contrasts between Infinitival and *That* Complement Clauses in English" and parts of sections 4.1 through 4.3 appeared in *Studia Neophilologica,* volume 57, 1985, pp. 145–155 under the title "Towards Classifying Verbs Governing Object-Controlled Infinitival Equi in Modern English." I thank the two periodicals for their kind permission allowing the reprinting of materials that originally appeared in article form.

I also express my sincere thanks to E. J. Brill for the kind permission to reproduce lists of verbs and illustrations of English usage from selected paragraphs of F. Visser's *An Historical Syntax of the English Language.*

I also express my sincere thanks to the following bodies and institutions: the Alexander von Humboldt Foundation, the Academy of Finland, the University of Tampere, the Foundation of the University of Tampere and the Scientific Foundation of the City of Tampere. All these bodies promoted the completion of this book.

I am happy to record that I was able to attend the 1985, 1986 and 1987 LSA Linguistic Institutes at Georgetown, CUNY and Stanford, respectively. I want to thank all officers of the LSA and of these three universities who organized these magnificent Linguistic Institutes.

At the 1985 Linguistic Institute at Georgetown, Walter Cook of Georgetown University kindly read through an earlier version of what are now sections 2.5.1 through 2.5.3 of this book and provided me with valuable comments, as is recognized in these sections. At the 1987 Linguistic Institute at Stanford, Luigi Rizzi of the University of Geneva kindly read through chapter 6 of the book and likewise provided me with valuable comments, as is recognized in that chapter. Readers for the publisher provided valuable comments as well. No doubt my book would have been improved further if I had incorporated more of their suggestions into the text.

I thank David Robertson, Robert MacGilleon and Ian Gurney, all of Tampere University, for reading through earlier versions of the book, for offering valuable suggestions with respect to English usage, and for acting as informants. Additionally, I am grateful to Ian Gurney for clarifying my thinking on verbs of negative volition. Further, I thank Robert Cooper, James Crichton, Dawn Jensen, Roy Parker, Robert Penhallurick and Nicholas Royle, all of Tampere University, for their patience when acting as informants. Hannele Miettinen deserves thanks for typing a large part of the book. Kari Huhtala helped me with some late revisions. Last but not least, I want to express my appreciation for the assistance that I received from Katriina Halonen. Her conscientiousness in checking the manuscript saved me from many an inaccuracy. Of course, I alone am the sole author of the book and the originator of all arguments not specifically attributed to others.

Juhani Rudanko
Tampere, March 1988

Chapter *1*

INTRODUCTION

In broad terms, the present book is an inquiry into the syntactic and semantic structure of English. It is not possible to claim that the two are identical, but we hold that the two can be investigated together and that generalizations can be found to cover their relationship. To the extent that regularities emerge, we satisfy what has recently been termed the 'grammatical constraint on semantic theory', which seeks to minimize, though not to eliminate, the differences of syntactic and semantic structure in favor of a regular relationship between the two (see Jackendoff (1985: 14)). There are obvious differences between the present investigation and Jackendoff's, especially with respect to the data considered. Even so, we recognize the relevance of the grammatical constraint and take it to provide a methodological underpinning for the present book.

In more specific terms, the purpose of the book is to isolate and to identify syntactically a number of types of sentences in English, seven in all, and to attempt to list and to distinguish semantically and to classify verbs that govern any one or more of these types. The types in question may be illustrated with the sentences of [1a–g]:

[1] **a.** Harry desires to talk to you alone.
 b. Harry likes talking to you.
 c. Harry preferred for you to leave early.
 d. Harry noted that you had left early.

    e. Harry induced you to leave early.
    f. Harry talked you into making a premature commitment.
    g. Harry relied on you to do your duty.

A property shared by the sentence patterns listed is the presence in each of two sentences. While that much is clear, the proper structural representation and bracketing of the sentences of [1a–g] raise a number of problems, some of them of considerable intricacy. Several of them will be considered in the individual chapters below. At this point, we note that, if we make certain simplifying assumptions, the sentences of [1a–g] may, at one level of abstraction, be assigned the partial schematic representations of [2a–g]. In [2a–g], and throughout the book, the symbol S_1 is used to refer to the higher, matrix sentence and the symbol S_2 is used to refer to the lower sentence. S_2 is embedded in S_1. One simplifying assumption made in [2a–g] is our decision to represent sentences with the symbol S only, and not to employ the symbol S' used in much recent work since Bresnan (1970, 1972). We justify our decision below.

[2]   **a.** $[NP_1 \ [Verb_1 \ [to \ Verb_2 \ . \ . \ .]_{S_2}]_{VP}]_{S_1}$
      b. $[NP_1 \ [Verb_1 \ [Verb_2ing \ . \ . \ .]_{S_2}]_{VP}]_{S_1}$
      c. $[NP_1 \ [Verb_1 \ [[for \ NP_2 \ to \ Verb_2 \ . \ . \ .]_{S_2}]_{NP}]_{VP}]_{S_1}$
      d. $[NP_1 \ [Verb_1 \ [[that \ NP_2 \ Verb_2 \ . \ . \ .]_{S_2}]_{NP}]_{VP}]_{S_1}$
      e. $[NP_1 \ [Verb_1 \ NP_0 \ [to \ Verb_2 \ . \ . \ .]_{S_2}]_{VP}]_{S_1}$
      f. $[NP_1 \ [Verb_1 \ NP_0 \ Prep \ [Verb_2ing \ . \ . \ .]_{S_2}]_{VP}]_{S_1}$
      g. $[NP_1 \ [Verb_1 \ [Prep \ NP_0]_{PP} \ [to \ Verb_2 \ . \ . \ .]_{S_2}]_{VP}]_{S_1}$

In [2a–g] and throughout this book the symbol NP_1 is used to represent the subject of the higher sentence. $Verb_1$ stands for the verb of the same sentence. $Verb_2$ stands for the verb of the lower sentence.

    In [2a–g] the lower sentence may be termed a 'complement sentence'. In the usage adopted here (cf. Rosenbaum (1967)), a complement sentence is marked by the property of being closely connected with the verb of the higher sentence. (A complement sentence may be connected with an adjective as well, but the present treatment is limited to verbal predicates.) Complement sentences include those that are subjects in deep structure, but these will not be the focus of attention here. Further, complement sentences may be objects, and this is relevant to [2a–d]. The complement sentences in patterns [2e–g] are not objects, but each is still closely connected with the verb of the higher sentence, in the sense that the verb in question is subcategorized as taking—that is, as co-occurring with—its embedded sentence. As is indicated in the individual chapters below, several types of adverbial sentences, which may be superficially close in form to [2a–g], are excluded by the requirement that S_2 be a complement clause, and therefore subcategorized by $Verb_1$.

    In [2c] and [2d], representing sentences [1c] and [1d], respectively, S_2, the lower sentence, has an expressed subject. In [2c–d], as elsewhere in this book, NP_2 designates the subject of S_2. The lower sentences of [2a, b] and [2e–g] do not have expressed subjects in surface structure, but they do have understood subjects. The description of such understood subjects has undergone changes in relatively recent work on syntax. Within transformational grammar, an early approach (see Postal (1970)) was to assume that NP_2 is a full lexical NP, which is coreferential with an NP of the matrix clause, and then subject to a deletion rule, called Equi or Coreferential Complement Subject Deletion. In later work (Jackendoff (1972: chapter 5)), Equi was considered a rule of interpretation. In Jackendoff's formulation, NP_2 is empty in deep structure and indeed in surface structure, but is interpreted as coreferential with an NP of the matrix sentence. A still more recent approach is to represent NP_2 as PRO, symbolizing a pronominal element that is empty in the sense of being phonetically unrealized, but which carries the features of person, number and gender (Chomsky (1981: 61)). PRO is then interpreted as coreferential with an NP of the higher clause, or is controlled by it, to use Chomsky's (1981: 57) term. In the present context, it is not very important whether the rule is considered one of deletion, of interpretation or of control. For the sake of convenience, we will use the name Equi for the rule in question. Similarly for the sake of convenience, we will use the symbol PRO.

[1a, b] and [1e–g] may then be represented as in [2a', b'] and [2e'–g'].

[2]   **a.'** $[NP_1 \ [Verb_1 \ [[PRO]_{NP_2} \ to \ Verb_2 \ . . .]_{S_2}]_{VP}]_{S_1}$
     b.' $[NP_1 \ [Verb_1 \ [[PRO]_{NP_2} \ Verb_2ing \ . . .]_{S_2}]_{VP}]_{S_1}$
     e.' $[NP_1 \ [Verb_1 \ NP_0 \ [[PRO]_{NP_2} \ to \ Verb_2 \ . . .]_{S_2}]_{VP}]_{S_1}$
     f.' $[NP_1 \ [Verb_1 \ NP_0 \ [Prep \ [[PRO]_{NP_2} \ Verb_2ing \ . . .]_{S_2}]_{PP}]_{VP}]_{S_1}$
     g.' $[NP_1 \ [Verb_1 \ [Prep \ NP_0]_{PP} \ [[PRO]_{NP_2} \ to \ Verb_2 \ . . .]_{S_2}]_{VP}]_{S_1}$

The patterns of [2a'] and [2b'] will be discussed in Chapter 2. What is crucial about them is that S_2 is an infinitival clause (as in [2a']) or an *ing* clause (as in [2b']) and that NP_2, which is PRO, is understood to be coreferential with NP_1. If we use the notion of control, we may say that PRO is controlled by NP_1.

The patterns of [2c] and [2d] will be discussed in Chapter 3 and an attempt will be made to compare them with the patterns of Chapter 2. In [2c], NP_2 is not PRO, but rather a full lexical NP. The full lexical NP cannot be coreferential with NP_1, as we see in *Harry preferred for him to leave early*, where *him* cannot refer to *Harry*. In [2d] the subject NP_2 is again not PRO, but rather a full lexical NP. The full lexical NP may or may not be coreferential with NP_1, as we see in *Harry noted that he had left early*.

In pattern [2e'], to be covered in Chapter 4, NP_2 is PRO, but this time controlled by the direct object of the matrix verb. In pattern [2f'], to be covered in Chapter 5, NP_2 is again PRO and it follows a preposition in the sequence of constituents. It is controlled by the direct object of the matrix verb. That is, relevant matrix verbs govern both a direct object NP and a sentential prepositional phrase. In pattern [2g'], to be covered in Chapter 6, NP_2 is again PRO. The matrix verb of this pattern governs both a prepositional object and an infinitival clause. PRO is the subject of the infinitival clause and it is controlled by the object of the preposition of the higher clause.

The NP_0s of [2e'] and of [2f'] are objects of their $Verb_1$s and the NP_0 of [2g'] is the prepositional object of its $Verb_1$. [2e'–g'] are in the active voice. The matrix sentences of these control patterns may be turned into the passive voice, as in [3a–c]:

[3] **a.** You were induced by Harry to leave early.
    b. You were talked by Harry into making a premature commitment.
    c. You were relied on by Harry to do your duty.

In [3a–c] NP_0 is the subject of the passive matrix sentence. It is still the controller of PRO as well.

Following Chomsky (1980: 32; 1981: 75ff.) and other work, we have used syntactic notions such as 'subject' and 'object' to designate the controllers of PRO in the patterns of [2a', b'], [2e'–g'] and the passive counterparts of [2e'–g']. (In traditional terminology, the understood subjects of the lower sentences of these five patterns are understood to be subjects or objects of the matrix sentences in question, see, for example, Quirk et al. (1985: 1215, 1216, especially note a), Visser (1973: 2250 ff.).) An alternative, semantic theory of control has been developed by Foley and van Valin (1984). Our pattern of [2e'] may serve to illustrate their approach. In their description, the NP_1 of [2e'] would be called the actor ("the argument of a predicate which expresses the participant which performs, effects, instigates, or controls the situation denoted by the predicate") and the NP_0 of [2e'] would be called the undergoer ("the argument which expresses the participant which does not perform, initiate, or control any situation but rather is affected by it in some way") (Foley and van Valin (1984: 29)). Thus, in pairs of sentences such as their (1984: 307) *The burglar forced Larry to open the safe* and *Larry was forced by the burglar to open the safe,* and in [1e] and [3a] and in analogous pairs, a semantic theory of control permits the statement that the undergoer is the controller in each case, irrespective of whether the sentence in question is in the active or in the passive voice. Such a semantic approach to control assignment is of interest and may even be in some ways attractive (cf. Foley and van Valin (1984: 310 ff.)). It may be recalled that we recognize the relevance of the grammatical constraint on semantic theory. Therefore, while we neither expect nor, we would add, even seek to eliminate differences of syntactic and semantic structures, we aim, as far as possible, to establish a regular relationship between the two (cf. Jackendoff (1985: 14)). To this end, rather than start from a semantic description of the control patterns listed, we prefer in the present book first to isolate and to identify patterns of complementation on a basis that is primarily syntactic. Only after we have provided a primarily syntactic underpinning for our discussion of complement patterns will we discuss their semantic properties. Our decision to proceed from a primarily syntactic identification of patterns of complementation and of control is made easier by the predictability of the passive patterns of control of [3a–c] on the basis of their active counterparts of [1e–g].

The types of complement sentences listed and sketched above in a preliminary way are all central in present-day English. Only type [2c] may be argued to be a possible exception. It is a type perhaps more common in American rather than in British English, but it is by no means confined to the former. Moreover, its use seems to be expanding, and this may serve to justify its inclusion in the present treatment.

The types of complement sentences selected for discussion in this volume are important in present-day English, but we cannot claim that all the important patterns of complementation in present-day English are covered here. Omissions include Raising and WH patterns, which are not covered, except for some passing references to predicates triggering Raising. Even if we set aside considerations of space, our decision to exclude these particular patterns is not arbitrary. Postal (1974, especially chapter 9) provides an account of predicates that trigger Raising. As for WH complements, Baker (1968, especially 102 ff.) and Grimshaw (1977) provide useful discussions of matrix predicates that take WH clauses. From another point of view, the selection of the patterns listed above for discussion in this volume is motivated by our desire to include at least most of the more important Equi patterns of complementation in present-day English. As will be argued in Chapter 3, *that* and *for to* clause patterns afford useful points of comparison for the Equi type of [2a].

Each type of complementation will be discussed separately, which allows the characteristics peculiar to the type in question to emerge. Of course, comparisons will be made as well, where relevant. In each chapter, each type is isolated and distinguished from constructions that may look similar, but, on a closer examination, exhibit different syntactic properties that set them apart from the pattern in question. After each type has been isolated syntactically, an attempt will be made to provide representative lists of verbs governing the type in present-day English. In this connection, Visser's (1972, 1973, 1978) lists prove to be helpful, indeed indispensable, but it also turns out that they cannot be accepted uncritically. We will discuss and illustrate the point in more detail in Chapter 2 and in later chapters, where actual verbs are considered, but it is worth noting here that our use of Visser's collections, and of other data, is guided and governed by two general considerations. The first of these is analytical and theoretical. Our notion of 'relevant patterns' does not always entirely coincide with Visser's. We will seek to bring methods of rigorous syntactic analysis to bear on the description of the verbs and classes of verbs that he has collected. The same holds for the description of other data. The specific problems encountered and the solutions devised to solve them will be presented and discussed in early sections of individual chapters.

The second consideration guiding our use of data collected by Visser, and of other data, relates to the notion of present-day English, as employed in this book. Visser lists and illustrates verbs from all periods of the history of the language, from Old English to Modern English, the latter reaching up to the 1950s and the 1960s. He marks a large number of verbs as obsolete, but his concept of 'not obsolete' does not entirely coincide with our notion of present-day English. The term 'present-day English', as employed in this book, focuses on contemporary English, on twentieth-century English, on English within living memory of speakers, of varying ages, who are alive today. This notion of present-day English, which will be discussed further in section 2.3, where the first batch of actual verbs are considered, provides the basis for the inclusion and exclusion of verbs in the present book.

The collecting and classification of verbs is necessary, but it is only a first step. In each chapter an effort is made to characterize the verbs of each pattern, especially in terms of their semantic properties. Ideally, such characterizations should embody predictions about the types of verbs likely to occur in a given class. Such predictions cover verbs that might be discovered in the patterns considered in present-day English if a larger sample of sources were taken into account. Also, such predictions are relevant to future trends, at least in some instances, as noted in the individual chapters below.

One of the main concerns of the book will be an attempt to apply case grammar as a tool for analyzing the patterns of complementation that are isolated. Specifically, the mutual relationship of NP_1 and NP_2 will be investigated in a systematic way from the point of view of case grammar. In this connection we take note of such earlier studies as those by Růžička (1983) and Comrie (1984). These and the present study share the basic idea that case grammar—or a system of thematic relations—provides a framework which is useful for a statement of at least some of the constraints that hold with respect to the selection of NP_1 and NP_2. This conceptual similarity should be recognized, but, in spite of it, our study is somewhat different. Specifically, what is novel about our approach is that it is conceived and conducted as a follow-up to, and in the context of, the classifications and discussions of matrix verbs that we set up in this volume. Also, given that a prerequisite for the use of case grammar is a specification, as explicit as possible, of the case roles adopted, it should be pointed out that our approach incorporates a view of case roles and of case grammar that differs from earlier case grammar studies of complementation. We will outline our view of case roles and of case grammar in section 2.5.

Finally, a brief comment is appropriate on the theoretical stance and framework adopted in this book. Apart from case grammar, some parts of the arguments are expressed in the terminology of transformational grammar. A deliberate effort is made throughout the book to eschew technicalities. Among the technical questions eschewed is the status of the S′ node. In the version of transformational grammar that is predominant at the present time, namely, the government and binding theory, the S′ node is prominently and crucially employed. S′ dominates the nodes Comp and S (van Riemsdijk and Williams (1986: 59 ff.)). For example, [2c] is then represented as in [2c′]:

[2c′] $[NP_1 \ [Verb_1 \ [[for]_{Comp} \ [NP_2 \ to \ Verb_2 \ . \ . \ .]_{S_2}]_{S_2'}]_{VP}]_{S_1}$

We will not employ the S′ node, restricting ourselves to the more traditional analysis with the S node only, as in [2c]. There are a number of reasons for our decision. First, employing the S' node might tie our treatment too intimately to one particular framework of description and to issues defined by, and internal to, that framework. Second, it seems that the patterns selected can be discussed without the S' node at a level of sophistication that is sufficient to yield a number of generalizations. Also, the conversion of [2c] into [2c'] and vice versa is trivial and raises no theoretical issue. This is true of all the patterns selected for discussion here, with the possible exception only of [2g'].

We will not employ the S' node, but our decision does not imply any disparagement of it or of contributions to a resolution of issues that surround it. These issues are important to the government and binding framework. They include the very existence of the S' node in one or more of the patterns of [2a', b'], [2c, d] and [2e'–g'] in the government and binding framework. In spite of Chomsky (1981: 107 ff., 204 ff.), Manzini (1983: 424 ff.) and other work, it is perhaps no longer possible to take the presence of S' for granted in all of the patterns listed, even within the government and binding framework, in view of an S'-deletion rule proposed by Bouchard (1983: 172; 1985: 472 ff.). Bouchard's (1985) rule relates directly to pattern [2a'] only, but, if it is accepted, analogous rules may follow for a number of the other patterns, though not for [2c] and [2d]. From S' deletion it seems to be but a short step to the proposal that S' is never present (cf. Hornstein and Lightfoot (1987: 27, note 4)). The conversion referred to above may then turn out not to be relevant to all of the patterns listed, even in the government and binding framework. In any event, the present book is not designed directly to contribute to a resolution of issues that surround, or involve, the S' node in the government and binding framework.

What this study is designed to do is to make a contribution to the analysis of a number of patterns of complementation. These patterns and their contrasts are central facts of English. It bears stressing that they are not artifacts of any particular model of linguistic description, such as transformational grammar. As a consequence, we will make explicit and frequent use of nontransformational— and, in particular, traditional—attempts to formulate and to solve such questions as arise in the description of the patterns selected for consideration. Overall, the generalizations that emerge here are offered as a contribution to the grammatical description of English, independently of any particular framework of linguistic description.

Chapter 2

VERBS GOVERNING SUBJECT-CONTROLLED FORWARD EQUI

2.1 THE SCOPE OF THE PATTERN

Consider sentences [1a, b]:

[1] **a.** Harry desires to talk to you.
 b. Harry likes talking to you.

As argued in Chapter 1, [1a, b] have the partial bracketings of [1a′–b′]:

[1] **a.**′ [[Harry]$_{NP_1}$ [desires]$_{Verb_1}$ [[PRO]$_{NP_2}$ [[to talk]$_{Verb_2}$ · · ·]$_{VP}$]$_{S_2}$]$_{S_1}$
 b.′ [[Harry]$_{NP_1}$ [likes]$_{Verb_1}$ [[PRO]$_{NP_2}$ [[talking]$_{Verb_2}$ · · ·]$_{VP}$]$_{S_2}$]$_{S_1}$

Equi makes crucial reference to two NPs. The lower one is the subject of a complement clause and designated here as PRO. The higher NP may be termed the 'controller' or 'antecedent' of PRO. In somewhat older usage (cf. Soames and Perlmutter (1979: 220)), the terms 'victim' and 'trigger' are often found for PRO and the controller of PRO, respectively. With these terms taken for granted, we may note that forward Equi refers to sentences such as [1a, b] where, in the sequence of constituents, the controller precedes PRO. Sentences where this is not so, as, for instance, in *To live here would trouble him,* are outside the scope of the present inquiry.

A second general limitation on the scope of the present chapter is that it will confine itself to cases where the antecedent of PRO is the subject of the matrix sentence. This excludes cases where it is the object, as in [2a], or the indirect object, as in [2b]:

[2] **a.** Joe ordered me to go.
    b. Joe shouted at me to go.

Third, it bears stressing that the applicability of Equi in complement clauses only will be considered. This excludes from consideration several types of constructions where forward Equi may be applicable. We will list some such constructions here.

First, note that cases such as *Bill hated the sight of his apartment* (Wasow and Roeper (1972: 54)), where it is necessarily Bill who sees the apartment, contain neither infinitival nor gerund clauses and will not be considered.

Second, adverbial clauses of purpose, as in *He got up to ask a question* (Zandvoort (1966: 10)), which may involve forward Equi and yield the same surface sequence of constituents as [1a', b'], are also outside the scope of this inquiry. This exclusion is methodologically advisable because such adverbial clauses are syntactically different from complement clauses in that they often admit the insertion of *in order to* and *so as to* in place of plain *to* (*He got up in order to/so as to ask a question*), while complement sentences do not, as witness **Harry desires in order to/so as to see you*. For additional syntactic differences between the two constructions, cf. Kajita (1967: 19).

Third, sentences of the type *He awoke suddenly to find the car had stopped outside the hotel* (Visser (1972: 1010 ff.)) will be excluded. In them, the infinitive expresses an activity that (more or less) immediately follows that of the higher sentence and may be called an 'infinitive of result' (Palmer (1974: 210); cf. also Poutsma (1904: 552 ff.), who, in his discussion of relevant instances, refers to the relation of attendant circumstances). Such constructions differ from those considered here in that in the former the two parts of the utterance are practically coordinate: *He awoke suddenly and found . . . ,* cf. Visser (1972: 1010); cf. also Söderlind (1958: paragraph 471) and Palmer (1974: 166, 210). Unlike Palmer, though, we keep *awake* and *wake* strictly apart from verbs taking complement sentences, such as *manage* and *remember*. Palmer (1974: 206) suggests that *I remembered to see him* means *I saw him—I remembered* and is therefore apparently parallel, except for the unexplained reversal of the clauses, with Visser's *awake* sentence cited above. However, we submit, first, that *awake* and *wake* never take complement sentences, second, that *manage* takes complement sentences, but not infinitives of result (in the pattern of [1a], in other patterns it of course may, as in *He managed it, (only) to find that it was too late*), and third, that *remember* may take both complement sentences and infinitives of result superficially resembling the pattern of [1a]. On the normal interpretation, Palmer's *I remembered to see him* may be viewed as containing a complement sentence, as opposed to constructions where *remember* is used intransitively with an infinitive of result, as in *For a long moment the actor forgot that he was to speak next. He remembered (only) to realize that it was too late.*

Fourth, consider *He came talking* (cf. Visser (1973: 1906 ff.)), *He sat talking* (cf. Visser (1973: 1912 ff.)), *He answered choosing his words very carefully* and *He died brandishing his battle-axe* (Alexander and Kunz (1964: 53)). In these sentences the *ing* clause is a participle clause, and not a gerund clause (cf. Poutsma (1904: 729 ff.), Mustanoja (1960: 556 ff.) and the references in Visser (1973: 1912, 1916)). Nor is it a complement clause in the terminology used here, which is close to that of Rosenbaum (1967). Such types, though they may involve Equi, are outside the scope of the present inquiry.

Fifth, consider such infinitive clauses of time (from Poutsma 1904: 550 ff.) as those in *I doubt whether one of these will live to be free, He rose to be an inspector of the force* and *I could not but smile to hear her talk in this lofty strain.* As Poutsma perspicaciously points out, in the first two the infinitive clauses approximate subordinate clauses opening with *until,* and in the last one, the infinitive clause approximates a subordinate clause opening with *when.* As Poutsma (1904: 550) further points out, clauses corresponding to those introduced by *when* or *as* may imply a further relation of cause. (This is relevant to the *smile* example cited.) Indeed, in connection with instances where a *when* paraphrase is appropriate, Visser (1972: 1005 ff.) speaks only of the infinitive expressing ''the cause or the motive of the action mentioned in the main syntactical unit,'' citing such examples as *I laugh to see what ignorant persons you are, to take upon you so tedious a journey* (Bunyan, *The Pilgrim's Progress*). A *when* paraphrase is certainly possible here as well, even if the element of cause may predominate semantically. In the present context the point is that, even though such infinitives of time and cause may involve forward Equi, they are not complement sentences and they are therefore outside the scope of this inquiry.

The purpose of this chapter is to examine the applicability of Equi as thus delimited. More precisely, on the other hand, an effort is made to establish classes of verbs to whose complements the rule is applicable. This is a task which, as far as can be determined, has not as yet been undertaken, in spite of the attention paid to Equi within transformational grammar since Postal's (1970) pioneering study. On the other hand, going beyond classification, we will seek to characterize the classes that emerge, at least in a preliminary way. Section 2.3 is devoted to verbs governing infinitival Equi and section 2.4 to verbs governing gerundive Equi. As a preliminary, in section 2.2 the class of Equi verbs is briefly delimited against the class of A-type Raising verbs (Postal (1974: 28 ff.)), with which they display some superficial similarity and with which they have been occasionally classed. It is hoped that the arguments in section 2.2 will serve to show that the class of Equi structures under consideration constitutes a well-defined set whose members have their own distinctive syntactic properties.

Even though the discussion will be couched mostly in terms of transformational grammar and of a transformation of Equi, it should be emphasized that the properties of Equi structures and their range in terms of the verbs to which they are relevant must, as noted in Chapter 1, be accounted for in any description of

English complementation. Therefore, this inquiry is meant to be a contribution to the study of English grammar in general, independent of any particular framework. In traditional, nontransformational terms, this chapter concerns infinitive and gerundive clauses that function as objects or adjuncts that complete the meanings of their governing verbs with which they share their subjects, e.g. Mätzner (1885: 20 ff.), Zandvoort (1966: 9, 13 ff., 26), Meyer-Myklestad (1968: 207 ff., 230 ff.), Schibsbye (1970: 28, 63), Makkink (1978: 109, 114) and especially Scheurweghs (1959: 185 ff., 205 ff.).

2.2 EQUI AND RAISING STRUCTURES

In order to bring out some contrasting properties of Equi and A-type Raising verbs, it is helpful to consider the Equi verb *desire* and the A-type Raising verb *seem:*

[3] **a.** He desires to see you.
    b. He seems to like you.

Desire and *seem* are similar in that both may occur as $Verb_1$ in the sequence NP_1—$Verb_1$—*to* $Verb_2$ . . . , but their similarity is only superficial. We are not laying claim to originality here and therefore we will review only briefly two kinds of evidence showing that *desire* and *seem,* representing their respective classes, are fundamentally different. The two arguments are based on Postal (1974: 369 ff.); see also Soames and Perlmutter (1979: 106 ff.).

First, the weather *it,* as in [4a], is compatible with Raising verbs (cf. [4c]), but not with Equi (cf. [4b]) verbs:

[4] **a.** It is raining hard now.
    b. *It desires to be raining hard now.
    c. It seems to be raining hard now.

Second, such NPs as only occur in idiom chunks, for example, *advantage* in *take advantage of, cognizance* in *take cognizance of, heed* in *pay heed to,* are compatible with Raising, but not with Equi, verbs:

[5] **a.** *No advantage desires to be/to have been taken of their inexperience.
    b. No advantage seems to have been taken of their inexperience.

[6] **a.** *No cognizance desires to be/to have been taken of his exit.
    b. No cognizance seems to have been taken of his exit.

[7] **a.** *Not much heed desires to be paid/to have been paid to that.
    b. Not much heed seems to have been paid to that.

For additional properties of Equi verbs, cf. Postal (1970; 1974, chapter 12) and Soames and Perlmutter (1979, 106 ff.).

2.3 THE *TO* PATTERN

2.3.1 Gathering Data: Visser's Classification

After the brief references in section 2.2 to the distinctive syntactic properties of Equi verbs as opposed to A-type Raising verbs, an attempt will be made in this section to provide lists of verbs that pattern like *desire*. As far as can be ascertained, no such lists have been worked out by transformationalists, but it seems to the present author that Visser's lists of verbs taking infinitival complements, conceived of in a nontransformational framework, can serve as a good starting point. Of relevance here are all the classes where Visser (1978: 1309 ff.) suggests there is no subordination of the first verb to the second, save the last (e.g., *He commanded to go*), where in present-day English there would be an NP between the verb and the infinitive. (Subject-controlled Equi is not relevant to the verbs of this class, cf. [2a].) Additionally, of relevance are a number of verbs that Visser treats under Slight Subordination (of the infinitive to the main clause verb). On the other hand, the class of verbs of aspect (*begin* etc., cf. Visser (1978: 1372 ff.)) will be omitted from consideration, because, even though Equi derivations for them have been proposed occasionally (Perlmutter (1970)), these proposals are problematic and open to question (cf. Fischer and Marshall (1969), Newmeyer (1969), Fodor (1974)).

The method of procedure adopted is as follows: Visser's classes are examined closely, and as a first step only those verbs will be adduced which Visser suggests are not obsolete today, save in the odd case where the present author disagrees with Visser and holds that a verb marked by Visser as obsolete is in point of fact still current in present-day English. Rather more frequently, the lists will be modified in that additional verbs will be omitted as obsolete, even though Visser did not mark them as such. Each individual case is noted and the aim is to do justice to the English usage of today. Also, in a number of cases, the syntactic properties of individual verbs are examined, in order to ensure, as far as possible, that remaining verbs belong to the syntactic pattern of complementation under consideration. The collecting of verbs in this section is only a preliminary to section 2.3.2. In the latter, an attempt is made to regroup the relevant verbs into fewer categories than those that Visser set up. Another difference is that while all of Visser's classes are on a level footing, those of the present classification are arranged so as to bring out at least some of the semantic interconnections among them.

Visser's classes are a natural starting point because of their comprehensiveness and their breadth of documentation. They are the most comprehensive lists of relevant verbs currently available. Other efforts to list relevant verbs, such as that by Alexander and Kunz (1964), fail to yield any significant number of additional verbs. The few additional verbs that do emerge as relevant will be taken into account in the classification.

Visser's (1978, 1311 ff.) first class is that of verbs expressing desire, liking, preference. As regards spelling variants of verbs, only the more modern forms are given. (All references to Visser in this section are to Visser (1978).)

ache	gape	prefer
care	hanker	rage
chafe	insist	reck
choose	languish	select
claim	like	sigh
covet	list	thirst
crave	long	want
desire	love	whine
die	pant	wish
elect	pine	yearn
fret		

The list requires comment. As regards some of the verbs listed, it may be questioned whether they really occur with infinitival complements in present-day English. At this point, of course, there arises the question of what criteria should be decisive. Not unnaturally, recorded usage, which may be claimed to have been Visser's chief criterion, should be considered. In an inquiry concerned with present-day English, such recorded usage should, to be relevant, be of recent occurrence. Additionally, the intuitions of native speakers of English may be admitted as a criterion. In some areas of syntax intuitions may indeed be the predominant, or even the only, criterion and source of data, but in the present case the two criteria should be kept in balance and checked against each other: neither isolated instances of recorded usage that are felt to be deviant by native speakers (in this connection, cf. Wasow (1979: 3)), nor idiosyncratic intuitive judgments can form a reliable basis for a study of infinitival complementation of the type in question. (For a discussion of the data of linguistic description, cf. also Leech (1968: 88 ff.)) An effort will be made here to take both criteria into account; for recorded usage, the obvious sources are the OED and data collected by Visser. Illustrations in these two sources include material from the present century; Visser has material even from the 1950s and the 1960s. However, the bulk of their illustrations of usage are pre-twentieth century. Numerous verbs are illustrated with pre-twentieth century examples only. Such usages need to be assessed as to their currency in present-day English. In general, the acuteness of the need for assessment and the age of the most recent illustrations of usage are interdependent: the older the illustrations of a verb, the more acute is the need for assessment and evaluation of the verb in question.

Any assessment of verbs as to their currency in present-day English is guided by the interpretation that is assigned to the concept of 'present-day English'. By present-day English we mean contemporary English, twentieth-century English, of speakers who are alive today. To explicate the notion further, it is helpful to consider types of variation in present-day English. Such types, interrelated up to varying degrees, include variation according to region, social group, field of discourse and attitude (cf. Quirk et al. (1985: 16 ff.)). For practical reasons, our treatment of regional variation will be limited to references to British and American English. Even here, our focus will not be on regional variation. Social variation, in Quirk et al.'s (1985: 18) words, includes "an important polarity between uneducated and educated speech in which the former can be identified with the nonstandard regional dialect most completely and the latter moves away from regional usage to a form of English that cuts across regional boundaries." Our concern is clearly not with uneducated English. It is rather with educated English, with English that is potentially used by, and acceptable to, educated speakers of English. (On an aspect of acceptability, cf. Wolfram and Fasold (1974: 18 ff.)) The description of variation according to field of discourse includes the labeling of usages as 'religious', 'legal' and so on (Quirk et al. (1985: 24)). There is no obvious limit to the number of fields of discourse. As Quirk et al. (1985: 24) put it, "there are indefinitely many fields depending on how detailed we wish our discussion to be." References will be made at times to fields of discourse, but our focus is not on verbs that are only permissible in the language of one narrow field of discourse, such as legal English. Our focus is more on literary English, provided that this concept is understood in a broad sense, to relate not only to literature, but also to other fields, such as nontechnical essays (cf. Quirk et al. (1985: 24)). The description of variation according to attitude employs such concepts as 'formal', 'neutral', 'informal' or 'colloquial' (Quirk et al. (1985: 26 ff.)). Here we will not set out to look for formal or colloquial verbs, but we cannot restrict our scope to neutral verbs only.

We will take note of varieties when they are clearly relevant. Even so, the concept of present-day English, as used in this book, focuses on the kind of educated English that, on the whole, transcends regional variation and that, for the most part, is not strictly limited to one narrow field of discourse only. It is from this point of view that verbs will be assessed and evaluated.

Given these methodological considerations, it will be seen that it is possible to drop a number of verbs from Visser's lists even without the benefit of examples. We will be fairly cautious in this respect, however. Rather more frequently, we will produce a sentence to help evaluate the currency of a verb in present-day English. Of course, when we speak of the currency of a verb in present-day English, we mean the currency of the verb in the pattern under review and not in some other pattern. This qualification should be understood throughout the book, even if it is not repeated every time that a verb is dropped. Numerous verbs that we drop here are current, or have senses that are current, in other patterns in present-day English.

Three kinds of sentences will be used for the purpose of evaluating verbs. First, authentic sentences, from Visser, the OED, or, less often, from other dictionaries; second, sentences modified from an authentic source and third, sentences that have been freely invented. The sources of authentic examples will be indicated, and the examples will be cited in their original forms, apart from the omission of Visser's italics and of final periods in the body of the text and apart from the occasional modernization of certain features of spelling, etc. (If something has been modernized, this will be mentioned.) Examples modified from a source will likewise be indicated. The use, as data, of sentences that have been freely invented is a reflection of our reliance on intuitions of native speakers.

Evaluative marks, such as stars and question marks, will not be assigned to authentic examples. If such authentic examples are judged to be obsolete, this is indicated in words. On the other hand, stars and question marks, when they are judged to be necessary, will be assigned to examples that have been modified from a source and to examples that have been freely invented.

To repeat, when evaluating verbs, we will apply two overall criteria: the criterion of CURRENCY in present-day English, as described above, and the criterion of SYNTACTIC ANALYSIS, as described in sections 2.1 and 2.2 for the infinitival pattern under consideration here and as described above in the discussion of other patterns appearing later in this book. In general, we apply the two criteria in this order, but this decision is for the sake of convenience and is made possible by the availability of sources such as Visser.

In general, the criterion of syntactic analysis yields a clear-cut decision: a verb occurs or does not occur in the relevant pattern. For the majority of verbs, the criterion of currency in present-day English similarly allows a clear-cut decision. We will then limit ourselves to one of two choices: we either accept a given verb or we drop it. For most verbs, the decision can be made with a fair degree of confidence. However, given the nature of language, including its dynamic, nonstatic property, there will inevitably be verbs for which a clear-cut decision is more difficult, especially with respect to their currency in present-day English. We are sensitive to this, but we will still apply our binary description to such verbs as well. (Sometimes it is more accurate to speak of 'senses' of verbs.) We will then not include question marks in our later lists of verbs that we accept. However, comments that are made in our discussion of individual verbs—such as the labeling of verbs as 'marginal' or 'acceptable only with a degree of hesitation' and such as are implied by the use of question marks—should be borne in mind even if a verb has been retained in the face of misgivings. Analogous considerations hold for verbs that are dropped with a degree of hesitation.

Given the methodological considerations presented, some verbs may be dropped from Visser's list. For *list,* the most recent entry in the OED is from 1814 (Scott, *The Lord of the Isles*), and it sounds clearly archaic today: *If you list to taste our cheer.* For *reck,* there is an entry in the OED from 1873 (Symonds, *Greek Poets*) that is archaic as well: *Old eyes forlorn Scarce reck the very sunshine to behold.* Further, the OED recognizes explicitly that the infinitival construction with *insist* represents former usage. *Rage* seems archaic as well, as in ??*Violent men were raging to pursue the offender,* modified from Visser, as does *gape,* as in ??*John was gaping to say something. Select* may be dropped as well (cf. Bolinger (1978: 14)). As for *chafe, covet, crave,* and *languish, crave* is possible and not subject to doubt, but the other three are somewhat doubtful, as in *John was ?chafing/?coveting/craving/?languishing to take part.* The decision is a marginal one and it is not valid for all speakers, but we will retain the three doubtful verbs. As for *claim,* the usage in question, where *claim* has the approximate sense of 'demand as one's due' (cf. the OED), as in *Every townsman could claim to be tried by his fellow-townsmen* (OED, 1876, from Green, *Short History*) does not represent the most common sense of the verb in the infinitival construction. We will retain it, though again with some hesitation.

To recapitulate, we have dropped *gape, insist, list, rage, reck* and *select* from the list. These omissions reduce the class of thirty-one to one of twenty-five verbs. We add two verbs to the list: *burn* and *gasp,* the latter as in *I am gasping to taste your homemade wine.* (We thank David Robertson for the example and for pointing out *gasp* to us. We thank Nicholas Royle for pointing out *burn* to us.)

Visser's (1315 ff.) second class is that of verbs of emotion.

abhor	glory	rejoice
blush	grudge	scorn
delight	hate	shudder
disdain	loathe	wonder
enjoy	marvel	

Enjoy should be dropped from this list, because the infinitive with it is clearly a marked form, as the OED and even Visser himself (1316) recognize. *Glory* seems archaic as well, as in ??*He gloried to think how . . . ,* modified from Visser. *Glory in thinking . . .* would be more current. *Grudge* is at best very marginal in the pattern: ??*He grudged to give me my share.* The negative ?*He did not grudge to give me my share* is perhaps slightly better, but still somewhat archaic. An *ing* form is preferred: *He grudged/did not grudge giving me my share.* With some hesitation, we omit *grudge.*

More fundamentally, Visser (1316) notes that with a number of the verbs cited, such as *blush, delight, rejoice, shudder, wonder,* the infinitive strongly resembles the adverbial of cause. As noted in section 2.1, this term refers to cases such as *I could not but smile to hear her talk in that lofty strain.* As further noted there, such adverbials as a rule also allow a *when* or an *as* paraphrase, indicating the possibility of a temporal interpretation. Interestingly, the infinitival constructions with *blush, rejoice, shudder* and *wonder* cited by Visser all pass this double test. To take one example at random (1317, from G. A. Beck, ed., *The English Catholics*): *They shuddered to see how closely the Cardinal was prepared to grapple with social evils* allows *They shuddered when they saw how . . . .* Such paraphrase possibilities indicate that the constructions in question are more felicitously considered adverbial clauses of time or cause than complement clauses. Accordingly, *blush, rejoice, shudder* and *wonder* should be dropped from the list, along with *marvel* (cf. *I marvel to (when I) see such things*). On the other hand, *delight* seems to be altogether less susceptible to this analysis. The sentence *This system delights to honour that kind of man* (to change Visser's sentence a little) does not comfortably allow a relevant paraphrase: **This system delights when it honours that kind of man*. Accordingly, *delight* is retained in the list, which is now changed to the following: *abhor, delight, disdain, hate, loathe, scorn.*

Visser's (1317 ff.) third class is that of verbs expressing fear: *dread, fear, scruple.* Of these, *scruple* is perhaps slightly marginal for some speakers, as in *He did not scruple to stretch a point,* but can be retained.

Visser's (1318 ff.) fourth class is that of verbs of refusing, failing, forgetting, omitting etc.:

abstain	forget	refuse
decline	neglect	shun
fail	omit	spare
forbear	refrain	stick

Visser (1318) notes that *spare* and *stick* are now rare with the infinitive, judgments that are confirmed by the OED, and they are accordingly dropped from the list as being obsolete. The same goes for *abstain,* which, as Visser (1318) notes, now usually takes *from* Verb + *ing,* and for *refrain,* which also takes *from* Verb + *ing,* rather than the infinitive. Visser does not make this second point, but Jespersen (1961: 195) does, and the judgment is backed by the OED. *Shun* seems obsolete in the pattern as well, as witness ??*John shunned to tell me the whole truth. Forbear* is somewhat archaic as well and possibly on its way out, but may still be retained, as in Visser's example from c. 1930 (Aldington, *Seven against Reeves*) *Mr. Reeves sighed, and forbore to speak of his dream.*

Visser's (1321) fifth class is that of verbs of feigning and affecting: *affect, feign, pretend.*

Visser's (1321 ff.) sixth class is that of verbs of contriving and managing: *afford, arrange, contrive, find in one's heart, manage.*

Visser's latest instance of *find in one's heart* is from the eighteenth century: *They . . . cannot find in their Hearts to relinquish it* (from 1711, Steele, *The Spectator*). The construction exists in present-day English, but generally in the form *find it in one's heart,* as in *He could not find it in his heart to refuse her.* The origin of the *it* is perhaps syntactic and traceable to an application of the rule of Extraposition (cf. Rosenbaum (1967: 35 ff.)), and it is then not necessary to cite it in the dictionary entry of the construction. More fundamentally, the construction is problematic in the present context from another point of view. The focus of our treatment is on verbs, including phrasal verbs (such as *set out*), taking infinitival complements. The construction *find in one's heart* is syntactically different and more complex. It is easy to think of other complex constructions co-occurring with infinitives. They include *have a mind, have a purpose, have a plan,* etc. (We thank Ian Gurney for bringing *have a mind* to our attention.) A construction such as *consider beneath oneself* is perhaps closer to *find in one's heart,* for this construction takes an *it* as well, as in *He considered it beneath himself to respond to the accusation.* Some aspects of our analysis of verbs, to be given below, seem relevant to some such more complex constructions. However, it should be noted that, strictly speaking, such more complex constructions do not conform to the patterns of [1a', b'] of section 2.1. Further, their description raises issues that are not relevant to the description of verbs in infinitival Equi complement constructions, including the origin of the *it* that occurs with *find in one's heart* and with *consider beneath oneself*. For these reasons, we omit from consideration here such complex constructions, including *find in one's heart*.

Visser's (1323 ff.) seventh class is that of verbs of knowing, doubting, supposing, guessing etc.: *believe, ken, know how, remember, think.*

Of the five verbs given, *ken* is totally dialectal or obsolete, and therefore does not have a place in the list. Neither does *believe: *He believed to be rich/to have done it* vs. *He believed that he was/would be rich, that he had done it.* How may be considered to be a WH complementizer (see Bresnan (1972: 28 ff.)), and it is therefore doubtful whether the construction *know how* belongs here. The inclusion of *think* is also questionable, cf. Poutsma (1904: 584), Ellinger (1910: 517), Kruisinga (1925: 146) and Hornby (1966: 19), and even though there are occasional counterexamples (cf. Poutsma 1904: 541 and the OED), on balance, it seems appropriate to drop *think* from the present list. The decision is based on such contrasts as that between **He thinks to have done it* and *He thinks that he has done it.* In other words, the class is reduced to *remember*. As Visser notes, the sense of the verb that is current in the infinitival construction in present-day English is that of 'not to forget'. To express the meaning of 'have the memory of', an *ing* form is preferred: *He remembered having been flattered* is preferred to *??He remembered to have been flattered,* modified from Visser.

Visser's (1324 ff.) eighth class is that of verbs of deserving: *deserve, merit.* Of these, *merit* should be dropped. For instance, we may compare *merit* and *deserve* in the following, modified from Visser: *Does he deserve/*merit to be so happy?*

Visser's (1325 ff.) ninth group is that of verbs of suffering and bearing: *abear, abide, bear, endure, stand.*

Of these, *abear* should be dropped from the list (cf. the OED).

Visser's (1326 ff.) tenth group is that of verbs of declaring, vowing, promising:

avouch	declare	say
avow	menace	swear
boast	pretend	threaten
brag	profess	vow
confess	promise	warrant

Visser (1327) notes that most of these verbs more usually have a *that* clause as object. It seems possible to go one step farther and totally exclude *declare* and *say* from the list, cf. **He declared/said to be interested* vs. *He declared/said that he was/would be interested.* (The use of *say* in constructions such as *He said* *(for you) to go* is outside the scope of this chapter, as defined in section 2.1.) Similarly, *boast* and *brag* (cf. the OED) are at best questionable or obsolete in this pattern, cf. ??*He boasted/bragged to have done it.* *Confess* is now generally constructed with *to* and Verb + *ing*, as Visser (1327) indeed notes, or with a *that* clause. *Avouch* is obsolete as well. Visser produces no example of it from Modern English and an example such as ??*He avouched to confirm the sentence,* modified from the OED, is obsolete. *Avow,* as in ??*They avowed to die for their country,* modified from Visser, is archaic and restricted to archaic texts and contexts. Contrary to Visser's presentation, *menace* should be dropped as well. It may be compared with *threaten* in the following, modified from Visser: *The solitary dissenter was *menacing/threatening to leave the meetinghouse.* The inclusion of *warrant* may also be considered questionable; in support, cf. the OED. On the other hand, *claim,* in its primary sense of 'assert', should be accommodated here. *Vow* is fairly formal, but certainly current. Visser's class of fifteen is thus changed to a class of seven: *claim, pretend, profess, promise, swear, threaten, vow.*

Visser's (1328 ff.) eleventh class is that of verbs of granting, agreeing, deigning, etc.: *accede, agree, concur, consent, deign, vouchsafe.*

Visser marks the verb *condescend* as obsolete in this pattern, but this judgment seems without foundation. Its frequent use in books on English grammar (e.g., Rosenbaum 1967: 93) testifies to the contrary. Therefore, it should remain a member of this class. On the other hand, *accede* should be dropped, cf. ??*He acceded to give me help.* *Vouchsafe* is too archaic, almost liturgical, to be retained. As for *concur,* as in *Several things concurred to make it perfect,* modified from Visser, the usage in question is certainly current. However, the subordinate clause seems to have an adverbial force, as an adverbial of result, for the sentence has the approximate meaning of 'several things came together with the result that it became perfect'. Consequently, we drop *accede, concur* and *vouchsafe.*

Visser's (1329 ff.) twelfth class is that of verbs of asking and requiring: *ask, beg, demand, entreat, pray, request, sue.*

As Visser notes (1329), *sue* with the infinitive is now archaic, so that the verb should be dropped from the list.

Visser's (1330 ff.) thirteenth class is that of verbs of intending, aiming, designing, deciding, etc.:

aim	deem	purpose
aspire	design	reckon
bandy	determine	resolve
compass	intend	scheme
conclude	mean	set out
conspire	plan	think
decide	plot	

Some changes should be made to bring the list into line with present-day English. In Visser's list, the status of two items is somewhat indeterminate: he marks *aim* with a dagger in parentheses (a dagger standing for 'obsolete') and *deem* with a square bracket. Clearly, *aim* should be a member of the class. By contrast, *deem* should be dropped. (Raising sentences such as *Works . . . which have been deemed to fulfill their design fairly* (OED, from 1875, Jowett, *Plato*) are of course irrelevant here.) *Bandy* should, on balance, also be dropped from the list (cf. the OED). The same holds for *compass* and *conclude*. Visser has instances of each from the middle of the nineteenth century: *??If any persons should compass to depose our Queen,* modified from Visser, and *My wife concluded to hire a balcony* (1858, Hawthorne, *French and Italian Journals*). Neither of these reflects current usage, and the verbs will be dropped. By contrast, *think* is among the sixteen that will be retained.

Visser's (1334 ff.) fourteenth class is that of verbs of expecting, hoping and trusting: *despair, elect, expect, gape, hope, look, reckon, think, trust.*

We drop *gape* from the class, as we dropped it from class 1. *Despair* seems archaic as well, as in *??He despaired to ascend the throne,* modified from Visser. (The original is from the eighteenth century.) In present-day English, *despair* prefers *of,* as in *He despaired of ascending the throne.*

Visser's (1335 ff.) fifteenth class is that of verbs of trying, attempting, undertaking:

assay	offer	sweat
attempt	seek	travail
endeavor	strive	try
essay	struggle	undertake
make	study	

Visser (1336) notes that *study* and *travail* with the infinitive are now archaic. Therefore they should be dropped from the list. Visser has both *assay* and *essay*. *Essay* is clearly current, but *assay,* in the pattern, seems formal and even unfamiliar to some native speakers of English. The OED (under III. 17.b., with the sense of 'to make the attempt', 'to endeavour (the issue being uncertain)', 'to do one's best'), has an example from 1868 (Freeman, *History of the Norman Conquest* (1876)), *The King's strength was failing, but he assayed to show himself in the usual kingly state,* but it is only with a great deal of hesitation that we retain the verb.

It seems possible to add two verbs to the list: *strain,* as in *They were straining to reconcile their differences,* modified from the OED (sense 19), and *battle,* as in *The Prime Minister was battling to preserve his credibility.* (We thank Robert MacGilleon for drawing our attention to *strain.*)

Visser's (1340 ff.) sixteenth class is that of verbs of risking, venturing: *hazard, presume, venture.*

Next come classes that Visser presents under the title of 'slight subordination' but to which forward Equi is relevant. Class number 17 (Visser, 1367 ff.) is that of verbs of hastening: *dispatch, hasten, speed.*

Dispatch should be dropped from this list (cf. the OED), e.g., **He dispatched to do it.*

Class number 18 (Visser, 1368 ff.) is that of verbs of hesitating, wavering, delaying, etc.: *delay, hesitate, tarry, waver.*

Here the inclusion of *waver* (cf. the OED) and *tarry*, as in ??*He tarried to take action*, may be questioned and we drop both verbs. *Delay* is likewise somewhat doubtful in the pattern (cf. Jespersen (1961: 200)). Sentences such as ??*He delayed to send for a taxi* are conceivable, but not acceptable to most speakers. (*He delayed sending for a taxi* is preferred.) However, negative imperatives, such as *Don't delay to send in your answer in time*, sound better. (We thank Robert Cooper for this sentence.) On balance, we retain *delay*, given that the observation made is to be borne in mind, even though the verb is not cited as *not delay*.

2.3.2 An Alternative Classification

In this section an alternative classification will be presented. Our classes will accommodate all the verbs that were not dropped from Visser's lists and a number of additional ones, most of which are from the list by Alexander and Kunz (1964: 76). The additional verbs could no doubt also be accommodated by Visser's classes, but there are two reasons for attempting a reclassification. First, the overall number of classes can be reduced. Second, and more important, it is possible to bring out at least some of the interconnections among the classes. Visser's classes are all on a level footing and his classification is not designed to express interconnections among them.

In our classification the first division is effected by the nature of the antecedent of PRO, that is, of NP_1 of the sequence $[NP_1—Verb_1—[PRO—to\ Verb_2—]_{S_2}]_{S_1}$.

For the majority of the verbs appearing as $Verb_1$ in this sequence, NP_1 must necessarily be +animate, or perhaps even +human. (Metonymic or metaphoric usages are of course possible, but they will be set aside in the present context.) For some other $Verb_1$s, NP_1 need not be +animate. The second class further divides into those predicates that necessarily take an inanimate trigger and those whose trigger may be either animate or inanimate. The former class comprises *serve* (cf. Kajita (1967: 17)), *contribute*, and *suffice*, the latter, *deserve* and *fail*, as witness [8a–e]:

[8] **a.** His words/*he contributed/served/sufficed to show the depth of feeling on the issue.

b. He deserves to win the prize.

c. The news deserves to be on the front page.

d. The bomb failed to explode.

e. He failed to notice me.

[8d] has the approximate meaning of 'the bomb did not explode'. A similar meaning is relevant to [8e].

Proceeding to the much larger class of Equi verbs that require their triggers to be +animate, we may distinguish the following classes:

(1) Verb$_1$ expresses volition, positive or negative, roughly meaning 'want or wish for something (not) to be realized or to hold'.

(1.1) Verb$_1$ expresses positive volition, roughly meaning 'want or wish for S$_2$ to be realized or to hold'.

(1.1.1) Verb$_1$ expresses a degree of volition, desideration.

(1.1.1.1) Verb$_1$ has the rough paraphrase 'to want or wish':

care	like	want
desire	prefer	wish
hope		

(1.1.1.2) Verb$_1$ has the rough meaning 'to want or wish intensely or impatiently':

ache	fret	pine
burn	gasp	sigh
chafe	hanker	sweat
covet	languish	thirst
crave	long	whine
delight	love	yearn
die	pant	

(1.1.2) Verb$_1$ expresses intention in addition to volition (desideration): NP$_1$ intends to realize S$_2$.

(1.1.2.1) Verb$_1$ implies that NP$_1$ communicates his intention.

(1.1.2.1.1) Verb$_1$ refers to the action of NP$_1$ only:

agree	promise	undertake
consent	swear	volunteer
offer	threaten	vow
pledge		

(1.1.2.1.2) Verb$_1$ implicitly refers to a second person:

apply	claim	plead
ask	demand	pray
beg	entreat	request

(1.1.2.2) Verb$_1$ expresses a decision or an intention not necessarily communicated for the realization of S$_2$:

afford	deign	plan
aim	design	presume
aspire	determine	propose
choose	elect	purpose
condescend	intend	resolve
contract	look	think
decide	mean	trust

(1.1.3) $Verb_1$ expresses a degree of endeavor in addition to volition (desideration) and intention:

arrange	hazard	seek
assay	labor	set out
attempt	learn	speed
battle	make	strain
bother	manage	strive
conspire	move	struggle
contrive	plot	trouble
endeavor	proceed	try
essay	push	venture
hasten	scheme	

(1.2) $Verb_1$ expresses negative volition with respect to the realization of S_2.
(1.2.1) $Verb_1$ has the rough meaning 'not to want' or 'not to wish':

abhor	hate
cannot abide/bear/endure/stand/suffer	loathe
dread	regret
fear	scruple

(1.2.2) $Verb_1$ expresses negative intention.
(1.2.2.1) $Verb_1$ expresses communication: *decline, refuse*.
(1.2.2.2) $Verb_1$ expresses negative intention not necessarily communicated:

delay	hesitate	omit
disdain	neglect	scorn
forbear		

(1.2.3) $Verb_1$ implies that NP_1 endeavors not to realize S_2: no verbs.
(1.3) Others: *forget, remember*.
(2) $Verb_1$ does not express volition.
(2.1) $Verb_1$ has the rough meaning 'pretend': *affect, feign, pretend*.
(2.2) $Verb_1$ has the rough meaning 'assert': *claim, profess*.
(2.3) $Verb_1$ has the rough meaning 'anticipate the occurrence of': *expect, reckon*.

Above, as a first step, one very large class, in terms of its members, viz. class 1, has been distinguished from three very small classes, viz. 2.1, 2.2, 2.3. The large class is clearly the core of our classification. The small classes call for little comment, except perhaps for 2.3. *Expect*, of 2.3, may be felt to be close to verbs of class 1.1.2.2, especially perhaps to *intend*. Judgments are moderately subtle, but *expect* does not really express intention on the part of NP_1 to do something, but rather the anticipation of NP_1 (cf. the OED) that S_2 will be realized. For this reason, *expect* has not been included in 1.1.2.2. Similar considerations apply to *reckon*.

Proceeding to the large class of 1, we set aside the very small class of 1.3 for the moment. With 1.3 set aside, the major division within class 1 derives from the attitude of NP_1 toward the action or state of affairs referred to in the lower sentence, that is, S_2. (We will speak of 'NP_1' even when we mean the entity designated by NP_1, and of 'S_2' when we mean the content of S_2.) The attitude, or disposition, may be positive (class 1.1) or negative (class 1.2). This division seems clear: for instance, *I want/wish to go there*, with *want* and *wish* representing class 1.1, may be contrasted with *I hate to go there*, with *hate* representing class 1.2. More basically, though, it may be asked why we call the members of class 1 verbs of volition in the first place and not, for example, verbs of intention. The question is of some significance because, provided that the classification is even approximately adequate, it concerns the characterization of the largest class of Equi verbs under discussion.

The choice of the term 'volition' can be justified on the basis of semantic relations obtaining between statements containing typical or core verbs of the major subdivisions of 1.1 and 1.2. Both 1.1 and 1.2 are structured along parallel lines. They are both divided into three major subdivisions. The first two of these are based on the notions of 'volition' and 'intention'. The verbs of classes 1.1.1 and 1.2.1 basically express desideration, a degree of volition, but do not express intention. The verbs of classes 1.1.2 and 1.2.2 express intention in addition to desideration. The third major subdivision of both 1.1 and 1.2 is based on the notion of 'endeavor': the verbs of classes 1.1.3 and 1.2.3 imply a degree of endeavor or effort on the part of NP_1 for the realization or the nonrealization of S_2. The description is vacuous in respect of class 1.2.3, since no verbs were found that belong to this class (see below).

In order to shed light on semantic relations holding between the three hierarchical classes, it is profitable to consider typical verbs of the major subdivisions. We will consider such typical verbs of the positive side of the division, that is, of 1.1. It is easy to choose *intend* as the typical and straightforward verb expressing intention and *endeavor* as the typical verb expressing endeavor. These choices are easy, because neither of these verbs carries irrelevant other senses or distracting connotations. The choice of a core verb expressing desideration, a degree of volition, is somewhat less easy. Volition relates to willing and to will. According to a relevant sense of the noun *will* formulated by Webster's 3rd (1976: sense 4a), *will* means "a mental power or a disposition or the sum of mental powers or dispositions manifested in such operations and functions as wishing, choosing, desiring, intending." Of the four verbs cited in Webster's, we will discuss *intend* in more detail below. *Choose* carries the implication of a conscious decision and is therefore not a suitable choice to be a core verb, or, still less, to be the core verb of volition. *Desire* is worth considering (cf. Searle (1983: 29 ff.)), but it has the prominent sense of 'wish for earnestly' (Webster's 3rd (1976: sense 1)). The adverb *earnestly* implies a high degree of intensity. Because the sense is prominent, we do not adopt *desire* as a core verb of desideration. *Wish* has distracting and irrelevant senses as well, including that of 'express a wish for' (Webster's 3rd (1976: sense 3b)). Even so, it may come close to being a core verb of desideration. It is worth quoting Random House (1981: under *wish*), which compares *wish, desire* and *want*: "*To wish* is to feel an impulse toward attainment or possession of something; the strength of the feeling may be of greater or less intensity. . . ." The description is meant to cover the meaning of *wish* in the infinitival construction as well. It is the last part of the description that recommends *wish* as a core verb of desideration, for we are looking for a verb that expresses a basic degree of desideration. *Want* is not in Webster's list. It has irrelevant senses as well, including those of 'wish earnestly' (1976: sense 2a (1)), and 'feel a profound yearning for' (1976: sense 2a (2)). These senses express too high a degree of intensity and we ruled out *desire* as a core verb of desideration because it has a similar sense. However, a sense of this kind is less prominent in *want* than in *desire*. Further, Webster's Third (1976: discussion of *want* under *desire*) notes that *want* generally "implies a need or lack" and according to Random House (1981: discussion of *want* under *wish*), *want* "suggests a feeling of lack or need which imperatively demands fulfillment." 'Imperatively' again implies too high a degree of desideration for a core verb and the suggestion of a 'lack or need' does not recommend *want* as a core verb of desideration either. In view of these considerations, *want* may perhaps come close to being a core verb of desideration only if we can interpret it in a broad sense. By a broad sense we mean a sense where *want* expresses a basic degree of desideration only, insofar as it can, without an implication of earnestness or of profundity of yearning and with the suggestion of a lack or need pushed into the background as far as possible. (A reference to Davidson's (1985: 101) "very broad sense of want" may not be altogether misplaced at this point.)

In view of their irrelevant senses, neither *want* nor *wish* is completely straightforward or satisfactory as a core verb of desideration and still less as *the* core verb of desideration. Both *intend* and *endeavor* are more satisfactory as the core verbs of intention and endeavor, respectively. *Want* and *wish* may serve as core verbs of desideration only to the extent that it is possible to put aside irrelevant senses and meanings. In order to exclude at least some of the senses of each that are irrelevant in the present context, we will cite both verbs side by side, as in *want/wish,* as core verbs of desideration. Citing them thus side by side serves to focus on the broad sense of basic desideration that is shared at least up to a point by both verbs.

Desire will not then be used as a core verb of classes 1.1.1 and 1.2.1. Nor will these classes be called 'verbs of desire'. Instead, the noun 'desideration' is used as a heading for these classes. It is notable that this noun, related to the verb *desiderate,* carries a less intense meaning than the noun *desire*. Verbs of desideration are verbs expressing a broad sense of wanting/wishing, a basic degree of volition.

The semantic relations between the three subdivisions of 1.1 and 1.2 that we have in mind can be epitomized by the relation of ENTAILMENT. It will be recalled that for a statement X to entail a second statement Y means that if X is true, so is Y, and if Y is false, so is X (cf. Lyons (1977: 165); Kempson (1977: 142)). A relevant point of departure is provided by Miller and Johnson-Laird's

(1976: 509) statement that *"I am willing to write a novel* does not entail *I intend to write a novel,* though the converse inference does seem to follow." Miller and Johnson-Laird discuss neither *want* nor *wish,* as opposed to *be willing to,* but of the two statements (A) *I want/wish to write a novel* and (B) *I intend to write a novel,* A again clearly does not entail B, for it may be true that I want or wish to write a novel, but quite false that I intend to do so. On the other hand, B again does seem to entail A, provided that we can interpret *want* and *wish* as having a sense of basic desideration, setting aside such other senses as that of 'wish earnestly' of *want.*

The argument as presented presupposes noncontrastive stress patterns of sentences of the form of A and B. In the noncontrastive stress patterns the main stress in each sentence falls on the last word *novel.* The argument is not equally valid if *intend* and *want/wish* are stressed contrastively, as in A' and B', where capitalization indicates contrastive stressing.

A' I WANT/WISH to write a novel.
B' I INTEND to write a novel.

The verb *intend* has the major sense of 'have in the mind as a fixed purpose' (OED: sense 18, the "chief current sense"). The verb, like other verbs of intention, leaves it open as to why the purpose came to be formed or induced. As an approximation, we may say that it may be of one of two types: (1) either autonomous, spontaneous, unprompted, not directly induced by another purpose or by other purposes, or (2) it may be instigated, prompted, induced by another purpose or by other purposes. We will use the terms UNPROMPTED and PROMPTED for the two types, respectively. Regardless of which is relevant, *intend* carries the meaning that there is a degree of volition or desideration involved (cf. Searle (1983: 34)). We can then speak of prompted or unprompted volition (desideration). However, neither *want* nor *wish* is neutral with respect to the source of the volition that they express. Both focus on unprompted, rather than on prompted desideration. (The adjectival construction *be willing to* expresses both prompted and unprompted desideration.) In B' it is natural to think of unprompted desideration. Consequently, the truth of B' suggests that A' is true. However, there is an entailment relation between B' and A' only on the reading of unprompted volition of *intend.* To put it another way, B' may then be glossed as 'I INTEND to write a novel for the sake of writing a novel'. The predicate *write a novel* encourages this interpretation, but the likelihood of such a reading is not constant. Rather, it is a function of the lower predicate. It is instructive to consider a lower predicate that favors the prompted interpretation of volition, such as *pay one's taxes.* (We thank an anonymous reviewer for drawing our attention to this predicate.) We may then construct analogs to A, B, A' and B':

C I want/wish to pay my taxes.
D I intend to pay my taxes.
C' I WANT/WISH to pay my taxes.
D' I INTEND to pay my taxes.

The predicate *pay one's taxes* favors the reading of prompted volition. D' does then not entail C' on the reading of prompted volition of D'. The reading of unprompted volition is unlikely in D', but, if it were possible to imagine such a reading, D' would entail C'.

Want/wish and *intend* are contrastively stressed in C' and D'. If we remove the contrastive stressing, as in C and D, and let the stress fall on *taxes* in the ordinary way, an entailment relation exists between D and C, without regard to the source of volition of *intend* in D, provided, of course, that *want/wish* are interpreted to express broad volition, as described above.

It is instructive to combine such pairs of sentences or statements by means of *but* and to consider contradictions that may or may not arise. (On the use of *but*, cf. Bendix (1966: 23 ff.); on problems of the method cf. Fillmore (1969) and Lipka (1972: 60 ff.)) Thus *I intend to write a novel, but I don't want/wish to write a novel*, with the main stresses on *novel*, is a contradiction. So is *I INTEND to write a novel, but I don't WANT/WISH to write a novel*, on the reading of unprompted volition of *intend*, but not on the reading of prompted volition. *I intend to pay my taxes, but I don't want/wish to pay my taxes*, with main stresses falling on *taxes*, is a contradiction. (The contradiction may be removed by changing the *but* sentence into *but I don't want/wish to pay my taxes now*, with the stress falling on *now*, but this only supports the analysis, since there is no *now* in the first part.) Finally, *I INTEND to pay my taxes, but I don't WANT/WISH to pay my taxes* is not a contradiction on the reading of prompted volition, which is the predominant reading.

To sum up the argument, B entails A and D entails C with noncontrastive stressing, provided that *want/wish* have a broad sense of volition. If *intend* and *want/wish* are stressed contrastively, the entailment relation is limited to the reading of unprompted volition of *intend*. This reading is not a necessary reading of *intend*. The likelihood of such a reading is a function of the lower predicate.

Going back to the choice of terms for the major classes, we take note of the direction of the—admittedly conditional—entailment relation between pairs of statements such as A/B and C/D. It is then appropriate to have *intend* in a list of verbs with the component, and under the heading, of volition, whereas having *want* and *wish* in a list under the heading of (verbs expressing) intention would be inadequate.

Core verbs of the major verb classes are important and they serve to anchor our classification firmly in actual English data. It is notable how fully the notions of intention and of endeavor are carried by the actual verbs *intend* and *endeavor*, respectively. However, the classification is not solely—or even primarily—based on core verbs. It is more abstract, being based on components of meaning that are theoretical entities. Actual verbs, or, more precisely, senses of actual verbs, carry and realize such components of meaning. However, it is not being claimed that the verbs of class 1.1.1 or of 1.2.1 or of any other class of the classification are synonymous in all, or even in any, of their senses. The classification does not provide—and it does not have the purpose of providing—an exhaustive analysis of the senses and meanings of the verbs that are classified. It is not designed to act as a substitute for a dictionary. What the classification is designed to do is to establish a framework for the description of some of the dominant senses of verbs that occur in the infinitival pattern in question. With respect to 1.1.1, it should be noted that several verbs of the pattern have a fairly general additional component of meaning in addition to expressing volition. We will call it the PLEASURE COMPONENT: NP_1 derives pleasure from the realization of S_2. For several verbs of 1.1.1, including *want* and *wish,* the pleasure component appears to be less prominent, optional or perhaps even absent, but it is a necessary part of the meaning of at least *delight, like* and *love.* For instance, we observe that *John wants/wishes to fish in troubled waters, but he does not get any pleasure out of it* is less of a contradiction than *John loves to fish in troubled waters, but he does not get any pleasure out of it.* It is the pleasure component of *love* that gives rise to the contradiction.

The pleasure component is undoubtedly present in *love* and in at least the two other verbs cited. It is a prominent component. Indeed, it would be conceivable to set up a separate class for such verbs, a class of verbs meaning that NP_1 experiences pleasure, or displeasure, in realizing S_2. However, it should be observed that of the two statements (E) *John loves to fish in troubled waters* and (F) *John wants/wishes to fish in troubled waters,* E entails F, for the following is a contradiction: *John loves to fish in troubled waters, but he does not want/wish to do so.* Analogous contradictions arise with the other two verbs. For instance, we may consider *delight* and the following: *In summer John delights to walk in the fields, but he does not want/wish to do so.* Because of such entailment relations, it seems appropriate to cite *love* and the other two verbs as verbs of volition, and not to distinguish a separate class for them. In this connection, it is perhaps of interest to observe the absence of a contradiction in analogous sentences with *expect.* For instance, there is no contradiction in *John expects to get up early tomorrow, but he does not want/wish to do so.*

Class 1.2.3, of verbs of negative ˙desideration, intention and endeavor, forms one part of our descriptive framework. In our survey, we did not find any verb in present-day English that belonged to 1.2.3. In spite of this negative finding, it is worthwhile to postulate the class. The main reason is that 1.2.3 affords a point of comparison with its positive counterpart, class 1.1.3. We also leave open the possibility that verbs belonging to 1.2.3 may be found in a larger survey. More importantly, in the history of English, class 1.2.3 has not always been empty, or nearly empty. Apart from verbs that have become totally obsolete, a number of verbs that are still current in other patterns, especially the *ing* pattern of section 2.4, have been members of class 1.2.3 at an earlier stage of the history of English. Such verbs include *avoid, eschew* and *evade* (cf. Visser's (1978: 1318 ff.) illustrations). The decline of class 1.2.3 is a fact, but it strikes us as a significant fact (see section 2.3.3). In our discussion, we will then retain class 1.2.3.

The verbs of classes 1.1.3 and 1.2.3 imply some endeavor on the part of NP_1 for the realization or the nonrealization of S_2. At this point, an interesting set of additional entailment relations can be pointed out. For instance, the statement *He endeavored to do it* entails both the statement *He intended to do it* and the statement *He wanted/wished to do it,* whereas neither of the latter entails the first. More generally, and this is a main feature of the classification, any statement whose Verb$_1$ is from an 'endeavor' class entails the corresponding statement whose Verb$_1$ is from one of the corresponding 'desideration' or 'desideration and intention' classes, except when a Verb$_1$ of the latter carries a major extra element of meaning in addition to desideration or intention and desideration. (Such major extra elements of meaning include the pleasure component of the *delight* class and the component of communication in 1.1.2 and 1.2.2 discussed below.) To put it another way, a person cannot endeavor to do anything without intending to do it and without wanting/wishing to do it.

By way of a summary, it is possible to say that the three major subdivisions of the two major classes 1.1 and 1.2 embody hierarchies of volition. Verbs of desideration express the weakest or lowest degree of volition. Verbs of intention express a higher degree of volition, which includes desideration and intention. Verbs of endeavor express a still higher degree of volition, embracing desideration, intention and endeavor.

Given the entailment relations that were established, the 'endeavor' class has no bearing on the choice between volition and intention as the heading of class 1. However, if neither class 1.1.1 nor class 1.2.1 existed, the remaining classes of verbs could be called verbs of intention.

Smaller classes within the six subdivisions of class 1 call for some comment. Regarding 1.1.1, the difference between its two subdivisions is one of degree only: the verbs of class 1.1.1.2 are felt to express a higher level of desideration than those of 1.1.1.1. As noted, some verbs of class 1.1.1 contain an additional semantic component implying that NP$_1$ experiences pleasure when S$_2$ is realized. Pleasure covers such emotions as delight, enjoyment and exultation.

Within class 1.1.2, verbs that express communication have been distinguished from those that do not. For instance, *vow* necessarily implies a verbal act, while *intend*, say, does not: *He intended to go there* may be true even if he never communicated his intention to anyone, whereas *He vowed to go there* is not true under such circumstances. (Communicating to oneself, as in *vow to oneself*, is perhaps to be considered an extension of communicating to others. Even here, **intend to oneself* is not possible.) The point is of some interest because Austin (1962: 158) classed *vow* and *intend* in the same group. (For a somewhat similar critique of Austin, cf. Searle (1979: 9).)

The two classes within 1.1.2.1 differ in that a Verb$_1$ of 1.1.2.1.1 implies that NP$_1$, in effect, commits himself to bringing about a new state of affairs. Class 1.1.2.1.1 may be compared to Fraser's (1974: 144 ff.) and Searle's (1979: 22 ff.) classes of 'commissives'. For a sentence such as *I promise to pay you the money* Searle (1979: 22) provides the deep structure I Verb (you) + I FUT Vol Verb (NP) (Adv), with Equi subsequently deleting the repeated subject. Searle's description is relevant to class 1.1.2.1.1, but less so to class 1.1.2.1.2, because a

Verb$_1$ of the latter implies the presence of a second NP in the matrix sentence in addition to NP$_1$. It is instructive to compare *He vowed to go there* with *He begged to go there*. In the latter sentence the realization of S$_2$ is viewed as depending not only on NP$_1$, but on the cooperation of an unspecified additional entity.

Since the verbs of class 1.1.2.1 express communication, it is only natural that the addressee of the communication may be expressed, in addition to the content. With some verbs the addressee can be expressed more readily than with others. Most often, the addressee is designated by a prepositional phrase. It is the addressee on whose cooperation the realization of S$_2$ depends in the case of verbs of 1.1.2.1.2. Verbs of 1.1.2.1.1 generally allow the addressee to be expressed as well, but the realization of S$_2$ is viewed as independent of the addressee. The difference in respect of the part played by the addressee is to a degree reflected in the selection of prepositions. Certain verbs of 1.1.2.1.1, where the realization of S$_2$ is not dependent on the addressee, allow the addressee to be expressed by a PP introduced by the preposition *to: He swore/vowed to me to come back and win*. For a reason that is not clear to us, some verbs of the pattern, notably *consent*, though they unquestionably express communication in the pattern, are quite incompatible with a PP introduced by *to* or indeed with any equivalent expression, as cf. **He consented to me to do his share of the work. Promise* is less impossible. Even so, most people do not like *He promised to me to come back and win*. There are others, apparently a minority, who accept it, however. Palmer (1974: 187) has *I offered to John to go* and observes additionally that *agree* and *undertake* take *with: I agreed/undertook with John to go*, but not all speakers of English are entirely comfortable with these either.

By contrast, most verbs of 1.1.2.1.2, where the realization of S$_2$ requires the cooperation or agreement of the addressee, take the preposition *of*, though only in a fairly formal style, as in *John asked/begged/demanded/requested of the King to be allowed to go free. Apply* and *pray*, which take *to*, as in *John applied to the King to be released/John prayed to God to be released*, and *plead*, which takes *to*, or, preferably, *with*, as in *John pleaded with the King to be released*, diverge from the pattern. A tentative explanation may be offered for these verbs on the basis of the omissibility of the *to* clause. A *to* clause cooccurring with *apply to, pray to* and *plead with* is more readily omissible than one governed by *ask of, beg of* etc. Thus compare the imperatives *Apply to/plead with the King!/Pray to God!* and **ask/*beg/*demand/*request of the King!* The difference is not limited to imperatives, of course. *He applied to/pleaded with the King/He prayed to God* are good as compared with *He *asked/*begged/*demanded/*requested of the King*. It may be then that it is more felicitous to consider the infinitival construction which cooccurs with *apply, plead* and *pray* an infinitive of purpose rather than a complement clause. This conclusion is lent some additional plausibility by the acceptability of *in order to/so as to*, instead of *to* only, with *apply, plead* and *pray*, with approximately the same meaning: *He applied to/pleaded with the King in order to/so as to be released/He prayed to God in order to be released*. There is then some reason to drop *apply, plead* and *pray* from 1.1.2.1.2. Most of the remaining verbs of 1.1.2.1.2 exhibit a degree of regularity in that they take a prepositional phrase introduced by *of* as the designator of the addressee.

The *to*-NP and *of*-NP patterns are of interest from another point of view. The resulting sequence of constituents is the following:

$$[NP_1 \quad Verb_1 \quad [Prep \quad NP_0]_{PP} \quad [PRO]_{NP_2} \quad to \quad Verb_2 \ldots]]_{S_2}$$

| John | vowed | to | me | PRO | to | come back and win |
| John | demanded | of | the King | PRO | to | be released |

This structure and sequence of constituents are the same as in the pattern of complementation discussed in Chapter 6, as in *John depended on me to do my duty.* However, while with *vow* and other verbs of 1.1.2.1 NP_1 is the controller of—that is, coreferential with—NP_2, with *depend on* and the other verbs of Chapter 6, it is NP_0, the NP of the PP, that is coreferential with NP_2.

A second difference relating to control arises with *promise*. There are few speakers for whom *promise* allows the addressee to be expressed by a prepositional phrase. However, quite universally, it allows the addressee to be expressed by a plain NP, as in *He promised me to come back and win*. *Promise* seems to be the only verb of 1.1.2.1 to allow this construction without strain in the present pattern. For instance, *beg*, as in *He begged the King to be released* produces a sentence so awkward as to be unacceptable, at least as a complement construction (cf. Postal (1970: 495, note 31)). If the *to* clause is viewed as an infinitive of purpose, it is possible, or at least much better: *He begged the King, in order to/so as to be released.*

Promise, then, allows this pattern:

$$[NP_1 \quad Verb_1 \quad NP_0 \quad [[PRO]_{NP_2} \quad to \quad Verb_2 \ldots]_{S_2}]_{S_1}$$

| John | promised | me | PRO | to come back and win |

This structure and sequence of constituents are the same as in the pattern of complementation discussed in Chapter 4, as in *John induced me to do my duty*, which is that of object-controlled Equi. Notably, though, in the pattern of *induce*, it is NP_0, the object of the higher sentence, that is the controller of NP_2, while with *promise* it is NP_1, the subject of the higher clause.

The difference between the patterns of *promise* and *induce* is reflected in what has come to be called 'Visser's generalization', a term coined by Bresnan in 1976 (cf. Bresnan (1982: 402)). As stated by Visser (1973: 2118), "a passive transform is only possible when the complement relates to the immediately preceding (pro)noun." Visser offered this generalization to account for the admissibility of such passives as *John is regarded by me as pompous* from (a string of the form of) *I regard John as pompous,* as contrasted with the inadmissibility of such passives as **I was impressed by his comments as unfortunate,* from (a string of the form of) the well-formed active *His comments impressed me as unfortunate.* (Active and passive sentences of this type were originally considered by Chomsky (1965: 229).) The generalization is equally relevant to complement sentence patterns. In the terminology that is employed here, the generalization is that passivization is possible when PRO is controlled by the direct object of $Verb_1$, as in the pattern of *induce,* but that it is excluded when PRO is controlled by NP_1, as in the pattern of *promise.* For instance, *I was induced by John to come back and win,* from (a string of the form of) *John induced me to come back and win,* is good, but **I was promised by John to come back and win,* from (a string of the form of) *John promised me to come back and win,* is bad. There may be some exceptions to Visser's generalization, but they may be more apparent than real (cf. Bresnan (1982: 404)). In any case, the generalization is significant and affords a method for distinguishing the patterns of *promise* and *induce.* (It may be noted that a number of accounts have been proposed as to how Visser's generalization may follow from other principles. These include Wasow (1977: 352 ff.), and Williams (1980: 211) in a transformational framework, Bach (1979: 520 ff.) in a Montague framework, Bresnan (1982: 401 ff.) in her lexical-functional framework, and Koster (1984: 431 ff.), which includes a critique of Bresnan (1982).)

Visser's generalization is a strictly syntactic method for separating the patterns of *promise* and *induce.* There is a second syntactic method, but, because it focuses on the pattern of *induce,* perhaps more so than Visser's generalization does, we defer it to the beginning of Chapter 4, where the pattern of *induce* is discussed in its own right.

From a different point of view, Postal's *Ought* Modal Constraint seems to shed light on the different patterns of control encountered in this section. Postal (1970: 470) notes that in a sentence such as *John told Max that he was sick, he* may be coreferential with either *John* or *Max.* However, in *John told Max that he ought to visit Greta, he* can only be coreferential with *Max,* given that the modal is "the indicator of an imperative performance" and not simply the modal of a declarative performance (cf. Postal (1970: 499)). With respect to examples of the present argument, we note that in *John demanded of the King that he should be released,* the *that* clause equivalent of *John demanded of the King to be released, he* is coreferential with *John* rather than with *the King.* In *John promised Max that he would come back, he* is again coreferential with *John,* given the imperative performance reading of the modal (cf. Postal (1970: 499)). Neither *induce* nor *depend on* take the *that* construction very readily, but if it is forced on them (cf. Postal (1970: 475)), in the resulting sentences *John induced Max that he would do it* and *John depended on Max that he would do his duty, he* is clearly coreferential with *Max,* that is, with NP_0, rather than with *John,* that is, with NP_1. In other words, in the investigation of control, it is helpful to refer to corresponding *that* complement clauses, even if some violence is done to normal patterns of complementation, and to judgments of acceptability.

Finally, with respect to 1.1.2.1.2, it may be noted that the verbs of the class allow $Verb_2$ to be a passive. In the discussion above, passive forms were used frequently. If the active is chosen instead of the passive for $Verb_2$, there are three cases that should be kept separate. First, if the addressee is left unspecified, the pattern of subject-controlled forward Equi is observed. In *John asked/begged/claimed/demanded/entreated/requested to speak,* it is *John* that controls PRO. Second, if the addressee is specified by means of a direct object, *ask, beg, entreat* and *request* cease to belong to the present pattern of subject-controlled Equi and switch to the pattern of *induce,* which is that of object-controlled Equi. These verbs will be included in the discussion of the pattern in Chapter 4. *Demand* will be included as well, but will be dropped, as unidiomatic in the pattern. *Claim* will not be included there at all, for clearly it does not allow the addressee to be expressed in this way: *The prisoner asked/begged/ *claimed/*demanded/entreated/requested his jailer to release him.* It is worth observing that these verbs obey Postal's condition even in their switch to the object-controlled pattern. *He* in *The prisoner asked etc. his jailer that he should release him* is coreferential with *his jailer,* and not with *the prisoner.* Third, the combination of some of these verbs with a following *of* NP and an active Verb$_2$, where a separate pattern of control is involved, will be considered in Chapter 6.

Within 1.1.2.2 there can be distinguished verbs that imply a reaching of a decision, or an arrival at a decision, that is, refer to the forming of an intention (*choose, determine, decide* etc.) from those that refer to the intention only, not to its formation (*aim, intend* etc.). From another point of view, *condescend, deign* and *presume* stand apart from the rest of class 1.1.2.2 in implying an attitude of superiority on the part of NP$_1$.

The verbs of class 1.1.3 all express some effort on the part of NP$_1$ for the achievement of a new state of affairs, but the degree of effort ranges from *make,* which does not imply much effort, to *labor,* which does.

Within class 1.2 the verbs of 1.2.1 in general express some emotion (fear, indecision, loathing, etc.) that amounts to negative desideration towards the realization of S$_2$.

The notion of intentionality is relevant to the verbs of 1.2.2, but not in exactly the same way. *Forbear* is among the verbs that are most strongly intentional, or rather negative intentional. It has the approximate sense of 'stop oneself from'. (We thank Robert Cooper for this gloss.) By contrast, *neglect* and *omit* are less inherently intentional. *Omit* has been glossed as 'to forbear or fail to do . . .' in Random House (1981: sense 2) and a somewhat similar gloss seems relevant to *neglect.* The *forbear* part of the gloss implies negative intentionality and the *fail* part unintentionality. However, the relevance of *fail* to these two verbs should not be pushed too far, for both *neglect* and *omit* are quite inconceivable in sentences analogous to [8d] above, as in **The bomb neglected/omitted to explode.*

Our class of 1.3 consists of *forget* and *remember. Remember* has been glossed as 'not to forget' (OED: sense 1b; cf. also ALD). *Forget* has the sense of 'disregard intentionally', but generally only in the imperative *Forget it* (Webster's Third (1976, sense 4)). *Forget* has the other sense of 'omit or neglect through inadvertence' (OED: sense 2) or 'omit or disregard unintentionally', as in *I forgot to close the door* (Webster's Third (1976: sense 2)). However, even though the actual realization, or rather nonrealization, of S_2 may be inadvertent, the verb still expresses an intention: if I forget to lock the door, it is the case that I had the volition and the intention to lock the door. (We thank Ian Gurney for drawing our attention to this point.) For this reason, we list *forget* and *remember* as verbs of volition. In view of the element of unintentionality in the actual performance or nonperformance of the intention, we do not include them in 1.1 or in 1.2, but set up a separate class for them.

2.3.3 Conclusions

In this section we discuss two conclusions that emerge from the classification, provided that it is even approximately adequate and that the lists are even reasonably representative. (As indicated above, the lists are not claimed to be comprehensive and the classification is not claimed to capture all senses of all the verbs listed.)

First, it seems that by far the greatest number of verbs governing Equi of the type specified in section 2.1 require animate subjects: of the verbs considered 126 do and only 5 do not. Among the 126 the class of volitional verbs predominates, by 119 verbs to 7. Even though the verbs that may take inanimate subjects are obviously also nonvolitional, the volitional vs. nonvolitional ratio is still as lopsided as 119 vs. 12.

It is not our purpose here to give figures covering the actual occurrences of the different classes in a corpus. A priori it would be quite possible that the 12 nonvolitional verbs occurred more frequently than the 119 volitional ones. We may speculate, though, that this is not so. It seems rather that the class of volitional Equi verbs is also the most frequently occurring of those under consideration. In other words, a Verb$_1$ of the sequence NP$_1$—Verb$_1$—PRO—*to*—Verb$_2$ . . . (where PRO—*to*—Verb$_2$ . . . is a complement sentence) characteristically denotes volition, positive or negative, on the part of NP$_1$. Even though Visser (1978: 1312) is right to point out that the *to* of the pattern is devoid of its original meaning of direction or purpose (cf. also Mustanoja (1960: 514)), the preponderance of volitional verbs as Verb$_1$ in the pattern may be related to, or perhaps partly even arise from, the original force of *to*. It may be profitable to quote Curme (1931: 256):

> The original concrete meaning of movement toward a person or thing found in the preposition *to* is still discernible in the *to* of the infinitive in infinitive clauses which form an indispensable complement to a verb. . . .

Volitional verbs imply direction or movement toward, or away from, an abstract goal. They are therefore compatible with the original force of *to,* provided that we can interpret *to* more abstractly, as expressing a broader concept of movement, setting aside the direction of the movement.

Contrasting the major classes of verbs that express positive volition with those expressing negative volition, we observe that the former clearly preponderate: 96 to 21. The imbalance is at its most striking in the class of verbs expressing an effort on the part of NP_1 to realize or not to realize S_2: 29 to 0. Thus it seems that in English at least it is exceptional for a $Verb_1$ of the infinitival pattern under consideration to express an effort on the part of NP_1 not to realize S_2. In other words, the direction of the movement is overwhelmingly toward, not away from, a goal. This finding brings into sharper focus the hypothesis that there is a connection between the infinitival pattern in question and the original force of *to*, which is indeed still the predominant one even in present-day English. We may distinguish a broader and a more narrow, or more specific, connection, depending on the broader and the more narrow, more specific interpretation of the force of *to:*

	to	the infinitival pattern
broader:	'movement'	verbs of volition predominate
more specific:	'movement toward'	verbs of positive volition predominate

The connection between the original, and still predominant, sense of *to*, 'movement toward', and the preponderance of verbs of positive volition in the infinitival pattern under consideration is striking. It is hazardous to speak of cause and effect, but we may perhaps venture to speculate that the original force of *to* may have contributed to the decline of class 1.2.3. However, any resolution of this issue would require tracing the history of class 1.2.3 from Old English to Modern English and we will not undertake this in the present book.

Second, the lists of verbs presented are of interest from the point of view of the division of verbs into IMPLICATIVE and NONIMPLICATIVE, as proposed by Karttunen (1971), in that they afford some indication of the generality of the two classes. Karttunen did not focus on this question in his pioneering study.

Implicative verbs differ from nonimplicative verbs in several respects. To take three, consider [9]–[12], of which [12] represents the complement sentence of [9] to [11] (cf. Karttunen (1971: 341 ff.)).

[9] **a.** John managed to solve the problem.
     b. John intended to solve the problem.

[10] **a.** John didn't manage to solve the problem.
     b. John didn't intend to solve the problem.

[11] **a.** Did John manage to solve the problem?
     b. Did John intend to solve the problem?

[12] John solved the problem.

We may observe in a manner analogous to Karttunen (1971: 341 ff.) that [9a] implies the truth of [12], but [9b] does not. [10a] implies the negation of [12], but [10b] does not, being noncommittal in this respect. Finally, an affirmative answer to [11b] does not imply [12], while an affirmative answer to [11a] does.

These judgments can be tested and corroborated in various ways. For instance, as regards [10a, b], note that [13a] is a contradiction, but that [13b] is not (cf. Karttunen (1971: 343)).

[13] a. *John didn't manage to solve the problem but he solved it.
       b. John didn't intend to solve the problem but he solved it.

Throughout the discussion of implicative and nonimplicative verbs, here as elsewhere in this book, noncontrastive stress patterns should be understood. The main stress in [9a, b], then, falls on *solve*. In [13a, b] the main stress of the first sentence similarly falls on *solve*. If the matrix verb is stressed contrastively in such examples, the argument is not equally valid. For instance, if *manage* is stressed contrastively, as in *John didn't MANAGE to solve the problem,* we may get *John didn't MANAGE to solve the problem—he was given the answer* (from Horn (1985: 130)). A number of intricate issues arise in such sentences with contrastive stress patterns or marked intonation contours (cf. Karttunen and Peters (1979: 46 ff.), Liberman and Sag (1974: 423 ff.) and Horn (1985, 129 ff.)), but we will set them aside in this book, limiting the argument to noncontrastive stress patterns.

Given the implicative vs. nonimplicative dichotomy, the distributions of the two classes among Equi verbs may be examined. It seems that the clear majority of the verbs examined are nonimplicative. The verbs of the major class 1.1.1 are nonimplicative in their entirety. (Some of them, e.g., *delight,* may perhaps 'feel' less nonimplicative than others, but all are still nonimplicative. For instance, *He didn't delight to learn the paradigm but he learned it* is not a contradiction.) The verbs of 1.1.2 and 1.1.3 are also overwhelmingly nonimplicative. Within class 1.1.2 the class of 1.1.2.1 is nonimplicative in its entirety and within class 1.1.2.2 perhaps only the 'attitude' verbs (*condescend, deign* and *presume*) are implicative, that is, 3 out of 40. Within 1.1.3 *bother, manage, trouble* and *venture* are implicative, that is, 4 out of 29. Ignoring the verbs that are generally constructed with *cannot* (or *could not*) (*abide* etc.), all the verbs of 1.2.1 are nonimplicative. The status of *decline* and *refuse* of 1.2.2.1 (concerning the latter, see Karttunen (1971: 354 f.)) is somewhat indeterminate. Within 1.3 *remember* is implicative, *forget* negative implicative. On the other hand, the class of 1.2.2.2. is interesting inasmuch as most of its members are implicative, or rather negative implicative. For instance, *He forbore to do it* implies that he did not do it. This is the only largish class whose members are not overwhelmingly nonimplicative.

As regards some of the nonvolitional classes of 2, the verbs of 2.2 and 2.3 are nonimplicative, and those of 2.1 may perhaps be ignored here (cf. Karttunen (1970: 337)).

Overall, it seems that the great majority of verbs that appear as a Verb$_1$ in the infinitival subject-controlled forward Equi pattern are nonimplicative except if the $Verb_1$ expresses a decision not to realize S_2 or a failure to realize S_2, in which case the $Verb_1$ is negative implicative. Given that, in nontechnical terms, a nonimplicative verb leaves it open whether or not S_2 is realized, this finding ties in with the first conclusion that a $Verb_1$ characteristically denotes volition and positive volition in the majority of cases: generally it is left open whether the positive volition comes to fruition. More specifically, if the three classes of verbs of the entailment hierarchy, those of desideration, those of desideration and intention, and those of desideration, intention and endeavor, are considered, the numerical findings given above are highly suggestive: the incidence of implicative verbs is at its lowest in the class of verbs of desideration and at its highest in the class of verbs of desideration, intention and endeavor. (If class 1.2.3 had members, a fair number of them might well be negative implicative.) This is perhaps only to be expected on common sense grounds: in general, desideration in the mind of NP_1, be it ever so sharply felt (recall class 1.1.1.2), is hardly sufficient alone to ensure that S_2 is viewed as realized. When more than desideration is involved, S_2 may still not be viewed as realized, but at least the likelihood is greater.

2.4 THE *ING* PATTERN

2.4.1 Preliminary Observations

Having discussed infinitival complement sentences characterized by subject-controlled forward Equi in section 2.3, we will in this section proceed to corresponding gerundive structures. The method of procedure here will closely approximate that of section 2.3. We will first go through a number of relevant verbs brought together by Visser, modifying Visser's classes as we go along. As a second step, we will rearrange the verbs left, plus some additional ones, into a classification that, it is hoped, brings out at least some interconnections that exist among the classes.

Gerundive complements call for some preliminary observations. Consider [14] and [15]:

[14] **a.** I like to dance.
    b. I hate to sing.

[15] **a.** I like dancing.
    b. I hate singing.

In [14a, b] the implied subject of the infinitive is necessarily the same as that of the higher verb, but in [15a, b] this need not be so. As Quirk et al. (1974: 742) note, [15a, b] are ambiguous. In their paraphrases, [15a] means either that '' 'I like it when I dance' '' or that '' 'I like it when people in general dance'.'' The former reading is produced when the *ing* clause (*dancing*) is derived as a *poss-ing* complement, the latter when it is derived as an action nominal. (For these terms, we have drawn on work by Lees (1963: 64 ff.), Rosenbaum (1967), Fraser (1970: 83 ff.) and Newmeyer (1970).) This difference is actually only one of several between the two constructions. To take another one, only *poss-ing* complements are compatible with nonprepositional direct objects, cf. [15a′] from Quirk et al. (1974: 742). (For a full treatment of the two types of constructions, cf. Wasow and Roeper (1972: 44 ff.). They call them "two kinds of gerunds.")

[15] a.′ I like dancing the tango.

[15a′] means, unambiguously, that " 'I like it when I dance the tango' " (Quirk et al. (1974: 742)). Since this chapter is concerned with Equi, action nominals will not be relevant.

It should be pointed out further that there are verbs that do not allow *poss-ing* complements without subject-controlled Equi (cf. [16] and [17]), and others that do (cf. [18]) (cf. Wasow (1979: 131)).

[16] a. Sue avoided meeting me.
    b. *Sue avoided Jack's meeting me.

[17] a. Sue resisted revealing her sources.
    b. *Sue resisted Jack's revealing her sources.

[18] a. Sue welcomed/disliked winning the prize.
    b. Sue welcomed/disliked Jack's winning the prize.

In [15a′], [16a] and [17a] the implied subject of the *poss-ing* complement is the same as that of the main clause. This seems true of most *poss-ing* complements occurring as S_2 in a sequence of the form of [19]:

[19] $[NP_1 \text{ Verb}_1 [\text{Verb}_2 ing \text{ } (NP_2 \text{ . . .})]_{S_2}]_{S_1}$

Apparently quite exceptional are verbs occurring as a Verb_1 in a string of the form of [19] that take *poss-ing* complements whose implied subjects are not identical with NP_1. (To what extent these are exceptional will become clearer when we discuss lists of verbs in 2.4.2.) *Advocate, authorize* and *sanction* may serve as examples of such verbs, cf. [20] (cf. Alexander and Kunz (1964: 53)).

[20] Jack advocated/authorized/sanctioned appointing Jones to the committee.

In spite of the fact that [20] undoubtedly contains a *poss-ing* complement clause as object and conforms to the form of [19], Equi is not involved since the implied subject of the subordinate clause in [20] is not necessarily or even primarily coreferential with the subject of the higher sentence. Of course, S_2 still has an implicit subject in [20]. If we take it to be PRO, we may say that in [20] PRO has arbitrary reference (cf. Chomsky (1981: 76)). Verbs such as *advocate* are interesting in their own right, and they raise the question of how arbitrary the reference of PRO is in [20]. However, this question and verbs such as *advocate* are outside the scope of the present treatment. To put it another way, the present treatment is restricted to constructions where PRO is controlled by NP_1.

Finally, given that PRO is controlled by NP_1, it is worth noting a point made by Alexander and Kunz (1964: 53). They observe a class of $Verb_1$s that are generally not acceptable with *poss-ing* complement sentences, but that are acceptable if $Verb_2$ is a member of a restricted class of verbs such as *have, be, want* and *need*. For instance, **He protested singing* may be contrasted with *He protested having to sing*. While the contrast is clear, *protest* is not compatible with all of *have, be, want* and *need*. (Indeed, many, perhaps most, speakers of British English do not accept the pattern of *protest* $Verb_2ing$ at all.) In our discussion of Visser's classes, we will set aside verbs such as *protest*, but we will come back to some of them at the end of 2.4.2.

2.4.2 Gathering Data: Visser's Classification

With the preliminary points of section 2.4.1 taken for granted, in this section a number of verbs will be discussed which, it may be suggested, govern subject-controlled forward gerundive Equi. As in section 2.3.1, Visser's classes will serve as the point of departure. (All references to Visser in this section will be to Visser (1973).) Of relevance here are the types of Visser's paragraphs 1772–1784, where, Visser suggests, there is no subordination of the first verb to the second. Visser's type *Fanny, dear, do you hear singing?* (paragraph 1785) is not an instance of an Equi structure and will therefore not be discussed here. The type of paragraph 1786 *What are we doing talking about our problems in front of them?* is perhaps most felicitously seen as a kind of a dislocation sentence (cf. Ross (1967: 232 ff.), cf. also Quirk et al. (1974: 632 ff.)). From this point of view the comma found in several of Visser's examples (also possible in the instance cited between *doing* and *talking*), and apparently indicating an intonational break, is highly significant. It supports the analysis of the type as a dislocation construction. Visser's type *He has somewhat to doing* (paragraph 1787, 1885) is not known in present-day English. Visser's type *Things that simply will not bear talking of* (paragraph 1788, 1886) does occur in present-day English with verbs such as *bear, need, require* and *want,* but is peculiar in that the lower clause necessarily corresponds to a passive. The discussion here will be limited to cases where a passive is not obligatory in the lower sentence for Equi to apply. Proceeding to types where, Visser (1888 ff.) suggests, there is slight subordination of the first verb to the second, we already (in section 2.1) referred to and in effect excluded from consideration Visser's (1906) type (d), verbs of motion, including *come,* as in *He came talking,* and Visser's (1912) type (e), verbs of rest, including *sit,* as in *He sat talking.* We will also omit from further consideration the three classes of verbs of aspect: Visser's (1888) types (a), verbs of inchoation, including *begin,* as in *He began talking,* (b), verbs of continuation, including *continue,* as in *He continued talking,* and (c), verbs of termination, including *cease,* as in *He ceased talking.* As noted in section 2.3.1, Equi derivations are problematic for verbs of aspect. Of course, we also exclude from consideration Visser's (1916) type (f), verbs of modality, including *seem,* as in

He seemed (to be) waiting, for, as argued in section 2.2, Equi derivations are out of the question for *seem.*

Visser's types will be called classes 1, 2, and so on. As in section 2.3.1, we will in general not adduce verbs that Visser suggests are no longer current, unless we disagree with a particular judgment.

Visser's first class (1863 ff.) is that of verbs of wishing (*covet, desire, entreat, sue, will* and *wish*), but as Visser is right in stating that none of the verbs of this group has survived into present-day English in this construction, this class can be skipped without further comment.

Visser's second class (1864 ff.) is that of verbs of liking and hating:

abhor	fancy	regret
abominate	grudge	relish
adore	hate	repent
bother	hie	resent
despise	lament	respect
detest	like	revere
disdain	loathe	sanction
dislike	love	scorn
distrust	mind	tire
enjoy	prefer	value

Of these, *hie* and *respect* should be dropped, for they are not current in present-day English (in this construction; this proviso should always be understood). Thus cf. *You do not respect spilling his blood,* to change Visser's example a little. *Repent* generally (cf. Visser: 1867) takes *of: repent of doing something* rather than ??*repent doing something.* We drop it as well. A number of the other verbs do not govern Equi. These are *despise, distrust, revere* and *sanction.* We may consider instances collected by Visser: for *despise, I despise boasting* (1748, Smollett, *The Adventures of Roderick Random*); for *distrust, the nurse looked up and said a little crabbily, for she distrusted studying: "Time to put the books away."* (1960, M. Dickens, *Angel in the Corner*); for *revere, he did revere becoming drunk and world-striding* (1927, Sinclair Lewis, *Elmer Gantry*); for *sanction, He had sanctioned flogging the prisoner,* modified from Visser. Visser has one instance of *tire, Back home women never tire asking that question* (1964, R. De Rouen, *The Heretic*), but, given that the following *ing* sentence is a complement, and not an adverbial, construction, *tire* takes *of,* as in never *tires* of reading the Bible (Webster's Third (1976)). Consequently, we drop the eight verbs from Visser's list. We add *begrudge* to it. *He did not begrudge spending so much money on his home* is possible and it is even preferred by some speakers to *He did not grudge spending so much money on his home,* modified from Visser.

Visser's (1868 ff.) third class is that of verbs expressing fear: *apprehend, dread, fear, funk, scruple.*

Visser has two instances of *apprehend,* both from around 1700, but the usage is clearly not current today, cf. **He does not apprehend going out at night.*

Scruple is at best marginal. Visser's most recent example is from 1823 (Lamb, *Essays of Elia*), *no simple Justice of the Peace seems to have scrupled issuing a warrant upon them.* Jespersen (1961: 195) remarks: "*Scruple to do*, hardly *doing.*" Reactions of native speakers to a sentence like *??He did not scruple stretching a point* are overwhelmingly negative. (Besides *He did not scruple to stretch a point*, noted in section 2.3, *He did not scruple at stretching a point* seems to be more possible.) On balance, we drop *scruple* as well.

Visser's (1869 ff.) fourth class is that of verbs denoting avoiding, delaying, missing, forbearing, postponing, refraining, refusing and kindred ideas:

abstain	excuse	postpone
avoid	fail	put off
bar	forbear	refuse
decline	forestall	reject
defer	hinder	renounce
delay	hold off	resist
deny	lose	shirk
disclaim	miss	shun
disdain	neglect	spare
escape	omit	suspend
eschew	overlook	tarry
evade		

Visser (1869 ff.) recognizes that nowadays *abstain* often occurs with *from*. We drop it. (Visser fails to document *abstain* without *from*.) We also drop *fail* (cf. Visser: 1871), *lose* and *tarry*, as not current. The same goes for *spare* and *suspend* as in **I will not spare writing to you* and *??The thought made me suspend speaking for a moment*, both modified from Visser. Visser has one instance each of *excuse* and *reject*, but they seem obsolete as well: "*I think I remember some lines; but you do not understand the Gaelic language.*"—"*And will readily excuse hearing it.*" (from 1816, Scott, *The Antiquary*), and *She rejected hearing the extent of your guilt* (1765, Walpole, *The Castle of Otranto*). *Refuse* is somewhat marginal. *He could not refuse to pardon her* is preferred to *He could not refuse pardoning her*, modified from Visser, but it may perhaps still be retained. On the other hand, *bar, forestall* and *hinder* are dropped, being non-Equi verbs, cf. Visser's quotation *The policeman had stationed himself close beside Mr. Privett as if to forestall lynching* (from 1959, Norman Collins, *Bond Street Story*). So, of Visser's 33 verbs only 22 remain.

Visser's (1874 ff.) fifth class is that of verbs expressing shamming, simulating, feigning: *ape, affect, feign, mime, pantomime.*

Affect to Verb$_2$ is generally preferred to *affect* Verb$_2$*ing*, as in *John affected to take no notice of complaints* and *??John affected taking no notice of complaints*. Nor does the insertion of *have* help, pace Alexander and Kunz (1964: 54): *??John affected having to take no notice of complaints*. We drop the verb. Reactions to *ape*, as in *?Old men should not ape being young*, modified from Visser, are not very positive, and it is only with considerable hesitation that the verb can be retained. On the other hand, we add *pretend* to the class without any hesitation.

Visser's (1875 ff.) sixth class is that of verbs expressing a mental activity:

anticipate	forget	recollect
consider	hope	remember
deprecate	imagine	suspect
despair	mind	understand
doubt	question	
expect	recall	

The sense of *mind* in question is that of 'remember', and this being largely obsolete, as recognized by Visser (1875), we drop *mind* from the present list. We also drop *doubt, hope* and *suspect*. Visser (1875 ff.) has one example of each: *Nor do we doubt being able to satisfy the most curious reader* (1742, Fielding, *Joseph Andrews*); *The binding caution is, never to hope Renewing of the time* (1629, Jonson, *The New Inn*); and *we do not suspect raising any great terror on this occasion* (1749, Fielding, *Tom Jones*). These run counter to present usage. *Expect* should be dropped as well, so strong is the preference today for *I expect to take some action soon* over ??*I expect taking action soon. Despair* prefers *of* Verb + *ing* to Verb + *ing: He despaired of ascending the throne* is better than ??*He despaired ascending the throne,* to modify an example from 2.3. Consequently, we drop *despair* as well. *Understand,* as in Visser's example (from 1947, W. S. Allen, *Living English Structure*), *I can't understand neglecting children like that,* seems to be a non-Equi verb. The same holds for *deprecate,* as in *He deprecated removing traders from the streets,* modified from Visser. Visser's list of 16 verbs is then reduced to 8.

Visser's (1876 ff.) seventh class is that of verbs of suffering, bearing, and tolerating, which are mostly preceded by *cannot* or *could not:*

abide	endure	stick
bear	face	stomach
brook	stand	tolerate

Stick is somewhat colloquial. *Brook* is not acceptable to all speakers in the pattern. (Visser's one example of *brook* from this century is from the *New Yorker*.) On balance, we are inclined to retain both.

Visser's (1878 ff.) eighth class is that of verbs such as *intend, plan, consider, purpose:*

cast	mean	purpose
consider	meditate	understand
contemplate	plan	ruminate
envisage	project	
intend	propose	

Of these, we drop *cast* and *understand:* **He cast/understood doing it/going there.* Additionally, we drop *purpose* (cf. Jespersen (1961: 199)), cf. ??*He* *purposed coming along. Ruminate,* as in ??*He ruminated taking action,* may be dropped as well. (*He ruminated on taking action* is possible.) *Project,* as in *He projected hiring a horse for her,* modified from Visser, is not current either. The constructions *mean doing something* and *plan doing something* are marginal for many speakers of English today. (They prefer *mean to do something* and *plan to do something* or *plan on doing something.*) However, the feeling is perhaps not quite universal enough for us to drop these two verbs.

To sum up, Visser's class of 13 is reduced to 8.

Visser's (1880 ff.) ninth class is that of verbs of trying, attempting, under-taking. Few such verbs occur with the gerund. For instance, *strive* and *endeavor* (Visser: 1880) do not. Visser only cites *attempt,* which he terms 'rare' in the pattern, and *try,* which is frequent in the pattern, but has the special meaning 'to make an attempt with', as opposed to its meaning with the infinitive ('to make an attempt at') (Jespersen (1961: 196 ff.)).

Visser's (1881) tenth class is that of verbs expressing risking, venturing: *adventure, hazard, risk, venture.* Of these, we drop *adventure* as obsolete, cf. Visser's solitary illustration *I am loth to move my lord unto offence; Yet I'll adventure chiding* (from 1623, John Ford, *Love's Sacrifice*).

Visser's (1881) eleventh class is that of *cannot/could not help* Verb + *ing.* Contrary to what may be inferred from Visser's presentation, *not* is not necessarily a part of this sequence, as in questions: *How can/could I help doing it* and *How can/could I not help doing it* are both possible.

Visser's (1882 ff.) twelfth class is that of verbs of admitting, confessing, swearing, mentioning, reporting:

acknowledge	discuss	profess
admit	forswear	propose
advocate	intimate	report
boast	mention	suggest
confess	own	

As Visser (1882) notes, *intimate* is obsolete in this pattern, and so we drop it. We also drop *boast,* which in present-day English more appropriately takes *of,* even in Visser's solitary illustration (from 1828, Scott, *Fair Maid of Perth, Chronicles of the Canongate*): *We boast being the Court end of the town. Profess* seems likewise obsolete, as in ??*Why should I believe you, since you professed deceiving others,* modified from Visser. We also drop *advocate,* and *suggest,* because these are non-Equi verbs, cf. *He suggested making an offer.*

Visser's (1883) thirteenth (and last relevant) class is that of verbs of the type of *practice,* as in *He practiced waltzing in a room over the Egyptian Hall.* (We will cite the more recent verbs only.)

attribute	involve	include
accomplish	do	describe
practice	imply	precipitate
learn	entail	organize

(We have cited the verbs in the order in which Visser provides them.)

Of these, we drop *do*, first of all, for taking the 'wrong' kind of gerund: **He did copying the article*, as opposed to *He did the copying of the article*. We also drop *involve, imply, entail, include, precipitate, organize*, because these are non-Equi verbs, cf., for example, *This might entail encountering the admiral* (1884, from 1956, London *Times*). On the analogy of *attribute* (as in *May I know to what accident I must attribute not having the honor of your hand?* (Visser: 1883, from 1778, Fanny Burney, *Evelina*)), *assign* may be added to the class. Thus this class is changed to: *assign, attribute, accomplish, practice, learn, describe*.

Having completed our discussion of Visser's classes, we may add a coda on Verb$_1$s such as *protest*. At the end of section 2.4.1 we observed the difference between sentences such as **John protested attending the meeting* and *John protested having to attend the meeting*. Alexander and Kunz (1964: 53) list 31 verbs that, they suggest, behave in the same way as *protest*. (They furnish about half of the verbs with a star, to indicate that they are hesitant about the acceptability of these verbs in the construction.) We decided at the end of section 2.4.1 to set aside such verbs in the present discussion. However, we may examine whether any of the verbs that Alexander and Kunz (1964: 54) list are among those that we accepted above. There are several such verbs. They are *describe, disclaim, escape, fear* and *resent*. These are all possible with *have*. However, pace Alexander and Kunz, they do not seem limited to taking *have* (or *be, want, need* (cf. Alexander and Kunz (1964: 53))) only. Above, we had an example of *describe*. We may add some illustrations of the other verbs: *He escaped drowning* (modified from Visser), *He did not fear wetting his feet* (Visser: 1869, from 1814, Scott, *Waverley*), *He disclaimed working for the company, He resented paying for lunch/He did not resent paying for lunch*. We may then retain the five verbs. Additionally, we may take note of *blame*. Alexander and Kunz (1964: 54) mark it as belonging to the same pattern as *protest*, but this does not seem to be well motivated. For instance, sentences such as *He blamed finishing last on poor equipment* are possible and PRO is understood to be coreferential with NP$_1$ in the sentence. Consequently, we consider *blame* relevant to our classification.

2.4.3 An Alternative Classification

We will now present our own classification of the verbs found in section 2.4.2 to occur in the gerundive pattern in present-day English. As in section 2.3.2, the main consideration motivating the analysis is the desire to better bring out the interconnections among the various verb classes.

(1) Verb$_1$ means that NP$_1$ considers or anticipates the realization of S$_2$.
(1.1) Verb$_1$ has the rough meaning of 'contemplate': *consider, contemplate, imagine, meditate*.

(1.2) $Verb_1$ has the rough meaning 'anticipate the occurrence of': *anticipate, envisage, foresee.*
(2) $Verb_1$ expresses volition with respect to S_2.
(2.1) The attitude of NP_1 is positive with respect to S_2.
(2.1.1) $Verb_1$ expresses a degree of volition, desideration on the part of NP_1 for the realization of S_2:

adore	like	relish
enjoy	love	value
fancy	prefer	

(2.1.2) $Verb_1$ expresses volition (desideration) and intention on the part of NP_1 for the realization of S_2:

intend	plan	propose
mean		

(2.1.3) $Verb_1$ expresses volition (desideration), intention and endeavor on the part of NP_1 for the realization of S_2:

accomplish	learn	try
attempt	practice	venture
hazard	risk	

(2.2) The attitude of NP_1 is negative with respect to the realization of S_2.
(2.2.1) $Verb_1$ expresses a degree of negative volition, negative desideration against the realization of S_2:

abhor	dread	loathe
abominate	fear	mind
begrudge	funk	regret
detest	grudge	resent
dislike	hate	

$Verb_1$ additionally expresses communication: *lament.*
(2.2.2) $Verb_1$ expresses negative volition (desideration) and negative intention against the realization of S_2:

defer	hold off	put off
delay	neglect	scorn
disdain	omit	
forbear	postpone	

$Verb_1$ additionally implies that NP_1 communicates his negative volition (desideration) and his negative intention:

decline	refuse	renounce
question		

Negative volition is generally expressed by *cannot/could not:*

abide	endure	stomach
afford	face	tolerate
bear	help	trouble
bother	stand	
brook	stick	

(2.2.3) Verb$_1$ expresses negative volition (desideration), negative intention and negative endeavor against the realization of S$_2$:

avoid	evade	shun
escape	resist	
eschew	shirk	

(2.3) Others: *miss, overlook.*
(3) Verb$_1$ expresses communication.
(3.1) Verb$_1$ is concessive: *acknowledge, admit, confess, own.*
(3.2) Verb$_1$ contains a negative element: *deny, disclaim.*
(3.3) Other cases: *describe, discuss, forswear, mention, report.*
(4) Other cases.
(4.1) Verb$_1$ has the rough meaning '(not) to have the memory of': *recall, recollect, remember, forget.*
(4.2) Verb$_1$ has the rough meaning 'attribute': *assign, attribute, blame.*
(4.3) Verb$_1$ has the rough meaning 'pretend': *ape, feign, mime, pantomime, pretend.* ·

The classification consists of four main classes, of which the fourth is rather heterogeneous, failing to capture any significant generalization. As for the others, the verbs of class 3 primarily express communication. There are some verbs expressing communication in 2.2.1 and 2.2.2, but the latter imply negative volition toward S$_2$. Several of the verbs of class 3 carry extra meanings in addition to communication, as well. It is noteworthy that verbs of communication lacking a concessive or a negative element (*allege, assert, claim, maintain,* etc.) are generally incompatible with gerunds: ??*He alleged having done it.*

In a sense class 2.3 is the counterpart of class 1.3 of the infinitival pattern. Verbs of this class express an intention to realize S$_2$, but also an unintentional failure to realize the intention. (For a reason that is not clear to us, we have not found a verb that would express an intention and then an unintentional realization of the intention.) For instance, *He missed meeting her by ten minutes* means that he had the volition and the intention of meeting her, but that he unintentionally failed to meet her. *Overlook* has been glossed as 'to pass over without notice (intentionally or unintentionally)' (OED: sense 2), but the sense of unintentional nonrealization seems to predominate, as in *He overlooked saluting a Lieutenant,* modified from Visser (1973: 1873). Consequently, we include *overlook* in class 2.3 only, and not in 2.2.2.

The major classes of verbs of class 2, carrying the basic meanings of 'want'/'wish' (2.1) and 'not want'/'not wish' (2.2), are organized in essentially the same way as the corresponding verbs of section 2.3.2. It is of interest to compare the numbers of verbs in the three categories of the two volitional patterns:

	NUMBER OF VERBS WITH THE INFINITIVAL PATTERN	NUMBER OF VERBS WITH THE GERUNDIVE PATTERN
positive desideration	27	8
positive desideration and intention (no communication)	21	4
positive desideration, intention and endeavor	29	8
negative desideration	12	15
negative desideration and intention (no communication)	7	10
negative desideration, intention and endeavor	0	7

Equally significant is the incidence of verbs of volition that additionally express communication:

	NUMBER OF VERBS WITH THE INFINITIVAL PATTERN	NUMBER OF VERBS WITH THE GERUNDIVE PATTERN
positive desideration, intention and communication	10 + 9 = 19	0
negative desideration and communication	0	1
negative desideration, intention and communication	2	4

Due allowance should be made for the fact that the lists of verbs presented are not exhaustive. Further, some isolated verbs may present difficulties of classification. Even so, provided that our classification is even approximately adequate, the figures that emerge are suggestive. They indicate that in each category of positive volition verbs governing infinitival complements predominate, whereas in each category of negative volition gerundive complements predominate. Of course, further research, including corpus-based research, is needed to test the validity of the generalization that the figures presented suggest.

Finally, it is of interest to consider the extent to which *ing* complements are implicative. It seems that, like infinitival complements, gerundive complements are also overwhelmingly nonimplicative. The verbs of class 1 are non-implicative, as are those of 2.1.1. *Enjoy* perhaps 'feels' more implicative than the others, but even this verb is nonimplicative: *He didn't enjoy doing it, but he did it* is clearly not a contradiction. The verbs of 2.1.2 are also nonimplicative in their entirety. Of the verbs of 2.1.3 *accomplish, hazard, risk, try*.and *venture* seem implicative, because, for example, *??He didn't venture doing it, but he did it* is distinctly odd. (Notably, *try to* was argued to be nonimplicative while *try - ing* is here being argued to be implicative. For instance, cf. *Did he try to sleep/sleeping on the floor? Yes.* The *ing* form implies that he did sleep on the floor, while the infinitive does not.) The rest (*attempt, learn, practice*) are nonimplicative. The majority of the large class of 2.2.1 are neither implicative nor negative implicative. For instance, *He did not fear doing it* implies neither that he did do it nor that he did not do it. Of this class, *begrudge, grudge, lament, regret* and *resent* seem implicative, that is 5 out of 15. Of the verbs of 2.2.2, *forbear, neglect* and *omit* are negative implicative. For instance, *He omitted doing it* implies that he did not do it. (Note that?? *He didn't omit doing it, but he did not do it* is a contradiction.) The verbs of 2.2.2 expressing verbal communication are nonimplicative.

Of the verbs of 2.2.3, *avoid, eschew, escape* and *evade* seem negative implicative, the remaining three nonimplicative. The verbs of class 2.3 are negative implicative. The verbs of class 3 are all nonimplicative, as are those of the *remember* class: *I don't remember doing it but I have done it* does not seem to be a contradiction. By contrast, an analogous pattern with the infinitive ordinarily (cf. Karttunen (1971: 342)) does give rise to a contradiction: *??I didn't remember to do it but I did it* (a contradiction) and *I didn't remember doing it but I did it* (not a contradiction). (The difference in the meaning of *remember* was discussed in section 2.3.1.) The verbs of the small *attribute* class seem implicative; those of the *pretend* class are outside the discussion (cf. Karttunen (1970: 337)).

We may summarize the incidence of implicative verbs in the central classes of volitional verbs in the form of a table. In the table we lump positive implicative and negative implicative verbs together, distinguishing them from nonimplicative verbs. We ignore verbs generally constructed with *cannot/could not*.

	NUMBER OF IMPLICATIVE VERBS/NUMBER OF VERBS IN THE INFINITIVE PATTERN	NUMBER OF IMPLICATIVE VERBS/NUMBER OF VERBS IN THE GERUNDIVE PATTERN
positive desideration	0/27	0/8
positive desideration and intention	3/40 = 8%	0/4

positive desideration, intention and endeavor	4/29 = 14%	5/8 = 63%
negative desideration	0/7	5/15 = 33%
negative desideration and intention	5/9 = 56%	3/14 = 21%
negative desideration, intention and endeavor	0/0	4/7 = 57%

Quite generally, verbs expressing communication are neither implicative nor negative implicative. The table above includes them, but it may be of interest to add a table that excludes them.

	NUMBER OF IMPLICATIVE VERBS/NUMBER OF VERBS IN THE INFINITIVE PATTERN, VERBS EXPRESSING COMMUNICATION EXCLUDED	NUMBER OF IMPLICATIVE VERBS/NUMBER OF VERBS IN THE GERUNDIVE PATTERN, VERBS EXPRESSING COMMUNICATION EXCLUDED
positive desideration	0/27	0/8
positive desideration and intention	3/21 = 14%	0/4
positive desideration, intention and endeavor	4/29 = 14%	5/8 = 63%
negative desideration	0/7	4/14 = 29%
negative desideration and intention	5/7 = 71%	3/10 = 30%
negative desideration, intention and endeavor	0/0	4/7 = 57%

Due allowance should be made for some problems of classification. Even so, the tables given suggest a number of conclusions. In several respects, the pattern discerned in section 2.3.3 is confirmed by verbs taking gerunds. Overall, the number of implicative verbs is not very large. It is notable that the classes where they form a majority are small, with fewer than ten verbs each. Care should be exercised when such small classes are evaluated. In none of the larger classes do they form a majority. We may be a little more specific and recall that not a single implicative verb expressing only positive desideration was found in the infinitival pattern. This finding is reciprocated in the gerundive pattern. The incidence of implicative verbs tends to rise as we proceed from the class of verbs of desideration, the class of the lowest degree of volition, to verbs of desideration and intention and to those of desideration, intention and endeavor. There is a tendency for the largest incidence of implicative verbs to occur in the class of verbs of desideration, intention and endeavor. The tendency is more pronounced in the gerundive patterns of positive verbs. It is not shared by the infinitival halves to the same extent. Indeed, the number of implicative verbs of positive desideration and intention was found to be about the same as the number of implicative verbs of positive desideration, intention and endeavor in the infinitival pattern. Also, a number of implicative verbs of negative desideration were found in the gerundive pattern. Even so, the numbers of implicative verbs were found to be rather small. As for verbs of negative desideration and intention and those of negative desideration, intention and endeavor of the infinitival pattern, a comparison is not possible on the basis of the present discussion, since the latter class is empty. We may nevertheless hazard the suggestion that if such verbs are found in a larger survey, a fair number of them may turn out to be implicative or negative implicative, but this remains a speculation.

Beyond volitional verbs, class 1 of gerundive verbs fits into the general pattern. Its verbs express deliberation with respect to the realization of S_2. On commonsense grounds it is not to be expected that deliberation alone is sufficient to ensure that the realization of S_2 is viewed as taken for granted. It is no surprise, then, that the verbs of class 1 of gerundive verbs are nonimplicative.

2.5 CASE GRAMMAR AND SUBJECT-CONTROLLED FORWARD EQUI

2.5.1 Introduction

This section is an attempt to examine the two subject-controlled Equi patterns with tools of analysis provided by case grammar. First, an attempt will be made to identify the case roles that are possible for NP_1 and NP_2. Second, provided that the choice of roles for NP_1 and NP_2 turns out to be interdependent, an effort will be made to investigate the nature of the interdependency. In a wider sense, the section is a test for the classifications provided in 2.3 and 2.4 in that the coherence of the classes that were established will be either confirmed or called into question.

In the present context, case roles are understood to mean semantic case roles or case relations. Thus a framework of description is presupposed where the verb of a sentence imposes an array of case roles on the noun phrases of the sentence. Such case roles may be divided into inner and outer. The division depends on the closeness of the noun phrase in question to the verb of the sentence. Informally, an inner case role requires a close relation, while an outer case role does not. Outer case roles have been argued to include Time, Purpose and Manner (Cook (1979: 44 ff.)). For example, the time expression *last night* has an outer case role in *He attended a concert last night*. There do exist verbs—though not very many—that have, or may have, a closer relation to time expressions. These include *last* and *take*, as in *The concert lasted/took two hours,* where *two hours* bears an inner case role. This is, however, exceptional for Time, Purpose and Manner. In the present context the focus of attention will be on inner case roles.

2.5.2 On Case Roles

The history of case grammar would be a topic for a monograph, but it cannot be attempted here. The framework goes back to Fillmore (1968) and to earlier work by Gruber. It remains associated with Fillmore's name. In the present context, Fillmore's work will be made use of. In addition, ideas and proposals by Cook, Gruber and Chafe, among others, turn out to be useful.

There are at least two major unresolved questions in case grammar (cf. Fillmore (1977: 70 ff.) and Starosta (1978)). First, what is the number of cases, and second, can there be more than one instance of a case in a simple sentence? Any work on case grammar is guided by answers to these two questions. Regarding the second question, it will be assumed here that there can be only one instance of a given case in a simple sentence, except for the Object case (Cook (1979: 203)).

Regarding the first question, we should bear in mind that NP_1 of the pattern under consideration is virtually always +Human. (The few exceptions, such as are subjects of *serve, contribute* etc., will be ignored.) It is therefore possible to limit the discussion here to a subset of potential case relations. Of relevance seem to be the cases of the Agent, the Experiencer, the Benefactive and the Object. We will first seek to define these case relations.

Definitions of the Agent have been symptomatic of the volatility of terminology and classificatory approaches within case grammar. We will draw on work by a number of scholars, seeking to arrive at a definition as explicit as possible. Delimiting the discussion to the subject position, we suggest that Cruse (1973) offers a useful summary of previous research and a helpful point of departure for present purposes. He makes the general methodological point that a semantic feature should be postulated only if it is "intuitively convincing," "detectable contextually," including syntactically, and if it has "some explanatory value." We consider these assumptions sound and will accept them.

Regarding the Agent, Cruse (1973) distinguishes definitions based on the referential properties of the subject NP from those that are more strictly or more narrowly linguistic. An example of the former is Fillmore's (1968: 24) definition of the Agentive as "the case of the typically animate perceived instigator of the action identified by the verb." That is, in [21a] *John* is an Agent, or an Agentive—the two terms will be used interchangeably—but not normally in [21b]. ([21a] is from Fillmore (1968: 25).)

[21] **a.** John opened the door.
 b. John died yesterday.

A grammatical method is to apply tests of compatibility. Chafe (1975: 100) and Cruse (1973: 14 ff.), apparently independently of each other, refer to the *do something* vs. *happen to* test. Thus pseudocleft sentences and question-and-answer pairs (on question-and-answer pairs, cf. Anderson (1976: 42)) differentiate the *open* and *die* sentences of [21a] and [21b] as follows:

[22] a. What John did was open the door.
   b. Q. What did John do? A. He opened the door.
   c. *What happened to John was he opened the door.
   d. Q. What happened to John? A. *He opened the door.

[23] a. ??What John did was die yesterday.
   b. Q. What did John do yesterday? A. ??He died yesterday.
   c. What happened to John was he died yesterday.
   d. Q. What happened to John? A. He died yesterday.

Cruse (1973: 18) suggests, plausibly, that all Agents take the *do*, not the *happen to* paraphrase, but that the converse is not true. That is, not all verbs that take the *do* paraphrase in preference to *happen to* take Agents. To cite one of Cruse's (1973: 16) examples, *the bullet* of *The bullet smashed John's collar-bone* is not a very satisfactory, or intuitively convincing Agent, even though *What the bullet did was smash John's collar-bone* is no doubt preferred to ?*What happened to the bullet was that it smashed John's collar-bone.* Therefore, verbs taking Agents are a subset of those taking the *do* paraphrase.

Another criterion of agentivity is the permissibility of the progressive, a test suggested by Gruber (1976: 160 ff.). For instance, he contrasts *John is being witty* with **John is being intelligent,* where the former has an agentive sense. However, the usefulness of this criterion is limited in that while all agentives can occur in the progressive, it is not true that all verbs that can be turned into the progressive have agentive subjects. For instance, in *John is inheriting his father's money,* the verb is in the *ing* form, but the subject is not an Agent. It can perhaps be objected that in the sentence the *ing* form does not express anything in progress, but rather futurity. The objection does not carry over to sentences such as [21b], which allows *John is dying (slowly),* where *John* is not an Agent.

A further criterion that has been suggested by Gruber (1967: 943), (1976: 161) as relevant to agentivity is the permissibility of purpose adverbials, such as *so that, in order to* clauses. Gruber (1976: 161) cites contrasts such as that in [24a, b]:

[24] a. John remained in the room in order to see who would arrive.
   b. *John inherited the money in order to get rich.

Cruse (1973: 18 ff.) argues that the admissibility of a purpose adverbial is a test of volitivity rather than of agentivity. Volitivity is present, according to him (1973: 18), "when an act of will is stated or implied." He then goes on to argue against volitivity being a necessary part of agentivity. Thus he (1973: 21) suggests that *the fire* is an Agent in *The fire spread (itself) rapidly.* The referent of *the fire* obviously does not have volitivity, and therefore a purpose adverbial is excluded, as in [25]:

[25] *The fire spread (itself) rapidly in order to destroy the building.

It is of interest to recall Cruse's first general criterion, cited above, that a semantic feature should be "intuitively convincing." It is a matter of judgment whether the claim that *the fire* in Cruse's sentence is an Agent is intuitively satisfactory or convincing. The claim is a departure from definitions of the Agent that assume that the NP in question must be +Animate or at least be perceived as +Animate. If agentivity is interpreted in this latter way, the notion of volitivity is relevant, as is the permissibility of purpose adverbials.

A further criterion, suggested by Gruber (1967: 943), is the admissibility of manner adverbials such as *carefully*. In support, Gruber cites the contrast between *John looked through the glass carefully* and **John saw through the glass carefully*, where the subject of *look* is an Agent and that of *see* is not. The criterion also distinguishes *John opened the door carefully* from **John died carefully yesterday*, **John inherited the money carefully* and **The fire spread through the building carefully*.

It is unclear what other manner adverbials, if any, Gruber may have had in mind, apart from *carefully*. He speaks of "such manner adverbials which go with agentives," but cites only *carefully*.

The definition of the Agent accepted here is close to that of Fillmore (1968); cf. also Ross (1972: 106). We accept the tests of agentivity as necessary conditions. The verb of a sentence with an Agent admits of a *do* paraphrase, may be used in the progressive, may be followed by a purpose adverbial and can co-occur with *carefully*. Further, we accept Fillmore's (1968: 24) original specification that an Agent is the "typically animate perceived instigator of the action identified by the verb." Expanding on the notion of 'instigator', we take it to imply intentionality. This excludes all inanimate NPs and even many +Human NPs.

A slightly different view of the Agent has been put forward by Langacker (1975: 366) and Cook. To explicate the difference, we may consider [26a–d], discussed in Cook's class lectures (summer 1985), on which our exposition of Cook's view is based:

[26] **a.** The salt water will heal them.
   b. He swam from the end of the dock to the shore.
   c. A small bird came toward the skiff from the North.
   d. Tom fell off the chair.

Cook regards the subjects of sentences [26a, b] as Agents, those of [26c, d] as non-Agents. These judgments reflect ours as well, except for the one concerning [26a]. Cook's approach may be possible and even fruitful (on its application, cf. Cook (1979: 172 ff.)), but in our analysis we distinguish [26b] and [26d] by making use of the notion of intentionality. For us, the presence of intentionality makes the subject of [26b] an Agent while the absence of intentionality makes the subject of [26d] an Object. Since we thus use intentionality as a criterion of agentivity, we cannot consider *the salt water* of [26a] an Agent. The difference is worth noting, but it does not seem to make it impossible for us to adopt other aspects of Cook's framework. More briefly, our approach also differs from Anderson's analysis, which makes use of erg, where a subset of erg are Agents, cf. Anderson (1977: 115 ff.).

While definitions of the Agent vary among case grammarians, most of them, though not all, employ the term. Regarding other cases, there is less uniformity of terminological practice. A survey of different approaches cannot be attempted here. Above, we noted that our conception of the Agent was not quite the same as Cook's. The difference should be recognized, but it does not seem to affect the usefulness in the present context of the conceptions of the Experiencer, Benefactive and Object cases that Cook (1979: 52 ff.) proposes. In the following, we shall in the main adopt his analysis of these three case roles. We can take into account that NP_1 of the pattern under consideration is +Human, apart from very isolated verbs. (These will be ignored here.) This limits and governs the relevance of cases in the present context.

The Experiencer specifies "the undergoer of a psychological event of sensation, emotion, or cognition" (Cook (1979: 52)) and also that of communication (Cook (1979: 202)). With verbs taking an Experiencer, that is, with experiential verbs, the Object is the case specifying the content of, or the stimulus for, the experience (Cook (1979: 52)). Thus, *I* of [27a] is an Experiencer. So is *me* of [27b], while *it* of [27a, b] is an Object:

[27] **a.** I doubt it.
  b. It interests me.

For Cook (1979: 102), the Benefactive specifies "the one in the state of possession, or the one who undergoes gain or loss in the transfer of property." With verbs taking a Benefactive, the Object "specifies the thing possessed or the thing transferred" (Cook (1979: 102)). Thus, *to me* of [28a] and *I* of [28b, c] are instances of the Benefactive, while *this car* of [28a, b] and *a game of tennis* of [28c] are instances of the Object:

[28] **a.** This car belongs to me.
  b. I own this car.
  c. I lost a game of tennis yesterday.

The Object may also occur with an Agent, as in *Mother is cooking the potatoes* (cf. Cook (1979: 92)), or alone. If alone, it specifies the object that is in a state expressed by a state verb or the object that undergoes a change of state. In the former case, the object is given the subscript *s* (from state), in the latter case there is no subscript. Thus, *John* of [29a] is represented as O_s, *John* of [29b] as a *plain O*. (We thank Cook (personal communication) for pointing out the distinction to us.)

[29] a. John is tall.

    b. John died unexpectedly.

The class of verbs that take a +Human subject that is not an O_s, but a plain O, is apparently not very large. Apart from *die*, the verbs *grow, shiver, shudder, sleep, sneeze* and *yawn* may be culled from Cook's (1979: 208 ff.) list.

By way of a summary and for the sake of explicitness, it may be advisable to cite instances of each case relation discussed in the form of a list. The focus of attention is on noun phrases that have the syntactic function of a subject. Thus, the *John*s of [30]–[33] are all subjects. The *John*s of [30a–c] are Agents, those of [31a–c] are Experiencers, those of [32a, b] are Benefactives and those of [33a, b] are Objects, that of [33a] being an O_s:

[30] a. John wrote a letter to a friend.

    b. John expressed an incautious opinion.

    c. John talked me into the business.

[31] a. John knows the answer.

    b. John disliked the idea intensely.

    c. John experienced a new sensation.

[32] a. John received a letter from a friend in the morning.

    b. John owns two cars.

[33] a. John is tall.

    b. John died unexpectedly.

It is apparent from this list that, while predicates with Agents always allow a *do* paraphrase, not all predicates taking non-Agent subjects allow a *happen to* paraphrase. For some discussion, cf. Anderson (1976: 42).

2.5.3 Case Grammar Applied to the *to* Pattern

Taking the cases discussed and illustrated above for granted, it is possible to consider the case roles of NP_1 and NP_2 in the subject-controlled Equi pattern. For presentational convenience, and in order to avoid repetition, we shall first proceed inductively and then deductively. We will start by discussing verbs of positive volition and classes 2.1, 2.2 and 2.3 of the *to* pattern. On the basis of this discussion, we shall seek to arrive at conclusions in 2.5.4. We will then test these conclusions in 2.5.5, using other verbs of sections 2.3 and 2.4 as data. These are other verbs of volition of the *to* pattern, especially verbs of negative volition, and verbs of the *ing* pattern, especially verbs of positive or negative volition.

When verbs of positive volition of the infinitival pattern are considered, it seems clear that not every subdivision need be taken into account. For instance, verbs of classes 1.1.1.1, meaning 'to want or wish', and those of 1.1.1.2, meaning 'to want or wish intensely or impatiently', clearly impose the same case frames on their NPs. We shall therefore base the discussion here on the major divisions of the classification.

Class 1: Verb$_1$ means 'to want or wish' or 'to want or wish intensely or impatiently'. With a verb of this class as Verb$_1$, NP$_1$ cannot be an Agent, because of the inadmissibility of question-and-answer pairs such as the following:

> Q. What did John do?
> A. ??He wanted to write a letter to a friend.

More appropriately, NP$_1$ designates a person that experiences a sensation, and may therefore be considered an Experiencer. NP$_2$ may be an Agent, as in *John desired/wanted/wished to write a letter,* an Experiencer, as in *John desired/wanted/wished to know the answer,* a Benefactive, as in *John desired/wanted/wished to receive a letter,* an Object, as in *John desired/wanted/wished to grow old,* or an Object$_s$, as in *John desired/wanted/wished to be tall when grown up.* (In *know the answer, know* is to be interpreted as 'be aware of', not as 'become aware of' or 'learn'. This interpretation should be understood throughout the discussion when *know* is used.)

Class 2: Verb$_1$ expresses intention or decision on the part of NP$_1$ to realize S$_2$. This class includes such verbs as *choose, decide, intend, mean, plan, purpose* and *think.* Because of the element of intention or decision in Verb$_1$, NP$_1$ is agentive. The following question-and-answer sequence seems possible:

> Q. What did John do?
> A. He ?intended/decided to write a letter to a friend.

In the question-and-answer sequence *decide* is better than *intend,* indicating that it is more agentive than *intend.* We will, however, assign the Agent role to both.

Walter Cook (personal communication) has suggested that NP$_1$ may be an Experiencer in addition to being an Agent with verbs of this class. (For the concept of coreferential roles, see Cook (1979: 94, 163).) Cook's suggestion is plausible and helpful. NP$_1$ may be viewed as an Experiencer, experiencing the sensation, or perhaps the cognition, that he intends to do something. NP$_2$ of the pattern may be an Agent, as in the example cited. It is less possible for NP$_2$ to be an Experiencer, as in *John ?intended/??decided to know the answer,* or a Benefactive, as in *John ?intended/??decided to receive a letter from a friend,* an Object, as in *John ?intended/??decided to grow old slowly,* or an Object$_s$, as in *John ?intended/??decided to be tall when grown up.*

Class 3: Verb$_1$ expresses communication in addition to intention and decision. That is, NP$_1$ communicates his intention and decision to realize S$_2$. This class includes verbs such as *offer, pledge, promise, undertake, vow.* The element of communication implies agentivity on the part of NP$_1$.

Q. What did John do?

A. He undertook/vowed to write a letter to a friend.

As regards NP$_2$, cases other than the Agent are doubtful, or downright impossible, cf. *John undertook/vowed* ??*to know the answer/*to receive a letter from a friend/?to own two cars/*??to grow old/*to be tall when grown up.*

Class 4: Verb$_1$ expresses endeavor in addition to intention on the part of NP$_1$. This class includes verbs such as *endeavor, seek, strive.* NP$_1$ is clearly an Agent.

Q. What did John do?

A. In spite of adverse circumstances he endeavored/sought to write a letter to a friend.

NP$_2$ can be neither an Experiencer nor a Benefactive nor an Object, cf. *John endeavored *to know the answer/*to receive a letter from a friend/??to grow old/*to be tall when grown up.*

Even when NP$_2$ is necessarily +Human, it does not always necessarily express volition on the part of NP$_1$. Three such classes were isolated above. Verb$_1$ may have the rough meaning of either 'pretend' (*feign, pretend*), or 'assert' (*claim, profess*), or 'anticipate the occurrence of' (*expect*). With the first two classes NP$_1$ is clearly an Agent.

Q. What did John do?

A. He pretended/claimed to be writing a letter.

Indeed, these two classes may be related in that *feign* and *pretend* express, or may express, nonverbal pretending, while *claim* necessarily implies pretending by verbal communication. As regards NP$_2$ with these classes, an Agent is possible, as in the example cited, but so is an Experiencer, as in *John pretended/claimed to know the answer,* a Benefactive, as in *John pretended/claimed to have received a letter from a friend,* and an Object, as in *John pretended/claimed to have grown old/to be tall.*

With *expect,* NP$_1$ seems to be an Experiencer rather than an Agent, as witness the oddity of **John expected carefully to write a letter in order to receive an answer.*

As regards possible case roles for NP$_2$, all four roles seem quite admissible, as in *John expected to write a letter* (Agent), *John expected to know the answer* (Experiencer), *John expected to receive a letter from a friend* (Benefactive), and *John expected to grow old/to be tall when grown up* (Object).

2.5.4 Conclusions

Above we discussed case roles of NP$_1$ and NP$_2$ with positive verbs of the infinitival pattern, drawing on the classification in 2.3.2. Due allowance should be made for a degree of idiolectal variation and problems of classification, and consequently, care should be exercised when drawing conclusions from the discussion. It is clear, however, that there is no restriction in English to the effect that the case roles of NP_1 and NP_2 must be identical. This is shown by class 1 of 2.5.3 and the *pretend/claim/expect* classes, where the case roles of NP_1 and NP_2 may be different without any trace of illformedness.

While no identity of the case roles of NP_1 and NP_2 can be postulated, it is also clear that the choice of case roles is not free. The case role of NP_2, empty as PRO, is selected by the predicate of its clause, but the selection is affected and constrained by the nature of the higher verb, and, by extension, of the case role of NP_1. It is perhaps possible to be a little more specific regarding the influence that $Verb_1$ exerts on the choice of NP_2. It was suggested above that verbs occurring as $Verb_1$ characteristically express positive volition on the part of NP_1. The discussion here suggests that where a $Verb_1$ is of this kind, and when its subject, NP_1, is an Agent, NP_2 should be an Agent as well. We will call this requirement the AGENT RULE. We rephrase it as follows:

The Agent Rule, first version: An agentive NP_1 governed by a verb of positive volition requires an agentive NP_2.

So far, the Agent Rule has been discussed and motivated on the basis of verbs expressing positive volition in the subject-controlled infinitival Equi pattern. We will see as we proceed that it has greater generality. Early illustrations of effects of the Agent Rule are provided by classes 2–4 above. In them, NP_1 is an Agent and roles other than that of the Agent seem doubtful for NP_2, at least up to a point. The Agent Rule is not relevant to class 1 of 2.5.3. An NP_1 governed by a $Verb_1$ of that class is not an Agent, but an Experiencer only. Under such conditions, the choice of NP_2 is not limited by NP_1, for NP_2 may be either an Agent, an Experiencer, a Benefactive or an Object. Also, when $Verb_1$ does not express volition, NP_2 may again be any one of the four cases (*claim, pretend, expect*). It is perhaps helpful to sum up the conclusions reached in the form of a table:

		ROLES OF NP_2
$Verb_1$ is +volition	NP_1 is −Agent, +Experiencer	A, E, B, O
	NP_1 is +Agent, −Experiencer	A, *E, *B, *O
$Verb_1$ is −volition	NP_1 is −Agent, +Experiencer	A, E, B, O
	NP_1 is +Agent, −Experiencer	A, E, B, O

The second line of the table is the Agent Rule.

A caveat of a general nature should be made. In the discussion above it has been assumed in a rather cavalier fashion that relatively hard-and-fast decisions can be made with respect to case roles assigned to subjects of predicates. This is an oversimplification and an idealization. The four case roles should be thought of as points delimiting a space where predicates are located. Not every predicate is equidistant from the point nearest to it. They may differ with respect to the degree to which they impose roles on their subjects. While this is hard to formalize, the concept of a cline or of a graded series suggests itself. To take a question-mark-versus-star example like the ones above, we may consider the verbs *own*, as in *own two cars*, and *receive*, as in *receive a letter from a friend*. The sense of *own* is that of 'possess'. For an account of the meaning of *receive*, we may profitably quote the Webster's Third (1976) discussion of the verb: "although *receive* can sometimes suggest a positive welcoming or recognition ⟨*receive* the group with open arms⟩ ⟨the work has been *received* with enthusiasm—*Current Biog.*⟩ it usu. implies that something comes or is allowed to come into one's presence, possession, group, consciousness, or substance while one is passive. . . ." Care should be taken to distinguish the two main senses of *receive* indicated in the quotation. In *receive the group with open arms* and in *receive a visitor cordially, receive* has the approximate sense of 'welcome' and takes an Agent as its subject. This sense of *receive,* along with similar senses, should be set aside in the present context and elsewhere in this book, where *receive* is used to illustrate verbs taking a Benefactive and not taking an Agent. The sense of *receive* that is relevant in *receive a letter from a friend* and elsewhere where *receive* is used to illustrate verbs taking a Benefactive but not taking an Agent is the sense of the second part of the quotation. If we simplify it somewhat, we may perhaps say that the sense of *receive* in question is that of 'get while one is passive'.

The subjects of *own* (*two cars*) and *receive* (*a letter from a friend*) were classified as Benefactives. This remains true, but it must be added that the subject of the former is less purely a Benefactive. There is a very slight suggestion of agentivity involved in *owning*. The suggestion is very slight, but still perceptible. By contrast, it is hard to see any agentivity at all in *receiving* (*a letter from a friend*). (*Receiving a visitor cordially* is quite different.) Thus note that *own* in the following is slightly better than *receive: John endeavored ??to own two cars/*to receive a letter from a friend.*

Regarding the case role of O, as opposed to O_s, it may be that, as observed in 2.5.2, the class of verbs taking as a subject a pure O that is +Human is not very large. We have used *grow*, as in *grow old*, in the examples above and it seems to take an O in subject position. Some of the other verbs cited by Cook (1979: 208 ff.), such as *sleep*, may take a less pure O in that there may be present an agentive tinge. The tinge has an effect on the acceptability of the sentence in the Equi pattern. Thus, e.g., *John endeavored/tried to sleep* is not very bad, and is better than *John endeavored/tried to grow old.* The *sleep* sentence does not undermine the analysis, though. The reason is that in the sentence *sleep* is interpreted, or reinterpreted, agentively. Some other normally nonagentive verbs of bodily function are still easier to interpret agentively and are so interpreted even independently of the Equi pattern. Thus *cough* may take an Agent, as in

John coughed politely. (Given that an Object is always present (Cook 1979: 206), *John* is then both an Agent and an Object.) It is no surprise, then, that the corresponding Equi sentence with a verb of the endeavor class as Verb$_1$ is well formed, as in *John endeavored/tried to cough politely.* The concept of intentionality, referred to in connection with the definition of the Agent above, seems to be relevant when the reinterpretation is made.

Provision should then be made for the concept of reinterpretation. The concept does not render nugatory a case-grammar analysis of the predicates concerned. The opposite is true. The reason is that a reinterpretation presupposes an initial interpretation without a reinterpretation and both in the first place presuppose a framework of case grammar. For instance, only case grammar provides an account of the fact that, while *John* of *John coughed* may be either an Object or an Agent and an Object, PRO of *John endeavored to cough* is necessarily understood agentively. That is, it is an Agent and an Object, not an Object only. We will come across similar instances of reinterpretation in later chapters of this book and it is therefore useful to have a term to cover reinterpretations of this type. We will use the term AGENTIVE REINTERPRETATION. An agentive reinterpretation is a reading of PRO that is characterized by three properties:

> First, an agentive reinterpretation is caused by the agentive controller of PRO.
> Second, the ease or difficulty of an agentive reinterpretation depends on the predicate of which PRO is the subject.
> Third, the very concept of reinterpretation implies that there exists a reading without a reinterpretation. The reading without a reinterpretation is suppressed when the predicate in question is the predicate of a sentence that is embedded under a verb of volition whose subject (NP$_1$) is an Agent. However, the reading without a reinterpretation can be observed when the predicate in question is the predicate of a non-embedded sentence, as is *sleep* in *John slept for ten hours.*

The relative ease of the reinterpretation in *John endeavored/tried to sleep* and the relative difficulty of the reinterpretation in **John endeavored/tried to grow old* serves quite generally to highlight the underlying nature of the deviance marked by stars and question marks in this section and in other sections on case grammar in the present volume. We have been concerned with interrelating syntactic and semantic properties of complement clauses in English, often downplaying any sharp divide between these two classes of properties. It is clear, though, that the deviance of the sentences listed here is at the semantic—or even pragmatic—rather than at the syntactic end of the scale. The semantic nature of the deviance here, as elsewhere in case grammar sections, is of course only to be expected, since case roles are defined to express semantic relations in the first place. The Agent Rule, then, is semantic in nature as well.

It is possible to say that case roles, the Agent Rule and violations of it are semantic, but to some extent this may gloss over the relation between semantics and pragmatics. Of the several recent accounts of this relation (cf. for example, Gazdar (1979: 161 ff.), Leech (1983: 5 ff., 19 ff.), Levinson (1983: 12 ff.)), it is perhaps sufficient in the present context to quote Jacobsen (1986: 357 ff.) and Jackendoff (1985). The former discusses sentences such as *My father is pregnant again* and notes that ". . . the question often arises whether it is really possible to distinguish between our linguistic knowledge of co-occurrence restrictions holding among lexical items on the one hand and our pragmatic knowledge, i.e., our knowledge of the world, on the other." (To be fair, for Jacobsen the question does not always arise. For instance, for him (1986: 360) the deviance of *The fox is strolling through the wood* is semantic, not pragmatic.) For his part, Jackendoff (1985: 106) argues more broadly that "although a terminological distinction between 'semantic' and 'pragmatic' notions undoubtedly remains useful, it is an open question whether it is a bifurcation of particular theoretical interest." This seems a fitting comment on our discussion of case roles, the Agent Rule and violations of it: the distinction between semantic and pragmatic notions is useful, but it does not seem to be "of particular theoretical interest" in the present context.

Of equal, or even greater, systematic interest is the concept of coreferential roles. Above, coreferential roles were referred to in connection with class 2. It was suggested that subjects of *intend, decide,* etc. have the role of the Agent and that of the Experiencer simultaneously. It should be recalled that an Experiencer as the NP_1 of a volitive verb is permissive as regards potential roles of its NP_2, allowing all four roles. It may be, then, that the Experiencer role mitigates or alleviates the constraint imposed by an Agent NP_1 of a verb of volition on the selection of roles for its NP_2. For instance, compare *intend,* whose subject is an Agent and an Experiencer with a verb whose subject is an Agent only, such as *try.* Both, of course, allow their NP_2s to be Agents, but *try* is less permissive as regards the admissibility of the other three roles for its NP_2. Compare *John intended to write letters in the afternoon/?to know the answer/??to receive a letter from a friend/??to grow old/?to be tall when grown up* with *John tried to write letters in the afternoon/*to know the answer/*to receive a letter from a friend/*to grow old/*to be tall when grown up.*

The difference is perhaps so clear as to allow us to add another layer to the graphic representation:

		ROLES OF NP_2
Verb$_1$ is +volition	NP$_1$ is −Agent, +Experiencer	A, E, B, O,
	NP$_1$ is +Agent, −Experiencer	A, *E, *B, *O
	NP$_1$ is +Agent, +Experiencer	A, ?E, ?B, ?O
Verb$_1$ is −volition	NP$_1$ is −Agent, +Experiencer	A, E, B, O
	NP$_1$ is +Agent, −Experiencer	A, E, B, O

At this point, it is worth recalling the difference noted above between *intend* and *decide*. The subjects of both verbs are Agents and Experiencers. However, the subject of *decide* is more agentive than the subject of *intend*. Correspondingly, the subject of *intend* is more Experiencer-like than the subject of *decide*. Not unnaturally, then, the more agentive an NP_1 is, the more stringently it imposes the Agent role on NP_2.

We had no verbs of the *to* pattern that are −volition and take both an Agent and an Experiencer. If such verbs are found in a larger survey, we may speculate that they will all allow all four roles for NP_2, since the Agent Rule is not operative for them.

Coreferential roles and agentive reinterpretations, then, mitigate violations of the Agent Rule. In Chapter 3 this account will be somewhat refined and supplemented with the introduction of a further mitigating factor, but the new factor will not affect the discussion of the present patterns in an essential way. Here it is appropriate to inquire into the relation of coreferential roles and agentive reinterpretations. Given the framework of case grammar that was outlined above, which, in its essential aspects, is modeled on Cook (1979), the relation between the two concepts is clearly an intimate one. The reason is that agentive reinterpretations produce coreferential roles. For instance, PRO in *John endeavored to sleep* is an Agent, but it is an Object as well, for there is an Object in every sentence in Cook's (1979: 206) framework. It is then possible to consider agentive reinterpretations a subclass of coreferential roles. That is, there are coreferential roles of two types: those that involve an agentive reinterpretation and those that do not. In effect, then, there is only one factor mitigating the Agent Rule: coreferential roles. The one mitigating factor is divided into two classes. This is perhaps more a shift in terminology than a reflection of a new insight, for, in any case, the concept of an agentive reinterpretation remains a useful one. It is useful for a number of reasons. First, only fully successful agentive reinterpretations produce fully coreferential roles. That is, agentive reinterpretations may be a matter of degree, which property does not appear to be shared by other coreferential roles. In other words, partially coreferential roles do not seem to exist apart from, and independently of, agentive reinterpretations. For instance, we may compare *John* in *John intends to go* and in *John intends to own a house in the country,* with PRO in the latter sentence. *John,* the subject of *intend,* is always an Experiencer and an Agent and never an Experiencer or an Agent only. By contrast, PRO, the subject of *own,* in the second sentence, is a Benefactive, and a reinterpreted Agent. It should be noted that the subject of *own* may be a Benefactive only, as is *John* in *John owns a house in the country.* (Tests of agentivity show *John* not to be an Agent. We may first turn the sentence into the past tense: *John owned a house in the country.* The following are then bad: Q. *What did John do?* A. **He owned a house in the country. *What John did was (to) own a house in the country.*) The very idea of a reinterpretation arises from the existence of a second, non-reinterpreted case frame for the predicate in question, a case frame where there is no Agent present. The existence of a second, non-reinterpreted case frame gives rise to the varying degrees of agentivity that different predicates display—some predicates are easier to reinterpret agentively than others. By contrast, other types of coreferential roles do not presuppose the existence of a non-coreferential reading, and, as a consequence, the question of partially coreferential roles does not arise for them.

A second consideration allowing us to define the class of agentive reinterpretations, delimiting it against other coreferential roles, is that the concept of coreferential roles relates to both NP_1 and to NP_2, whereas agentive reinterpretations relate to the interpretation of NP_2 only. An NP_1 may have coreferential roles. If it does, then it always has them, independently of context, and there is no non-coreferential interpretation. By contrast, an NP_2 may have coreferential roles with or without an agentive reinterpretation. An example of the latter is afforded by verbs of movement, such as *run, walk*, etc. Subjects of such verbs— when they are +Human—are always both Agents and Objects. Consequently, PRO in *John tried to walk faster* has coreferential roles without an agentive reinterpretation.

We will then still use the concept of an agentive reinterpretation, but we will take it for granted from now on that agentive reinterpretations are only a subclass of coreferential roles. Coreferential roles are then a factor mitigating the Agent Rule.

Coreferential roles, then, alleviate the deviance resulting from violations of the Agent Rule. As a limiting case, they may eliminate it, nullifying the Agent Rule. The precise degree to which coreferential roles alleviate deviance is a further question. We will call it 'the question of degree'. Clearly, a great deal of work needs to be done on the question of degree. The judgments that were made above and those that will be made below reflect one set of answers to the question of degree. The question of degree is important. However, it is crucial to notice that it is the Agent Rule and coreferential roles mitigating it that give rise to the question of degree. Our primary point here is the Agent Rule and the concept of coreferential roles. Whatever judgments may be made on the question of degree in individual cases, the Agent Rule and the mitigating factor make two predictions that are general in nature. First, among sentences that are otherwise well formed, sentences that do not violate the Agent Rule are always better than sentences that do violate the Agent Rule. Second, among sentences that violate the Agent Rule but are otherwise well formed, those that contain a mitigating factor are always better than those that do not contain a mitigating factor.

2.5.5 Testing the Conclusions

Let us now consider verbs of the *to* pattern that express negative volition. Given the Agent Rule, that a verb of positive volition requiring only an Agent as its NP_1 also requires an Agent as its NP_2, it is natural to expect that a verb of negative volition requiring only an Agent as its NP_1 would impose the same condition on its NP_2. That is, it is natural to expect that the Agent Rule extends to verbs of negative volition. *Refuse* is a verb of negative volition that commonly and normally occurs in the pattern and it may serve as an example. Its subject is an Agent only.

> Q. What did John do?
> A. He refused to write a letter to Sue/refused to write a letter to Sue in order to gain time.

Consequently, if the prediction that can be derived from the Agent Rule is correct, the role of NP$_2$ should be that of the Agent, to the exclusion of the other three case roles. This is corroborated by the contrast between [34a] and [34b–d]:

[34] **a.** Under such circumstances, John refused to write a letter to a friend.
    b. *Under such circumstances, John refused to know the answer.
    c. *Under such circumstances, John refused to get a message of condolence.
    d. *Under such circumstances, John refused to grow old/to be tall when grown up.

Further, if a Verb$_1$ of negative volition whose subject is not an Agent but an Experiencer is chosen, the prediction is that all four case roles should be possible for NP$_2$. *Hate* is a case in point. Its subject is not an Agent.

> Q. What did John do?
> A. *He hated to write a letter to a friend.

The subject of *hate* is an Experiencer only, designating the person who experiences the emotion of hating. [35a–d], then, corroborate the prediction:

[35] **a.** Under such circumstances, John hated to write a letter to a friend.
    b. Under such circumstances, John hated to know the truth.
    c. Under such circumstances, John hated to get a message of condolence.
    d. Under such circumstances, John hated to grow old/to be tall when grown up.

Negative Verb$_1$s whose subjects are both Agents and Experiencers include *disdain* ('to think beneath one (*to do* or *doing* something)', OED) and *hesitate* ('to find difficulty in deciding', OED). Subjects of these verbs designate entities experiencing emotions, such as reluctance or indecision, but unlike the subject of *hate*, they are not only Experiencers but also Agents.

> Q. What did John do?
> A. He disdained/hesitated to write a letter to Sue./He disdained/hesitated to write a letter to Sue in order to gain time.

Hesitate is perhaps slightly better than *disdain* in A. The subjects of both verbs are Agents and Experiencers, but the subject of *hesitate* is perhaps more agentive than the subject of *disdain*.

With verbs of positive volition we observed that the Experiencer role mitigates the Agent Rule. In [36a, b] we see that the mitigating influence is less perceptible with verbs of negative volition:

[36] **a.** Under such circumstances, John disdained/hesitated to write a letter to a friend.

b. Under such circumstances, John ??disdained/*hesitated to know the truth.

c. Under such circumstances, John *disdained/*hesitated to get a message of condolence.

d. Under such circumstances, John ??disdained/*hesitated to grow old/to be tall when grown up.

Disdain is perhaps slightly better in [36b–d], on account of its more Experiencer-like subject. However, even *disdain* seems worse than verbs of positive volition and intention in corresponding constructions: *John intended ?to know the truth/?to get a message of condolence/?to grow old/?to be tall when grown up.* We therefore modify our graphic representation for verbs of volition slightly, in order to take account of the difference:

		ROLES OF NP_2
	NP_1 is −Agent, +Experiencer	A, E, B, O
Verb$_1$ is +volition	NP_1 is +Agent, −Experiencer	A, *E, *B, *O
	NP_1 is +Agent, +Experiencer	A, ?E, ?B, ?O (Verb$_1$ is positive) A, ??E, *B, ??O (Verb$_1$ is negative)

That is, coreferential roles governed by verbs of negative volition redeem violations of the Agent Rule somewhat less effectively than do coreferential roles governed by verbs of positive volition. On the other hand, coreferential roles arising by way of agentive reinterpretations are not affected by the positive vs. negative dichotomy of Verb$_1$. As noted, agentive reinterpretations relate to the case roles of NP_2s. Thus *John disdained/hesitated to sleep on the sofa/to own a house in the country* are completely (the *sleep* version) or to a large extent (the *own* version) redeemed as agentive reinterpretations and the negativity of Verb$_1$ seems irrelevant. More generally, even coreferential roles without agentive reinterpretations are an effective mitigating influence, even with negative Verb$_1$s, as long as the NP carrying coreferential roles is NP_2, and not NP_1. Thus, *John disdained/hesitated to walk faster* is good, and in the sentence PRO has coreferential roles, the roles of the Agent and of the Object, without an agentive reinterpretation. In other words, only coreferential roles of NP_1s governed by verbs of negative volition fail to effectively mitigate violations of the Agent Rule.

As regards *forget* and *remember*, their subjects are perhaps not entirely happy with all tests of agentivity. However, in view of the admissibility of question-and-answer sequences such as Q. *What did John do?* A. *He forgot to mail the letter* and of pseudocleft sentences such as *What John did was to forget to mail the letter*, the subjects seem to be Agents. We then find a predictable pattern: *He forgot to write the letter/*He forgot to know the truth/*He forgot to receive a message of condolence/*He forgot to grow old/to be tall when grown up.*

Proceeding to the *ing* pattern, we take *hate* as an example of a verb expressing negative desideration. The same prediction as in the *to* pattern is observed in the *ing* pattern. Since NP_1 is an Experiencer only, and not an Agent, all four case roles are allowed for NP_2:

[37] a. Under such circumstances, John hated writing a letter to a friend.
   b. Under such circumstances, John hated knowing the truth.
   c. Under such circumstances, John hated receiving bad news.
   d. Under such circumstances, John hated growing old/being tall when grown up.

Hate exemplifies verbs of negative volition. The class also includes *resent*. This is of interest because of Gruber's (1976: 162) claim that *resent* is a verb that does not allow the subject of its complement to be an Agent. In support (1976: 162), he cites the putative contrast between *John resented inheriting so little* and *John resented fetching so little money*, which latter sentence he marks as ill formed.

To judge from his examples, Gruber presumably meant for his claim to hold only when the subject of S_2 is empty, that is, a PRO in the terminology that we have been using. (If it is not empty, counterexamples abound, as in *John resented my writing to him*.) However, even if the subject of S_2 is empty and the pattern therefore relevant in the present context, it seems that NP_2 can be an Agent, contrary to Gruber's claim. Gruber's sentence *John resented fetching so little money* is rather strange, apparently, however, for a reason that is unrelated to the case role of NP_2, but has to do with *so little*. If the object of S_2 is changed to *the money*, say, the sentence becomes good: *John resented fetching the money*. Here is another example of an Agent as NP_2: *He resented doing me a favor*.

Going on to verbs of negative desideration and intention and of negative desideration, intention and endeavor, it is clear that their subjects are Agents, as in the infinitival pattern. *Put off* may serve as a case in point. Its subject, as in *He put off answering our letter*, is an Agent only. The prediction is then that roles other than that of the Agent are excluded for NP_2. This is confirmed by [38a–d]:

[38] a. John put off writing a letter to a friend.
   b. *John put off knowing the sad truth.
   c. *John put off receiving a letter from a friend.
   d. *John put off growing old/being tall when grown up.

Hate and *put off* represent verbs of negative volition. As argued above, verbs of positive volition taking *ing* do exist, though their number is not very large. *Enjoy* is an example of a verb with a subject that is −Agent and +Experiencer. All four case roles should be possible for NP_2, as indeed they are:

[39] **a.** John enjoyed writing a letter to a friend.
    b. John enjoyed knowing the truth.
    c. John enjoyed receiving a letter from a friend.
    d. John enjoyed growing old/being tall when grown up.

When we proceed to verbs of positive desideration and intention and to those of positive desideration, intention and endeavor, NP_1 becomes an Agent and roles other than that of the Agent are excluded for NP_2 by the Agent Rule, except if the mitigating influence of coreferential roles is operative. *Intend* and *try* may serve as examples:

[40] **a.** John intended writing a letter to a friend.
    b. ?John intended knowing the truth.
    c. ?John intended receiving a letter from a friend.
    d. ?John intended growing old/being tall when grown up.

[41] **a.** John tried writing a letter to a friend.
    b. *John tried knowing the truth.
    c. *John tried receiving a letter from a friend.
    d. *John tried growing old/being tall when grown up.

The difference in acceptability between [40b–d] and [41b–d] may be explained by the relevance of coreferential roles to the former, but not to the latter. Again, the Experiencer role mitigates the degree of the violation of acceptability, at least up to a point.

The coreferential roles of [40b–d] relate to NP_1 and they are coreferential roles without agentive reinterpretations. The predicates in the relevant sentences, *receive a letter, know the truth, grow old, be tall* are such as do not allow agentive reinterpretations of NP_2. Agentive reinterpretations do nevertheless produce coreferential roles in the same way as in section 2.5.4, that is, when a Verb₂ allows an agentive reinterpretation. The same class of predicates is relevant as in 2.5.4. For instance, we may compare *John tried owning a house in the country* and *John tried sleeping on the floor/coughing* with [41c] and [41d], respectively. The former are clearly better than the latter, confirming the mitigating influence of coreferential roles.

On the basis of this section we generalize the Agent Rule as follows:

The Agent Rule, revised version: An agentive NP_1 governed by a verb of volition requires an agentive NP_2.

Coreferential roles, with or without agentive reinterpretations, alleviate violations of the Agent Rule. The mitigating effect of coreferential roles is considerable when an NP_2, or an NP_1 that is governed by a verb of positive volition, carries the coreferential roles in question. The mitigating effect is less noticeable when an NP_1 that is governed by a verb of negative volition carries the coreferential roles in question.

Chapter *3*

ON CONTRASTS BETWEEN INFINITIVAL AND *THAT* COMPLEMENT CLAUSES

3.1 INTRODUCTORY OBSERVATIONS

The principal purpose of the present chapter is to shed some light on the properties of *that* in comparison with *for to* complement sentences, as illustrated by [1a, b]:

[1] **a.** Joe claimed that he was right.
    b. Joe preferred for me to leave early.

By way of getting at the properties of *that* complement clauses, the chapter will seek to account for such differences in meaning as are exhibited by [2a] and [2b] and by [2c] and [2d]:

[2] **a.** Jane pretended to be a professor
    b. Jane pretended that she was a professor.
    c. Jane forgot to be cautious.
    d. Jane forgot that she was cautious.

The chapter will also seek to account for the fact that while in some cases, as above, both infinitival and *that* complement clauses are possible, there are other cases in which only one of them is allowed, as witness [3a, b], where a *that* complement is excluded, and [3c, d], where an infinitival complement is excluded:

[3] a. Jane condescended to play with me.
    b. *Jane condescended that she played with me.
    c. *Jane thought to be right.
    d. Jane thought that she was right.

As noted in Chapter 2, sentences with the form of [2a], [2c], [3a] and [3c], where the subject of the lower sentence is that of the higher sentence, may be described through Equi. The three patterns cited may then be represented schematically as in [4]:

[4] a. $[NP_1 \ Verb_1 \ [[that \ NP_2 \ Verb_2 \ . . .]_{S_2}]_{NP}]_{S_1}$ for *that* complements.
    b. $[NP_1 \ Verb_1 \ [[for \ NP_2 \ to \ Verb_2 \ . . . \ ]_{S_2}]_{NP}]_{S_1}$ for *for to* complements.
    c. $[NP_1 \ Verb_1 \ [[PRO]_{NP_2} \ to \ Verb_2 \ . . .]_{S_2}]_{S_1}$ for infinitival Equi complements.

The scope of the inquiry is limited in several ways. First, the claims made are to be regarded as tentative. Second, they relate only to a subset of infinitival constructions in English. Raising (cf. Postal (1974) and Chapter 2 of the present volume) and *Tough* Movement (cf. Postal (1971), Berman (1974) and Nanni (1978)) structures are among those outside the scope of the present inquiry. With respect to *that* clauses, the discussion will focus on those without subjunctives. (Subjunctives may be illustrated with sentences such as *Congress has voted that the present law be maintained* and *I wish she were not married,* both sentences from Quirk et al. (1985: 1012 ff.).) We will not attempt to list $Verb_1$s taking subjunctive *that* clauses in the present context. However, we will refer to subjunctives and, more broadly, to subjunctive equivalents in section 3.3.2, where we discuss the semantic properties of the Equi pattern of [4c]. Further, it should again be stressed that only complement sentences will be considered in the present context. This excludes from consideration cases where S_2 is an adverbial clause expressing purpose. Such adverbial clauses may have the same schematic form as the three types cited and there may be some ambiguous or marginal cases, but the distinction is clear in principle, and therefore their exclusion is methodologically as well as presentationally advisable. For instance, compare *He preferred for Sue to go first* with *He placed himself at a corner of the doorway for her to pass him into the house* (Jespersen (1961: 304)). Only in the latter is it possible to substitute *in order to* for *for to:* *He preferred in order for Sue to go first* vs. *He placed himself at a corner of the doorway in order for her to . . .* Similar contrasts can be cited for the other patterns. Contrast *He knows that/*in order that Jack might examine him* with *He came (so) that/in order that Jack might examine him* and *He preferred to/*in order to go first* with *He arrived early to/in order to go first.*

The operational method of procedure in this chapter will be as follows: first an outline will be given of the main aspects of a previous attempt to formulate generalizations to cover the data, and the patterns [4a] and [4c], in particular. The inadequacy of this attempt will then be shown. More positively, there will subsequently be offered a description that is, it would seem, both more adequate and applicable to a wider range of data, including the pattern [4b].

The argument will be based solely on English. Parts of it have cross-linguistic implications, but these will be ignored in the present connection.

3.2 RIDDLE'S ACCOUNT AND ITS INADEQUACY

According to Riddle (1975: 467 ff.), whose account of the data will be considered in this section by way of exposition, [2a] means that Jane acted in a manner suggestive of that of a professor, while, most straightforwardly, [2b] means that Jane made the (false) verbal claim—perhaps only to herself in her mind—that she was a professor. Further, [2c] means that Jane forgot to act in a cautious manner, while [2d] means that she forgot the fact that she was cautious, that being cautious was part of her character.

Noting these paraphrases and, in particular, the element of 'activity' in the paraphrases of [2a] and [2c], Riddle (1975: 467) suggests that *to* complements express some notion of activity, while *that* complements refer to mental or physical states.

Riddle (1975: 468) supports her suggestion with two kinds of independent evidence. First, in English there are some verbs, such as *condescend* and *neglect,* that impose the requirement on their complement sentences that the latter express an activity. Riddle's presentation of the point is confusing. Her (1975: 468) sentence reads: "In all these sentences the meaning of the embedded verb requires that an action be predicated by the complement verb." We take it that there is a misprint in the sentence: instead of writing "the embedded verb" she intended to write "the embedding verb." The slip of the pen is regrettable because the point is crucial. With the correction taken for granted, it is explained why these complements must be infinitival of the form of [4c], and not *that* clauses. In other words, [3a, b] and [5a, b] are accounted for:

[5] a. Jane neglected to arrive on time.
     b. *Jane neglected that she arrived on time.

Second, there exist embedding verbs that, in Riddle's (1975: 469) words, refer "to a state of being in the complement" and therefore require a *that,* as opposed to an infinitival Equi clause (of the type of [4c]), as witness [3c, d] and [6a, b]:

[6] a. *Jane assumed to be a genius.
     b. Jane assumed that she was a genius.

However, in view of sentences such as [7a, b], Riddle (1975: 469) introduces another factor into her account:

[7] a. I have decided to have a temperature.
     b. I have decided that I have a temperature.

The complement verb of [7a] refers to a time posterior to that of the main verb, while [7b] implies an already existing state of affairs. That is, [7b] means that I had a temperature before I decided (or realized) that I had it.

Riddle (1975: 469) then argues that for some verbs the time reference factor rules out the use of a *that* complement, as shown by [8a, b] (Riddle's [27a, b]):

[8] **a.** I promised to be good.

  b. *I promised that I was good.

The next logical step for Riddle (1975: 469) is to try and collapse the two generalizations, at least partially. She says: "An action which has already occurred is reduced to a state." Further, she introduces the notion of 'controllability': embedding verbs requiring verbs of action as their embedded verbs also contain a controllability factor. According to her (1975: 469), "an action is controllable in a way that a state is not" and "an already past state of affairs cannot be."

To summarize Riddle's argument: an infinitival structure occurs if either the complement refers to a time posterior to that of the embedding verb or if the verb of the complement expresses a controllable action. On the other hand, a *that* structure occurs if either the complement verb is −controllable, expressing a state, or if it refers to a time not posterior to (that is, either prior to or simultaneous with) that of the embedding verb.

Riddle (1975: 470) then notes one exception to her rule. The sentence *He pretended to have been a spy* is good even though its embedded verb has a past time reference with respect to the embedding verb. She offers the explanation that the meaning of *pretend* "does not include a sense of control over the predication of the complement."

Riddle's analysis is to be welcomed as focusing attention upon an interesting and somewhat neglected area of the syntax and semantics of present-day English, but it seems doubtful whether it can stand. Regarding *pretend,* Riddle's very premise seems suspect: how does the meaning of *pretend* in *He pretended to have been a spy* not include a sense of control over its complement if that of *try,* e.g., in *Jane tried to be a parachutist* (Riddle 1975: 468) is supposed to do so? It seems rather that an individual has full control over what he may pretend to be or do.

Assuming, though, that Riddle is justified in her claim that *pretend* does not include a sense of control over the complement, how does this explain the infinitival pattern? Surely, her rules predict instead a *that* complement, since *that* introduces complements that are not controllable. To be sure, too much should not be made of this criticism based on *pretend,* because, as argued in Chapter 2, *pretend* is rather exceptional as an Equi verb.

More fundamentally, it seems that essential features of Riddle's system are shaky and unconvincing in the form in which she presents them as a basis for describing differences between *that* and Equi structures. First, consider her notion of controllability and the claim that if the complement verb is −controllable because it expresses a state a *that* construction occurs. That this is false can be shown for instance by [9a–c]:

[**9**] **a.** John wants to know French.
   b. John desires to own a car.
   c. John would not like to resemble his father.

In [9a–c] the lower verb is expressly stative (cf. for example, Lakoff (1966)) and S_2 refers to a state. Yet infinitival structures are quite good.

Riddle does not consider *for to* complements, but it may be noted in passing that they are good in sentences analogous to [9a–c] as well:

[**10**] **a.** John wants for Sue to know French.
   b. John desires for his wife to own a car.
   c. John would not like for his nephew to resemble his father.

We are not convinced, then, that controllability governs the incidence of *that* and Equi structures in the form that Riddle proposed. (However, the notion of controllability is relevant from a different point of view, cf. section 3.4.)
   Riddle's claim based on time sequences, viz., that if the time reference of S_2 is posterior to that of S_1, an infinitival structure is possible and a *that* complement is not, is also fallacious. Thus in *He decided that he would be a teacher* the time reference of the complement is posterior to that of the embedding verb and yet the sentence is good with a *that* complementizer.
   Establishing that Riddle's account of the data is inadequate is of course only a first step. It only shows the need for a new approach. That will be provided below.

3.3   A CONTRASTIVE ACCOUNT OF *THAT, FOR TO* AND EQUI PATTERNS

3.3.1   From the Point of View of Verb₁

In this section an account will be provided of the data raised above, especially the sentences of [1]–[3] and [5]–[8]. The account will also cover additional aspects of *that, for to* and subject-controlled Equi constructions.
   One aspect of the question raised should be separated from the others at the outset, viz., the case of *decide* and *promise*. Riddle used these verbs to motivate her claim that if the verb of the subordinate clause is +future with respect to the embedding verb, an infinitival structure must be chosen. The claim was disproved in section 3.2. More positively, *promise, threaten, intend, decide* (with the meaning 'come to a decision', as opposed to 'realize', which latter case is constructed differently and for example does not allow Equi *I realized/decided to be having a temperature*) are verbs whose subordinate clauses properly refer to the future as compared with the time reference of their embedding verbs. (On

constructions such as NP *intended to have* Verb+*ed,* cf. Horn (1905) and Visser (1973: 2420 ff.)) Thus not only is [8b] bad, but so is **I promised to have been good* with an infinitival form, while both *I promised that I would be good* and *I promised to be good* are well formed. It seems clear that such a specification is needed quite independently of any interaction of this condition with Equi and complementizers. Semantically, and pragmatically, the justification for such a specification is obvious: one can promise, threaten, intend, decide to do something or to be something only in the future, not in the past.

3.3.1.1 *That* Clauses

The remaining questions require more comment. It seems to the present author that their solution requires a consideration of the characteristic semantic functions of *that, for to* and Equi structures. It is expedient to discuss these functions from three points of view: first, from the point of view of Verb$_1$ in [4a–c], since, as was seen, not all embedding verbs embed all types of complements. Second, the complement structures in question can be viewed from the point of view of semantic functions and characteristics internal to them. Third, it will be recalled that case grammar was applied to the *to* infinitival pattern in Chapter 2. Here case grammar is applied to the *for to* infinitival pattern, though not to the *that* pattern, in a comparative way. In the remainder of this section we will consider [4a–c] from the first point of view. In section 3.3.2 we will apply the second, and in section 3.4 the third.

Starting with *that* complements of the form of [4a], it is helpful to refer to Poutsma's (1904: 537 ff.) statement to the effect that after verbs expressing judging or declaring, an infinitive is impossible or at least highly unusual and that English mostly requires a full subordinate clause after verbs of this description. Starting with Poutsma's verbs of declaring, it is more felicitous to call its members 'verbs of verbal communication', but Poutsma's generalization is significant. That this is so is clear from a consideration of a sample of such verbs. (In compiling the list, we have benefited from that of Alexander and Kunz (1964: 3 ff.).)

accept	decree	prophesy
acknowledge	deny	protest
add	determine	question
admit	disclaim	radio
advertise	disclose	reaffirm
affirm	divulge	reason
allege	emphasize	recommend
announce	explain	reiterate
answer	expostulate	relate
argue	express	remark

assert	forecast	repeat
assure	foretell	reply
aver	give out	report
boast	grant	respond
brag	hint	retort
bring up	insist	rule
broadcast	intimate	say
cable	let on	specify
call to mind	maintain	speculate
certify	make known	spell out
charge	make out	state
communicate	mention	stipulate
complain	note	stress
concede	opine	submit
confess	own	suggest
confide	phone	telegraph
confirm	point out	telephone
contend	preach	tell
contest	predict	transmit
convey	premise	underline
counsel	proclaim	urge
counterclaim	prognosticate	whisper
cry out	promulgate	wire
declare	pronounce	write

For to is incompatible with the great majority of the verbs cited, but as will be seen below there is a subclass of verbs of verbal communication with which it is compatible. As for Equi, it is also incompatible with the great majority of the verbs cited, but again compatible with a subclass to be given below. Apart from the subclass, there are some isolated verbs of verbal communication with which Equi is either marginally or totally acceptable. *Boast* and *brag* belong to the former class (??*He boasted/bragged to have done it*); *claim* and *profess* to the latter (*He claimed/professed to be a patriot*). These isolated verbs should be recognized as exceptions to the rule that, apart from the subclass to be discussed below, verbs of verbal communication take *that* complements only.

As for Poutsma's verbs of judging (recall also Riddle's reference to images in the mind), the concept should be defined more rigorously before the precise scope of the claims can be evaluated. It seems that three classes can be distinguished: verbs with the basic meanings (a) 'believe' (cf. Searle (1983: 29 ff.)), (b) 'understand' and (c) 'come to believe' or 'come to understand'. Here is a sample of each group. (Again we have benefited from the list by Alexander and Kunz (1964: 3 ff.).)

Group (a):

adjudge	expect	opine
anticipate	fancy	reason
assume	feel	reflect
believe	figure	suppose
conceive	foresee	surmise
conjecture	guess	suspect
consider	hold	think
dream	hypothesize	trust
envisage	imagine	
estimate	meditate	

There is some overlap between this and the previous class: for instance, cf. *opine, reason* (cf. the entries in the ALD, for example), and some others.

Verbs meaning 'know' ('believe for sure') or 'take for granted' can be regarded as a subgroup of (a): *know, posit, presuppose, take for granted*.

Group (b): *apprehend, comprehend, understand*.

Group (c):

ascertain	find out	observe
calculate	gather	overhear
compute	glean	perceive
conclude	grasp	realize
decide	hear	see
discover	infer	sense
divine	intuit	smell
establish	learn	uncover
find	notice	

Virtually none of the verbs cited in groups (a), (b) or (c) takes *for to* complements or Equi. Two exceptions, with respect to Equi, are *expect* and *learn,* as in *Jane expected/learned to trust me/to leave early.* Some speakers, especially of American English, also accept *expect* in the *for to* pattern, as in *Jane expected for me to leave early,* but others object to this, some rather strongly. (For the use of *think* in the Equi pattern, see below.) Apart from such very isolated exceptions, the rule is quite general, explaining the nonoccurrence of [6a], among others.

Above, a somewhat refined version of Poutsma's (cf. also Mätzner (1885: 451)) rule has been accepted. The conclusion is that *that* complements are in general called for if a Verb$_1$ of the pattern [4a] is a verb of verbal communication or means either 'believe', or 'understand', or 'come to believe or understand'. In addition, there are two other classes of verbs whose members may appear as a Verb$_1$ in the pattern. The first of these will be called 'verbs of demonstration': *bring out, bring to light, demonstrate, establish, indicate, prove, reveal, show, signal*. These verbs may involve verbal communication, but this is by no means necessary: it is possible to demonstrate something by some action. Consequently, this class must be kept separate from the verbs of verbal communication.

The verbs of the 'demonstrate' class also bear a relationship to the 'come to believe or understand' class. Indeed, Partee (1973: 324 ff.) considers the two as one class, calling its members 'verbs of inference'. However, even though the verbs of both classes relate to an act of perception, there is a clear difference between them. A Verb$_1$ of the 'come to believe or understand' class expresses an act of perception on the part of NP$_1$ while a Verb$_1$ of the 'demonstrate' class shifts the point of focus to the attempt to make someone else (that is, other than NP$_1$) perceive that something is something. This shift of focus is reflected in a difference concerning selectional restrictions: a Verb$_1$ of the former class necessarily requires a human NP$_1$ while the NP$_1$ of a verb of the 'demonstrate' class may also be an abstract NP (if it expresses evidence). (While noting that some verbs of her class of verbs of inference may take NPs expressing evidence as subjects, Partee (1973: 324) failed to consider this as a reflex of a division of her class of verbs of inference.) For instance, contrast *John/*That an object fell to the ground inferred that there exists a law of gravity* with *John/That an object fell to the ground showed that there exists a law of gravity*.

No member of the 'demonstrate' class takes *for to* or Equi complements.

The remaining class of verbs taking *that* complements of the type of [4a] is that of verbs of emotion (*fear, hate, hope, regret* etc.), which express an attitude on the part of NP$_1$ toward S$_2$ or a reaction of NP$_1$ to S$_2$. For *to* and, even more generally, Equi complements are also compatible with verbs of this class and such verbs will be discussed below.

In conclusion, it is argued here that verbs of verbal communication as well as those meaning 'believe' or 'understand' or 'come to believe or understand' or 'demonstrate' characteristically take *that* complements only.

3.3.1.2 *For to* Clauses

Two preliminary points should be made with respect to the *for to* pattern. First, the precise derivation of *for* in the pattern is not altogether uncontroversial. (The reader may compare the partly conflicting accounts of Bresnan (1972: 98), Chomsky and Lasnik (1977: 479 ff., especially p. 482), Brame (1980: 250 ff.), Chomsky (1981: 145, note 84, and 153 ff.) and Seppänen (1981: 1984.)) In the present context, it is sufficient to assume that sentences such as *I arranged/hoped for John to go away* exhibit the surface structure [NP$_1$ Verb$_1$ [[*for* NP$_2$ *to*b$_2$ . . .]$_{S_2}$]$_{NP}$]$_{S_1}$, with *for* in the subordinate clause and part of the *for to* complementizer.

Second, it should be noted that the construction, though certainly attested in older literature (cf., for example, Söderlind (1958: 119) and the references that he cites), was apparently rare till the nineteenth century or perhaps even the beginning of this century (cf. Krüger (1914: 1250 ff.), Söderlind (1958: 119) and, most pointedly, Visser (1973: 2245)). The construction occurs especially in American English (cf. Quirk et al. (1974: 739)). However, as Visser (1973: 2245 ff.), cf. also Quirk et al. (1974: 840) shows, the construction is not confined to American English, but has been steadily spreading to, and in, British English. Even so, it should be added that the construction in question is subject to a great deal of idiolect variation.

With these preliminary points made, we propose to list and characterize verbs occurring as Verb$_1$ in the pattern in question. The most comprehensive list compiled so far consists of the verbs provided and illustrated by Visser. That list will be given as a first step. As a second step, an effort will be made to classify the verbs given, in order to characterize Verb$_1$ of [4b]. It should be noted that Visser does not attempt to classify the verbs that he illustrates.

Visser (1973: 2244 ff.) cites the following verbs as occurring in the pattern:

agree	hate	press
aim	hope	remain
arrange	indicate	ring
ask	intend	say
cannot bear	like	send
beg	listen	shout
call	long	sign
care	look	signal
consult	love	stay
cry	mean	wait
desire	motion	want
die	pine	watch
dread	plan	wave
expect	pray	will
fish	prefer	wish

Of these *consult* should be dropped: Visser's example is from 1662 (from Pepys's *Diary*) and the usage does not seem current today (*So we consulted for me to go first to Sir H. Bennet*). We add the following eight verbs (from Quirk et al. (1985: 1194)) to the list: *ache, burn, burst, clamor, crave, itch, prepare, yearn*.

Given the approximately fifty verbs, it is possible to discern a factor that governs the acceptability of *for to* clauses, cutting across British and American regional variation and across idiolectal differences. In general, verbs that take nonsentential *for* NP constructions are compatible with sentential *for to* complements as well. (We thank an anonymous reviewer for pointing out this rule for us.) All the verbs listed from Quirk et al. take *for* NPs, as do a number of the other verbs listed, including *aim, arrange, call,* etc. They are then quite generally good with sentential *for to* complement sentences as well, independent of regional or other variation.

Among the verbs listed, a classification emerges fairly naturally. The verbs in question may be divided into those that express volition on the part of NP_1 for (or against) the realization of S_2 and those that do not. The latter class of verbs is very small and perhaps even marginal: *expect, listen, watch, send, remain, stay*. Of these six, it is questionable whether the last two belong among verbs taking complement sentences, as opposed to adverbial clauses of purpose, at all. Visser's examples all seem to allow the insertion of *in order to* instead of *to*. For instance, taking one at random, *My lord, they stay for you to give your daughter to her husband* (from 1599, Shakespeare, *Much Ado about Nothing*) does so: *My lord, they stay in order for you to . . .* is good (though not a line from Shakespeare, of course). Consequently, *remain* and *stay* can be dropped from further consideration. *Send*, as in *She sent for her to come and show herself before she set out* (Visser: 2247, from 1865, Mrs. Gaskell, *Wives and Daughters*), should be excluded because the *for . . . to . . .* sequence is not a sentence. We may refer to a sentence pointed out to us by an anonymous reviewer: **He sent for there to be flowers in the room. Prepare* does not seem very good in the pattern either, as in *?He prepared for there to be more trouble on the range.* If it is retained, it does not convey volition for or against the realization of S_2. As for *listen* and *watch,* it is somewhat questionable whether they are outside the class of volitional verbs in this pattern (cf. Visser's (1973: 2245 ff.)) examples and his discussion of *watch for NP to*). As for *expect,* it seems to express anticipation rather than volition (cf. the OED), but judgments on the point are moderately subtle.

Volitional verbs may be divided as follows:

(1) Verb$_1$ expresses positive desideration.

(1.1) Verb$_1$ has the rough meaning 'NP$_1$ wants for S$_2$ to be realized'.

(1.1.1) Verb$_1$ expresses a desire or a wish for S$_2$ to be realized:

ache	fish	pine
burn	hope	prefer
burst	itch	wait
care	like	want
crave	long	will
desire	look	wish
die	love	yearn

(1.1.2) Verb$_1$ expresses a desire or a wish for S$_2$ to be realized and an act of communication on the part of NP$_1$:

agree	indicate	shout
ask	motion	sign
beg	pray	signal
call	press	wave
clamor	ring	
cry	say	

(1.2) Verb$_1$ expresses intention in addition to desideration: *aim, intend, mean, plan.*
(1.3) Verb$_1$ expresses endeavor in addition to intention and desideration: *arrange.*
(2) Verb$_1$ expresses negative desideration against the realization of S$_2$: *cannot bear, dread, hate.*

What emerges is that apart from isolated exceptions, verbs taking *for to* express volition on the part of NP$_1$ for (or, more rarely, against) the realization of S$_2$. A large class of verbs also imply that NP$_1$ communicates his desire or wish for the realization of S$_2$. This class is noteworthy because, as was argued, one of the major classes of verbs taking *that* complements was that of verbs of verbal communication. Interestingly, all the verbs of 1.1.2 that express, or which may express, verbal communication also take *that* complements. For instance, compare *He shouted for me to go first* with *He shouted that I should go first.* Verbs expressing a desire or a wish on the part of NP$_1$ for (or against) the realization of S$_2$, then, constitute the subclass of verbs of verbal communication allowing *for to* complements in addition to *that* complements.

It is of interest to note that one or two of the verbs of 1.1.2 express nonverbal communication only, which places them outside the domain of the rule that verbs expressing verbal communication in general, apart from the subclass just noted, take *that* complements. Thus *He waved for me to go first* is good, but **He waved that I should go first* is not (as a complement construction). The prediction carries over to, and is confirmed by, verbs not on the list. For instance, *nod* does not express verbal communication only, and, as predicted, it is incompatible with a *that* complement, whereas a *for to* complement is quite conceivable, though not attested by Visser: **He nodded that I should leave* vs. *He nodded for me to leave.* The absence from Visser's examples of the latter construction is therefore only an accidental gap, whereas the former would not be expected to occur at all.

That complements are also compatible with some verbs of 1.1.1 (for instance, *hope* and *wish*) and with those of 2, which do not express verbal communication. We will come back to these contrasts in section 3.3.2.

On the other hand, *that* complements are not in general compatible with verbs of class 1.2: cf. *Jack aimed/intended/meant/planned for Sue to leave the party first.* Similar judgments hold for *arrange* of 1.3: *Jack arranged for a nurse to attend the baby,* as opposed to *Jack ?arranged that a nurse should attend the baby.*

3.3.1.3 *That* and *For to* Contrasted with Equi Patterns

As noted in Chapter 2, among Equi verbs the class of volitional verbs is clearly preponderant, at least in terms of the number of its members, and, as noted, the class of volitional Equi verbs divides into the three major subdivisions of, respectively, expressing desideration, desideration and intention, and desideration, intention and endeavor. Only isolated Equi verbs of the pattern of [4c] are outside the class of volitional verbs.

Of interest here is the relationship of this classification to the two presented above. As regards *that* complements, the most perfect overlap obtains with respect to class 1.1.2.1 of Chapter 2. All the verbs of this class seem to be capable of expressing verbal communication. (It should be noted in passing that cases such as *There threatened to ensue trouble* are not Equi constructions at all, but rather derived via Raising, and therefore they are outside the scope of the present treatment, cf. Perlmutter (1970) and for differences between Equi and Raising verbs, cf. section 2.2 of Chapter 2.) Not surprisingly, therefore, all of them can also take *that* complements. Some of the verbs may express nonverbal communication as well, and in such cases there tends to be a noticeable difference between *that* and Equi constructions, with the former always more closely implying a verbal act and the verbal content of that act. For instance, contrast *He pledged to defend his country* with *He pledged that he would defend his country.* Only the former is compatible with a continuation implying a nonverbal act (e.g., *by raising his right hand*). Equally noticeably, *volunteer* with a *that* complement, as in *He volunteered that he would do it,* virtually means 'say voluntarily', whereas *volunteer* with an Equi complement, as in *He volunteered to do it,* may be less specific (e.g., he may have done so by taking one step forward). The difference between the cases of *pretend* in [2a, b] seems to be of the same kind as these cases, even though *pretend* is exceptional in that it is not a verb of volition.

The verbs of class 1.1.2.1 of Chapter 2 that express 'more purely' verbal communication also obviously take *that* complements. What is exceptional about them is their governing Equi at all.

That complements are also compatible with some isolated verbs of classes 1.1.1 and of 1.2.1 of Chapter 2, some isolated verbs of 1.1.2.2 of Chapter 2 (*decide, determine, resolve;* these have the rough meaning 'come to a decision') and with *forget* and *remember* of 1.3 of Chapter 2. Some of these and the differences between the different types of complements will be considered in section 3.3.2. On the other hand, *that* seems incompatible with verbs expressing endeavor (1.1.3 of Chapter 2). The verbs of class 1.1.2.2 of Chapter 2 that mean 'come to a decision' (and thus 'form an intention') are few in number; *that* is incompatible with all the other verbs of 1.1.2.2. As for *think* of 1.1.2.2, the use in question is that of 'purpose', 'intend' (cf. Kruisinga (1925: 146), Poutsma (1904: 538) and Hornby (1966: 19)). We may contrast [11a, b], which are from Kruisinga (1925: 146), with the star added to [11b]:

[11] a. I thought to find your brother guilty but it seems he is not.

    b. *A quickened imagination so deceived me that I thought to hear the sea rolling.

Think in [11b] has the sense of 'believe' of the *that* pattern, for which Equi is not normally possible.

At this point it is appropriate to refer to Ellegård's (1971: 159) rule that a *that* clause is not possible when the meaning of a Verb$_1$ is such that its subject must be identical with the subject of Verb$_2$. Ellegård does not precisely specify the ingredient of meaning in question. (He cites such verbs as *refuse, hesitate, manage, try*.) Conceivably, the meanings of intention and of intention and endeavor might be suggested as such ingredients of meaning as necessarily require identical subjects and therefore, by Ellegård's rule, exclude *that* clauses.

To rephrase Ellegård's rule, he visualizes a two-step generalization of the form: (1) a Verb$_1$ with a meaning X requires identical subjects, (2) identical subjects require Equi, and exclude *that*, complements. This is a conceivable approach, but here a one-step approach of the following form is proposed: a Verb$_1$ with the meaning X requires Equi, and excludes *that*, complements. (The identity of subjects follows automatically from the nature of the Equi complements in question.) The approach is motivated primarily because of the existence of classes 1.2 and 1.3 of the *for to* classification of this chapter. The members of these classes permit nonidentical subjects, (cf., for example, *He aimed for me to leave first*.) Yet, as noted, *that* clauses are in general still not possible with these verbs. (Cf. **He aimed that I should go first*.) Therefore, verbs allowing nonidentical subjects do not necessarily allow *that* complements. Consequently, an effort has been made to characterize the various patterns with reference to semantic classes, without recourse to identical subjects, which latter are an automatic concomitant of Equi complements of the form of [4c].

Comparing classes of verbs taking Equi with those taking *for to*, we note the similarity in that the core class of both is the class of volitional verbs, and further that the main subclasses within the core class are similar. At present, fewer verbs occur in the *for to* pattern than in the Equi pattern, but if the former continues its advance, we may speculate that verbs cited above in the [4c] pattern will increasingly come to govern *for to* as well.

To sum up this section, we have reached the conclusion that a Verb$_1$ of the patterns [4a–c] with the meaning of verbal communication or that of 'believe', 'understand', 'come to believe or understand' or 'demonstrate' characteristically takes a *that* complement. A Verb$_1$ expressing verbal communication and desideration and intention for (or against) the realization of S$_2$ may also take an Equi or a *for to* complement, the latter more rarely. In such cases, Equi and *for to* complements are less strictly limited to verbal communication. A Verb$_1$ expressing intention or intention and endeavor but not communication, characteristically may take Equi or *for to* complement clauses only, but no *that* complement clauses, except if Verb$_1$ means 'come to a decision', in which case a *that* complement is also possible. The variation regarding verbs of desideration, of positive or negative emotion towards the realization of S$_2$, will be treated in section 3.3.2.

3.3.2 Inherent Properties of the Three Types

In section 3.3.1 we endeavored to characterize *that, for to* and Equi complements from the point of view of the verbs governing them. (Admittedly, the point concerning the more verbal character of *that*, as opposed to *for to* and Equi, complements necessarily brought in a first reference to the internal properties of the three complements.) It seems that most of the contrasts raised at the beginning of this chapter (cf. [2a, b], [3a, b], [3c, d], [5a, b], and [6a, b]) can be accounted for in terms of Verb$_1$, supplemented by the point about the verbal character of *that* complements.

In this section the point of view will be shifted wholly to the internal properties of the three types of complements. (It will be seen that the difference between [2c, d], say, follows from the description of these internal properties.) We may start from Jespersen's (1961: 304) observation that "in nearly all sentences the combination of *for* and an infinitive denotes some vague possibility or something imagined." By way of contrast, Bresnan (1972: 71 ff.) suggests that *that* complements are more specific and more definite. She illustrates her point with sentences that are properly outside the scope of this inquiry inasmuch as in them the higher predicate is an adjective, and not a verb. (Bresnan (1972: 72) notes that judgments vary regarding the acceptability of [12a]. She gives it one question mark.)

[12] **a.** ?It's rather odd for a man to be chairing a women's meeting.
   b. It's rather odd that a man is chairing a women's meeting.

[13] **a.** It's always rather odd for a man to be chairing a women's meeting.
   b. *It's always rather odd that a man is chairing a women's meeting.

Bresnan (1972: 74) paraphrases [13b] as follows: "There is a particular definite event x, in which a man is chairing a women's meeting, such that at all times t, x is odd at time t." As for [13a], Bresnan (1972: 74) paraphrases it as follows: "Every time you have an event in which a man is chairing a women's meeting, it's odd (an odd time, situation)." The anomaly of [13b] is then that "a single, definite thing or event is asserted to be odd for all time." Thus the *that* complementizer contributes the notion of definiteness while *for to* is less specific, allowing sentence [13a]. (In this connection, cf. also Aijmer (1972: 90).)

It is in accordance with the definiteness of *that* clauses, as noted by Bresnan (1972: 72), that they are impervious to modal operators, while *for to* complements, not being definite, are not. For instance, contrast the sentences of [14] (from Bresnan 1970: 302):

[14] **a.** It may not distress John for Mary to see his relatives.
   b. It may not distress John that Mary sees his relatives.

[14a, b] differ in their presuppositions (Bresnan (1970: 302), cf. also Bresnan (1972: 72 ff.)): [14b] presupposes that Mary does see his relatives,

while [14a] does not: *that,* being definite, seals off its domain from external modality. One might note, however, as does Menzel (1975: 14), that when the complement clause contains a perfective marker, even a *for to* complement is impervious to external modality, cf. *It may distress John for Mary to have seen his relatives.*

Bresnan (1972: 75 ff.) further supports her analysis with such sentences as those in [15] and [16]:

[15] **a.** John made a proposal for funds to be raised.

b. John made a proposal that funds be raised.

[16] **a.** John made one proposal after another for funds to be raised.

b. ?John made one proposal after another that funds be raised.

[16b] is worse than [16a] because the *that* complement pins down the proposal made, while the *for to* complement "provides a description non-specific enough to subsume several distinct proposals," to quote Bresnan (1972: 76).

Bresnan's account seems convincing. We propose to supplement it with two additional observations, which suggest themselves when we consider Verb$_1$s that take both *for to* and *that* complement clauses. We may consider contrasts such as those between the *for to* and *that* versions of [17a, b]:

[17] **a.** I hated for John to be unpunctual.

??I hated that John was unpunctual.

b. I loved for John to speak out at the meeting.

??I loved that John spoke out at the meeting.

The sentences of [17a, b], with Verb$_1$s from the class of verbs of desideration of the *for to* pattern, are again within the scope proper of the present inquiry. On the whole, they confirm Bresnan's suggestion that *that* clauses are more specific and more definite than *for to* clauses. It is noticeable that the *that* versions of [17a, b] are severely strained. However, they may be redeemed if a suitable NP—such as *it* or *the fact*—is inserted in front of the complement clause. (For the postulation of such NPs in front of *that* complement clauses, we have drawn on work by Kiparsky and Kiparsky (1970) and Menzel (1975: 63 ff.). Indeed, Menzel (1975) postulates a number of other NPs, apart from *it* and *the fact,* as well, but we leave these aside here.) By contrast, such additional NPs are less compatible with *for to* clauses:

[18] **a.** I hate ??it/*the fact for John to be unpunctual.

I hated it/the fact that John was unpunctual.

b. I love ??it/*the fact for John to speak out at the meeting.

I loved it/the fact that John spoke out at the meeting.

In [17a, b] and [18a, b] the truth of the *that* clauses is presupposed, while the corresponding *for to* clauses are less definite. When the truth of a *that* complement is presupposed, the NP *the fact* can quite generally be inserted in front of the *that* clause. (Of course, it is not possible to claim that all *that* clauses are presupposed to be true; for some discussion, cf. Kiparsky and Kiparsky (1970).) In the present context, it is of interest to note that when a *that* clause allows the insertion of the NP *the fact* directly in front of it, we can hardly say that a Verb$_1$ that governs the *that* clause expresses desideration. To put it another way, if S$_2$ is presupposed to be true—manifested by the potential insertion of the NP *the fact*—a Verb$_1$ cannot express desideration for, or against, the realization of S$_2$. *Hate* and *love* were listed above as verbs of desideration with a pleasure (displeasure) component. In the *that* versions of [18a, b], which are well-formed, *hate* and *love* express an emotive reaction on the part of NP$_1$ to the fact of S$_2$. It follows from this argument that when a Verb$_1$ of desideration does not carry such an extra ingredient of meaning, it is less easy to combine it with a *that* clause preceded by the NP *the fact*. For instance, **I desire the fact that John will speak out/spoke out at the meeting* seems worse than *I love the fact that John will speak out/spoke out at the meeting*.

Our second additional observation concerns sentences where the specificity or otherwise of the complement is neutralized, owing to the nature of the verb in it. Such neutralization occurs with stative verbs in the complement, which seem to allow little scope for one/many or specific/nonspecific contrasts. In such cases *for to* and *that* complements should be close synonyms. This seems to be borne out: contrast the sentences of [10], repeated here for ease of reference, with those of [19]. [19a–c] are somewhat strained for most speakers except perhaps in some dialects of American English:

[10] **a.** John wants for Sue to know French.
   b. John desires for his wife to own a car.
   c. John would not like for his nephew to resemble his father.

[19] **a.** John wants it that Sue should know French.
   b. John desires it that his wife should own a car.
   c. John would not like it that his nephew resembled his father.

To reiterate, we have endeavored to provide a contrastive account of the semantics of *that* and *for to* clauses. Our method has been to consider some Verb$_1$s that take both types of complement clauses. Drawing on work by Bresnan (1972), we have argued that when a Verb$_1$ takes both *that* and *for to* clauses, the *that*-clause variant is the more definite of the two. The *that*-clause variant is also more often compatible with the insertion of the NP *the fact*. When the NP *the fact* can be inserted in front of the *that* clause, a Verb$_1$ does not express desideration for (against) the realization of S$_2$, but only an emotion in respect of the content of S$_2$. Further, we have argued that when an S$_2$ allows little scope for the specific/nonspecific dichotomy, *that* and *for to* clauses are close synonyms.

As for the distinctive semantic property of Equi structures of the type of [4c], Vendler's (1968: 59 ff.) reference to the presence of a subjunctive or a subjunctive equivalent in what he calls the matrix is helpful. (In the terms used in schematic representations here, Vendler's 'matrix' corresponds to our S_2.) Vendler does not explicitly define what he means by a 'subjunctive equivalent', but it seems clear from his examples (cf. Vendler (1968: especially 60)) that he intends for this concept to refer to, or at least permits it to refer to, appropriate forms of *shall* and *will*. Vendler's suggestion apparently amounts to the proposal that all Equi structures of the form of [4c] should be derived from underlying structures with subjunctives or subjunctive equivalents. This proposal should perhaps be seen against the background of a framework where semantic interpretation takes place at the deep-structure level only. Since it is assumed here that surface structure may contribute to semantic interpretation, there is no a priori reason to adopt Vendler's view concerning the syntactic derivation of Equi sentences.

Irrespective of the role of subjunctives and subjunctive equivalents in the syntactic derivation of Equi sentences, the subjunctive-like semantic interpretation of Equi structures is corroborated by such pairs as those in [20] and [21] (Vendler (1968: 60)):

[20] **a.** I wish to be in Paris.
    b. I wish that I were in Paris.

[21] **a.** He preferred to do the job.
    b. He preferred that he do the job.

The subjunctive or subjunctive equivalent analysis is also relevant to *forget* (cf. [2c, d]), *remember* and the 'come to a decision' class, left in abeyance above. For instance, it explains why *I have decided to have a temperature* [7a] is interpreted as meaning that I should/would have a temperature and not that I had a temperature.

Decide, prefer, and *wish* are verbs that occur both with infinitival Equi and with *that* clauses. This makes it easy to consider their subjunctive equivalents. However, the usefulness of referring to subjunctive equivalents in the semantic interpretation of the sentence is not restricted to predicates of this type. We may consider verbs of the intention and intention and endeavor classes. As noted above, apart from the 'come to a decision' class, these do not take *that* clauses, but do take infinitives of the Equi pattern. A subjunctive equivalent may be discerned in the semantic interpretation of their complement sentences as well. For instance, *He intended/endeavored to do it* implies that in the view of NP$_1$ S$_2$ should be realized. Indeed, even though Vendler does not consider them, it seems that a subjunctive-equivalent interpretation is relevant to *for to* complement sentences governed by verbs expressing volition as well, for we may recall [10a–c] and [19a–c]. Overall, it seems that Vendler's suggestion is relevant to volitional verbs only, but not to other verbs, irrespective of whether the latter take *for to* or Equi complements. For instance, it would be gratuitous to assume the presence of a subjunctive or of a subjunctive equivalent in the semantic reading of sentences like *He claimed/pretended to have done it* or of *He claim-*

ed/pretended to be an expert. The correlation of the presence of a subjunctive interpretation with the class of verbs of volition lends independent interest to the classification of Equi and *for to* predicates adduced above, which was to a significant extent based on the notion of volition. To put it another way, our classification allows a more precise statement of the role of a subjunctive or of a subjunctive equivalent in the semantic interpretation of infinitive constructions, including both Equi and *for to* structures.

3.4 CASE GRAMMAR REVISITED

It seems that case grammar is more readily useful in the analysis of the *for to* pattern than in the analysis of the *that* pattern. With respect to the latter, the case role of NP_1 does not exercise any influence on that of NP_2. For instance, when NP_1 is an Agent, as with verbs of communication, NP_2 can still have any of the four case roles discussed in Chapter 2, subject to compatibility with $Verb_2$, of course. Thus all of *John noted that Sue had written a letter to him/that Sue had been feeling low/that Sue had received a letter from a friend/that Sue had grown old/that Sue was tall when grown up* are good. If NP_1 is an Experiencer, as with verbs of believing, all four case roles are again possible for NP_2, as can be ascertained if the *that* clauses just cited are embedded under *John believed*. Since it is therefore hard to discern a basis for NP_1 restricting case roles of NP_2 in the *that* pattern, the rest of this section will be devoted to the *for to* pattern.

The classes of the *for to* pattern are relatively simple to deal with. The version of case grammar that was used in Chapter 2 will be taken for granted here as well. Further, the conclusions of Chapter 2 provide a convenient point of departure. The main focus of interest in this section is to explore what similarities and differences there are between those conclusions and properties of the *for to* pattern.

With verbs of 1.1.1 of the *for to* pattern, NP_1 is clearly an Experiencer only.

Q. What did John do?
A. ??John longed/wanted for Sue to write a letter to him.

The prediction transferred from the patterns of Chapter 2 is that all four case roles should be possible for NP_2. This prediction is corroborated; cf. the sentences of [22a–d]:

[22] **a.** John longed/wanted for Sue to write a letter to him.
 b. John longed/wanted for Sue to know the truth.
 c. John longed/wanted for Sue to receive a letter from a friend.
 d. John longed/wanted for Sue to grow old/to be tall when grown up.

The element of communication in verbs of class 1.1.2 makes the subjects of verbs of this class Agents. The prediction, on account of the Agent Rule, is then that roles other than that of the Agent should be excluded for NP_2. This is borne out, as witness [23a–d]:

[23] a. John begged for Sue to do something about the matter.
   b. *John begged for Sue to know the truth.
   c. *John begged for Sue to receive a letter from a friend.
   d. *John begged for Sue to grow old/to be tall when grown up.

The other classes of *for to* verbs are small, but perhaps growing. The verbs of 1.2 are verbs of positive desideration and intention and their subjects are Agents and Experiencers simultaneously. The transferred prediction is then that an Agent should be perfect as NP_2 and that the other three case roles should be not quite perfect, but not very bad either:

[24] a. John intended/planned for Sue to write a letter to him.
   b. ?John intended/planned for Sue to know the truth.
   c. John intended/planned for Sue to receive a letter from a friend.
   d. ?John intended/planned for Sue to grow old/to be tall when grown up.

The predictions are confirmed for [24a, b] and [24d], but not for [24c], which is good and not doubtful. Other verbs taking Benefactive subjects confirm this finding: *John intended for Sue to own two cars/for Max to gain time.* This finding is of interest, because it is the first appreciable divergence from conclusions reached for the *to* and *ing* patterns in Chapter 2. The conclusion in question was motivated by sentences such as ?*John intended to receive a letter from a friend* and ?*John intended receiving a letter from a friend,* which were argued to be slightly doubtful. The degree of violation in the patterns of Chapter 2 was argued to vary, depending on the degree of agentivity of NP_2, that is, of PRO. If a NP_2 was capable of being interpreted agentively, the result was good. By contrast, in the *for to* pattern the construction is good even if NP_2 is not agentive.

We suggest that a crucial feature of the interpretation of [24c] is that the realization of S_2 is viewed as within the control of NP_1. To explicate the notion of 'controllability' and its relevance in the present context, we may profitably refer to Kuno (1970) and Berman (1970). Strictly speaking, Kuno (1970: 352) does not speak of controllability, but rather uses the terms [+self-controllable] and [−self-controllable]. He introduces and characterizes them in his footnote 9. We may quote the beginning of the footnote:

> [+self-controllable] is a semantic feature which is independent of [+active]. Both features play an important role in syntax. For example, roughly speaking, [+self-controllable] is required for forming imperative constructions, while [+active] is a deciding factor for progressive constructions. *Fall* and *encounter* are [+active], but [−self-controllable], and therefore,
>
> The capsule is falling down closer and closer to the earth.
> *Fall down.
> I am encountering great difficulties.
> *Encounter great difficulties.

Sleep, semantically, consists of two components: an act of falling asleep, and a state of being asleep. The former action is self-controllable, and, therefore, *sleep* as a whole is [+self-controllable]. On the other hand, *asleep* refers only to the state, and does not contain the "falling asleep" component. Therefore, *asleep* is [−self-controllable].

Kuno (1970: 352), then, visualizes predicates as being marked either as +self-controllable or as −self-controllable. −Self-controllable predicates include *fall, encounter* and *asleep,* while *sleep* is +self-controllable. In our opinion, the choice of *sleep* as a case in point of a +self-controllable predicate—and the semantic analysis of *sleep* offered by Kuno—may not be the most felicitous possible, but the notion of self-controllability that emerges from Kuno (1970: 352) is a coherent one. A predicate is +self-controllable if it can form an imperative construction. The permissibility of an imperative construction is a syntactic correlate of +self-controllable, but, in addition, we may perhaps discern a descriptive content in the meaning of the term 'self-controllable.'

The analysis of controllability is taken up by Berman (1970: 205 ff.). When discussing the concept, she argues that "we must establish that predicates are marked for a feature which reflects on the intention and volition of their subjects, and that there exist at least three syntactically relevant distinctions along these lines."

We are not persuaded that a reference to the notions of intention and volition is sufficient in the present context, for what is involved is the capability to control—controllability. Indeed, controllability plays a crucial role in the definition of the three classes that Berman sets up. In her numbering, the classes are [9a–c]. We quote her (1970: 205) below:

[9] **a.** Fully within the 'control' of the subject, e.g.: *go, come, wait, stay, write a letter,* etc.

b. Partly within the control of the subject, e.g.: *win/lose the race, arrive/finish on time,* etc.

c. Beyond the control of the subject, e.g.: *be tall, receive a letter,* etc.[8]

It is worth quoting part of Berman's (1970: 230) footnote 8 as well:

This last may really be two classes, to wit:

a. under the 'control' of someone other than the subject: *receive a letter, suffer ostracism, get a spanking*

b. under no one's control: *be tall, have visions*

I have no really compelling evidence for this, especially since there are so few non-passives where 'control' (in the intuitively clear, though very-hard-to-define-formally way I am using the term) is in the hands of someone other than the subject. It is evident that much more work needs to be done on these distinctions. . . .

Berman's observations are of relevance for our discussion of case grammar.

For the sake of presentational clarity, it is useful to coin some new terms. Predicates of Berman's class [9a] are fully within the control of their subjects and predicates of Berman's class [9b] are partly under the control of their subjects. We will use the terms INTERNAL CONTROL for such predicates. Predicates displaying internal control are either fully or partly (partially) under the control of their subjects. Berman's class [9c]-a designates predicates that are not under the control of their subjects, but are under the control of some other entity. We will coin the term EXTERNAL CONTROL for them. It is not very easy to make the full-versus-partial division with respect to the concept of external control and we refrain from making it. Predicates of Berman's class [9c]-b are not under the control of anyone. The term NONCONTROL may be used for them.

In the *to* and *ing* patterns, NP_2 is, of course, empty and coreferential with NP_1. The Benefactive case expresses the transfer of something from someone to someone else. (All parties to the transaction need not be expressed, of course.) NP_2 receives, or loses, something. If the transfer is intentional for NP_2, NP_2 is an Agent in addition to being a Benefactive. If the transfer is unintentional and beyond the control of NP_2, NP_2 is purely a Benefactive. It is the latter case that is of interest here. In the *to* and *ing* patterns of Chapter 2, NP_1 is NP_2. That is, if $Verb_2$ expresses something that is unintentional for, or beyond the control of NP_2, that something is unintentional for, or beyond the control of NP_1 as well, since NP_1 is coreferential with NP_2 in these patterns of Chapter 2. This is the source of the doubt attaching to Benefactive NPs with verbs of intention in the *to* and *ing* patterns. By contrast, in the *for to* pattern, NP_1 is noncoreferential with NP_2. There are two different entities involved. $Verb_2$ can still express something that is unintentional for, or beyond the control of NP_2. The transfer expressed by a Benefactive, while unintentional for, or beyond the control of NP_2, may be intentional for, or within the control of NP_1, and, consequently, the *for to* pattern is well formed when NP_2 is a Benefactive.

There is a slight modification still to be made. While the observations above, regarding the presence of one entity only in the patterns of Chapter 2, hold true of virtually all verbs of Chapter 2, there are one or two verbs that are exceptional in that they imply an understood additional entity. Given the understood additional entity, predicates of Berman's class [9c]-a are good in the complement sentence even though $Verb_1$ is a verb of volition and NP_1 is an Agent and NP_2 is not. *Arrange* is a case in point, as in *The team arranged to get a beating*. We note, incidentally, that the additional entity may be overtly expressed, as in *The team arranged with their opponents to get a beating*. Since the external control reading is relevant to so few verbs of the pattern of Chapter 2, and since it is more generally relevant to verbs of the *for to* pattern, we introduced it here, rather than in Chapter 2.

It may be helpful to reiterate our main argument in this section so far. Drawing on work by Berman (1970), we have adopted the following classification of predicates with respect to controllability:

PREDICATES

control-
lable

+subject
control

fully control-
lable: *write*

partly controllable:
win the race

−subject
control: *receive a letter*

−controllable,
noncontrol: *be tall*

There is clearly a close relation between controllability and case grammar, particularly with respect to the Agent role. The relation is especially close with respect to partly controllable predicates with subject control, on the one hand, and agentive reinterpretations, on the other. We recall that agentive reinterpretations are a subtype of coreferential roles. They presuppose a non-reinterpreted reading without an Agent, and a reinterpreted reading with an Agent. If $Verb_2$ allows it, PRO is interpreted agentively when NP_1 is an Agent and $Verb_1$ is a verb of volition. The degree of reinterpretation depends on the predicate of S_2. Regarding the relation of controllability and case roles, then, it seems clear that predicates that are fully controllable typically take Agents as subjects without any agentive reinterpretation. It is equally clear that predicates that are not controllable by anyone do not take Agents under any circumstances. Nor do they allow agentive reinterpretations. On the other hand, predicates that are partly controllable with subject control are typical examples of predicates that are subject to agentive reinterpretations. For example, we may consider *John endeavored to win the race/to cough.* When an agentive reinterpretation takes place, the PRO in question is assigned the role of the Agent. In addition, it still retains its non-reinterpreted role, at least given Cook's framework, which has provided the underpinning for much of the discussion of case grammar here. In *John endeavored to win the race,* PRO is an Agent, but it still retains its Benefactive role. In *John endeavored to cough,* PRO is an Agent, but it must still be an Object as well. This is so even by definition, since there is an Object in every sentence in Cook's (1979: 206) framework.

We may perhaps go so far as to say that the permissibility of agentive reinterpretations may be identified with predicates that are partly controllable with subject control. In general this identification seems possible. Even so, we still retain the term 'agentive reinterpretation' for its descriptive content.

Agentive reinterpretations produce coreferential roles and they can therefore be subsumed under coreferential roles. However, neither agentive reinterpretations nor readings of predicates that are partly controllable with subject control can be identified with coreferential roles. 'Coreferential roles' is a broader concept. Even when the NP concerned is NP_2 and one of the coreferential roles is

that of the Agent, coreferential roles do not necessarily involve agentive reinterpretations. For instance, in *John intends to walk faster,* the PRO preceding
walk is an Agent and an Object without an agentive reinterpretation. There is no
non-reinterpreted reading such that the subject of *walk* is not an Agent. Therefore, it does not make sense to speak of a reinterpretation, as it does with
predicates such as *win/lose the race, cough,* etc., which may be interpreted
nonagentively. It will be recalled that agentive reinterpretations may be a matter
of degree, depending on the predicate in question, more so than coreferential
readings that do not involve agentive reinterpretations. Therefore, while all
agentive reinterpretations, if successful, produce coreferential roles, not all coreferential roles, even when the relevant NP is NP_2, involve agentive reinterpretations. In terms of controllability, *decide* belongs to fully controllable
predicates with subject control.

The class of coreferential roles is then divided into those that involve agentive reinterpretations and those that do not. The class of coreferential roles
encompasses +controllable predicates that display +subject control, but they do
not encompass +controllable predicates that do not display subject control. For
instance, we may consider *John arranged to receive a letter* and, taking *arrange*
as the typical verb of class 1.3 of *for to* verbs, *John arranged for Sue to receive a
letter.* In both of them, the subject of S_2, PRO and *Sue,* respectively, is a
Benefactive. In neither of them is the subject of S_2 an Agent. It is not an Agent
without an agentive reinterpretation. Neither is an agentive reinterpretation possible. Consequently, the concept of coreferential roles is not relevant to predicates displaying external control.

To facilitate discussion, we will use the term EXTERNAL CONTROL READING
to refer to a reading of a predicate displaying external control.

External control readings are separate from coreferential roles. They are a
second factor mitigating the Agent Rule. Limiting the discussion to the complement sentence patterns covered here, we may say that in an external control
reading $Verb_2$ is not within the control of NP_2, but that $Verb_1$ is such that there is
an overt or understood NP in the matrix sentence that is interpreted as controlling
the realization of S_2. If NP_2 is PRO and coreferential with NP_1, as in the *to* and
ing patterns of Chapter 2, an external control reading is excluded except if $Verb_1$
implies the existence of an expressed or understood NP, in addition to the
subject, in the matrix sentence. For instance, we may consider *John arranged to
receive a letter,* where PRO is coreferential with NP_1. There is no overt second
NP in S_1 in this sentence, but just such a second NP is understood. We may
profitably quote the relevant sense of *arrange* from the OED: 'to come to, or
make, a settlement with other persons as to a matter to be done, so that all
concerned in it shall do their part'. Of crucial interest in the definition is of
course the reference to other persons. We conclude, then, that if NP_1 is coreferential with NP_2, an external control reading presupposes an overt or an understood second NP in the matrix sentence, the second NP being noncoreferential
with NP_1 and NP_2.

Proceeding to the *for to* pattern of the present chapter, where NP_1 is never coreferential with NP_2, we may observe that *arrange* of class 1.3 occurs in it, as in *John arranged for Sue to get a letter.* The relevant sense of *arrange* is of course much the same as above and implies a second NP. However, as is shown in [24c], this is not necessary, given that NP_1 and NP_2 are noncoreferential. Verbs occurring as $Verb_1$ may mean that NP_1 is in control of the realization of S_2, and no reference to another—overt or understood—NP is necessary or possible. [24c] may serve as an example.

To sum up our discussion of external control readings, we have argued that they have the following properties:

1. They may arise when $Verb_2$ is of the type +controllable, −subject control.
2. External control readings presuppose that there are two noncoreferential NPs in the sentence. If NP_1 is coreferential with NP_2, external control readings presuppose that $Verb_1$ implies the presence of an overt or an understood NP in S_1. If NP_1 is not coreferential with NP_2, the two NPs are sufficient to satisfy the two-NP requirement.

This account makes a prediction with respect to such predicates occurring as $Verb_2$s as take Agents and are fully within the control of their subjects. Since in the infinitival and *ing* patterns of Chapter 2 NP_1 is coreferential with NP_2, it follows that such predicates in S_2 are awkward with matrix predicates such as *arrange,* which imply that the realization of S_2 is not within the control of NP_1 directly, but of an understood or expressed second NP in S_1. More precisely, such combinations are awkward unless a second controlling party may be understood. For instance, consider ?*John arranged to write a letter, John arranged to buy a new house.*

Going back to the *for to* pattern, we note that NP_1 can then control or effect a transfer of something beyond the control of NP_2 [24c], but that it seems harder for NP_1 to control the realization of S_2 when S_2 expresses a process or a state that affects NP_2 and that is beyond the intentions and beyond the control of both NP_1 and NP_2, as witness [24d]. The same goes for cognition, as shown by [24b]. On the other hand, while a sensation or a feeling may be beyond the intentional control of NP_2, NP_1 can apparently control or effect it. Thus Experiencers as NP_2s are good when governed by verbs of sensation or feeling: *John intended for Sue to see the explosion/for Sue to experience a new sensation at the party.* These are external control readings, not agentive reinterpretations, for *Sue* is an Experiencer in both, not an Agent.

Verbs of class 1.3 of the *for to* pattern express endeavor in addition to desideration and intention and their subjects are Agents only. The class is small, consisting of *arrange* only. We already had occasion to refer to it when examining external control readings. Here is a fuller pattern:

[25] **a.** John arranged for Sue to write a letter to him.
　　　b. *John arranged for Sue to know the truth.

    c. John arranged for Sue to receive a letter from a friend.
    d. *John arranged for Sue to grow old/to be tall when grown up.

[25c] was discussed above. As for [25b] and [25d], they are neither exceptional nor surprising. Since the predicates of S_2s in them are outside the control of their subjects and of anyone else, neither agentive reinterpretations nor external control readings are possible. So the violations of the Agent Rule are not redeemed. If NP_2 is an Experiencer governed by a verb of sensation or perhaps by one of feeling, external control readings become mitigating factors, as in *John arranged for Sue to see the explosion/for Sue to experience a new sensation,* which are good. That is, it is possible for NP_1 to endeavor to effect a transfer, a sensation or perhaps even a feeling for NP_2, an entity different from NP_1, even though the transfer, sensation or feeling is beyond the control of NP_2. On the other hand, it is not possible for NP_1 to endeavor to effect a process or a state [25d] or a cognition [25b], which is beyond the control of both NP_1 and NP_2.

    Verbs of negative volition take Experiencers as their subjects. It is then predicted, not only on the basis of Chapter 2, but on the basis of class 1 of the *for to* pattern, that all four case roles should be possible for NP_2. This is corroborated by [26a–d]:

[26] **a.** John hated for Sue to write a letter to him.
      b. John hated for Sue to know the truth.
      c. John hated for Sue to receive a letter from a friend.
      d. John hated for Sue to grow old/for Sue to be tall when grown up.

    To sum up this section, the most general conclusion is that there are constraints on the selection of NP_2 that are related to the selection of NP_1. In most cases the constraints are similar to those observed with the *to* and *ing* patterns of Chapter 2 and expressible by the Agent Rule. However, verbs of desideration and intention and of desideration, intention and endeavor of the *to* and *ing* patterns do not allow NP_2 to be a Benefactive, while such verbs of the *for to* pattern do. The latter even allow NP_2 to be an Experiencer if $Verb_2$ is a verb of sensation or perhaps even one of feeling. The term 'external control reading' was introduced to describe combinations where NP_1 is viewed as controlling the realization of S_2. It was argued that coreferential roles and external control readings constitute factors that mitigate the Agent Rule. Coreferential roles may or may not involve agentive reinterpretations. Coreferential roles involving agentive reinterpretations mean that the subject of S_2 is viewed as an Agent, it being presupposed that when S_2 is not embedded, its subject is not necessarily an Agent. It may be possible to identify agentive reinterpretations with predicates that are partly controllable with subject control. Coreferential roles without agentive reinterpretations mean that either NP_1 or NP_2 is always an Agent in addition to bearing a second role. Coreferential roles, whether or not they involve agentive reinterpretations, cannot be identified with external control readings. The reason is simply that external control readings do not produce coreferential roles.

An external control reading may occur when the predicate of S_2 is not controllable by its subject, but is controllable by someone else other than its subject. Two cases of external control readings should be distinguished. If NP_1 is coreferential with NP_2, as in the *to* and *ing* patterns of Chapter 2, the verb of the matrix sentence must be such as to imply the presence of another NP in the matrix sentence, with this second—overt or understood—NP controlling the realization of S_2. If NP_1 is noncoreferential with NP_2, as in the *for to* pattern, an external control reading may be possible even when $Verb_1$ does not imply that there is a second—understood or overt—NP in the matrix sentence. $Verb_1$ must still imply, though, that the realization of S_2 is within the control of NP_1.

A prediction made by the postulation of external control readings is that if the *for to* pattern spreads further and comes to be used with verbs of negative desideration and intention and with verbs of negative desideration, intention and endeavor, these new patterns, too, should allow NP_2 to be a Benefactive or even an Experiencer with verbs of sensation or perhaps of feeling as $Verb_2$.

Our discussion above, and throughout the book, is focused on constructions whose $Verb_2$s are in the active voice. A full treatment of passive sentences cannot be attempted within the confines of the present book. However, given that our case grammar analysis of sentences with active $Verb_2$s has now been outlined, we may briefly glance at its potential applicability to sentences with passive $Verb_2$s. We will only sample constructions whose $Verb_2$s take infinitival complement sentences. Starting with $Verb_1$s expressing desideration, as in [27a, b], we recall that their subjects are Experiencers, not Agents, and that such sentences are therefore unaffected by the Agent Rule:

[27] **a.** John desired to be elected.
    b. John wanted to be consulted.

Proceeding straight to $Verb_1$s of endeavor, we may consider [28a–c]:

[28] **a.** John tried to be arrested.
    b. John tried to be elected.
    c. John tried to be noticed.

[28a–c] are directly modeled on sentences devised by Barbara Partee and discussed by Růžička (1983: 323, note 2), who notes that Partee has pointed out that they ''are all quite good in English.'' There are speakers of English who do not like [28a–c]. One common comment we elicited is that [28a], say, should be changed to *John tried to get himself arrested*. While this latter sentence is quite generally preferred to [28a], let us set these doubts regarding the acceptability of [28a–c] aside for the moment and regard [28a–c] as acceptable.

In [28a–c] NP_1 is an Agent. If we do not consider the possibility of a reinterpretation, NP_2 in [28a–c] is not an Agent, but rather an Object. [28a–c], then, do not conform to the Agent Rule.

The least sophisticated response to sentences such as [28a–c] might be to say that the Agent Rule is operative only when a Verb$_2$ is in the active voice. Such a conclusion is questionable, though, because of sentences such as [29]:

[29] *John tried to be handed/given the message in time.

The passive *John was handed/given the message in time* is good, but [29] is bad. This judgment seems subject to little or no variation or doubt. The illformedness of [29] suggests that the Agent Rule is operative even if a Verb$_2$ is in the passive voice. We are then led to look for a mitigating factor which is operative in [28a–c], but not in [29]. An account of [28a–c] in terms of a mitigating factor becomes more attractive when we recall that the acceptability of [28a–c] is subject to idiolectal variation.

It is perhaps helpful to consider the predicates *to be elected* and *to be handed/given the message*. We may compare the two predicates with active predicates that are semantically similar:

to be elected	to win the election
to be handed/given the message	to receive the message

The subject of *to win the election* is a Benefactive. The predicate displays partial subject control and the subject is then capable of an agentive reinterpretation. The subject of *to receive a message,* where *receive* again means 'get while one is passive', and not 'accept' or 'welcome', is a Benefactive as well, but the predicate displays noncontrol and the subject is not capable of an agentive reinterpretation. We may then consider [28b′] and [29′]:

[28b′] John tried to win the election.
[29′] *John tried to receive the message in time.

[28b] is parallel to [28b′] and [29] is parallel to [29′]. The parallelism suggests that the subject of *to be elected* is susceptible to an agentive reinterpretation, but that the subject of *to be handed/given the message* is not thus susceptible. What, then, is crucial to the analysis of sentences such as [28a–c] and [29] is whether or not the Verb$_2$ in question allows an agentive reinterpretation of its NP$_2$.

We have arrived at our analysis of [28a–c] and [29] in the context of our consideration of case grammar. Our account is not radically different from accounts of [28a–c] by Růžička (1983) and Comrie (1984). (As far as we can determine, they consider neither sentence [29] nor sentences analogous to it.) The former (1983: 323) points out that in sentences such as [28a–c] "the passive in the complement is not very 'passive.'" The latter (1984: 453) discusses sentences such as *Otto tried to be punished/picked up/X-rayed* and comments that "the interpretation that is assigned to the sentence is one in which the controlling noun phrase in fact has high agentivity with respect to the situation expressed by the infinitive construction." Růžička and Comrie thus assign [28a–c] and analogous sentences a degree of—or even a high degree of—agentivity.

This feature is shared by our account. The accounts are nevertheless not entirely identical. One apparent difference between their accounts, on the one hand, and ours, on the other, is that they assign the agentivity in question to the higher NP, NP_1 in our terms, not to NP_2, as we do. In the pattern NP_1 and NP_2 designate the same entity, of course, and the difference between the two accounts should not be exaggerated. However, it seems to us that in all of [28a–c] and [29] NP_1 is the subject of the same verb, *try,* and has high agentivity in all of them. What varies is the predicate of S_2 and the degree to which NP_2 is susceptible to an agentive reinterpretation. To put it another way, what varies is the degree to which NP_2 may exert partial control over the predicate of S_2.

The account of the relative wellformedness of [28a–c] and analogous sentences is motivated by an additional consideration. As hinted at above, quite often a *get* construction is possible as an alternative to sentences such as [28a–c]. Thus, all of [30a–c] are good:

[30] **a.** John tried to get himself arrested.
   b. John tried to get himself elected.
   c. John tried to get himself noticed.

To most people [30a–c] sound better than [28a–c]. This is no accident in the context of our account, for it is clear that the subjects of the non-embedded sentences of [31a–c] are appreciably more agentive than the corresponding subjects of [32a–c]:

[31] **a.** John got himself arrested.
   b. John got himself elected.
   c. John got himself noticed.

[32] **a.** John was arrested.
   b. John was elected.
   c. John was noticed.

The subjects of [31a–c] are agentive enough to pass tests of agentivity, while those of [32a–c] do not pass such tests. (We thank an anonymous reviewer for a comment relating to the point.)

[33] **a.** Q. What did John do? A. He got himself arrested.
   b. What John did was (to) get himself arrested.

[34] **a.** Q. What did John do? A. *He was arrested.
   b. *What John did was (to) be arrested.

Since the subjects of [31a–c] are more agentive than those of [32a–c], it is natural that the former are easier to interpret agentively, which explains why [30a–c] are appreciably better than [28a–c].

We have argued that [28a–c] and analogous sentences are accounted for on the basis of agentive reinterpretations. External control readings are relevant as a mitigating factor as well even when an S_2 is in the passive voice. We may consider [35a, b]:

[35] **a.** John begged to be arrested.
    b. John asked to be consulted.

As is typical of external control readings when NP_1 and NP_2 are coreferential, the $Verb_1$ of [35a, b] implies the presence of an understood additional NP in [35a, b]. As we noted, the additional NP may be expressed overtly, as in *John begged of the officer to be arrested.*

To sum up our brief discussion of passive $Verb_2$s, we have argued that the Agent Rule is relevant even when a $Verb_2$ is in the passive voice. Both agentive reinterpretations and external control readings may be operative as mitigating factors.

Chapter *4*

VERBS GOVERNING OBJECT-CONTROLLED INFINITIVAL EQUI

4.1 INTRODUCTORY OBSERVATIONS

The present chapter constitutes an attempt to classify and to characterize a subset of verbs that appear as $Verb_1$ in sentences such as [1], with the schematic form of [1'] in surface structure:

[1] John urged Jack to leave at once.
[1'] NP_1—$Verb_1$—NP_2—to—$Verb_2$ . . .

We will be guided by the assumption that the subset in question has underlying structures of the form of [1''], illustrated by [2]:

[1''] $[NP_1$—$Verb_1$—NP_0—$[NP_2$—$Verb_2$ . . .$]_{S_2}]_{S_1}$
[2] $[[John]_{NP_1}$ $[urged]_{Verb_1}$ $[Jack]_{NP_0}$ $[[PRO]_{NP_2}$ $[to\ leave]_{Verb_2}$ . . .$]_{S_2}]_{S_1}$

That is, verbs of this subset govern an NP object, designated NP_0 in [1''] and [2], and a lower, complement sentence. NP_2 is the phonetically empty pronominal element PRO and it is controlled by NP_0.

There are several limitations on the scope of this chapter, arising from the definition of the subject. First, sentences derived via subject-controlled Equi are excluded. In general, they do not even conform to the pattern of [1'] (cf. [3a]), but at least in the case of *promise* they do:

[3] a. I want to go now.
    b. I promised him to go at once.

Sentences such as [3c], with a prepositional object, do not conform to the pattern of [1'] and are therefore excluded:

[3] c. Joe shouted at me to leave at once.

Verbs of the pattern of [3a] are discussed in Chapter 2 and verbs of the pattern of [3c] are discussed in Chapter 6. *Promise* is discussed in Chapter 2 as well. As noted there, there do not seem to be many verbs like *promise* in English, that is, verbs that may occur as $Verb_1$s in a sequence of constituents of the form of [1''], but involve control by NP_1. The pattern of *promise,* involving control by NP_1, and the pattern of the present chapter, of verbs such as *urge,* involving control by NP_0 in [1''], were distinguished from a strictly syntactic point of view by means of Visser's generalization in Chapter 2. There is a second method that is strictly syntactic as well. The second method has come to be called Bach's generalization. It goes back to work by Bach (1979; 1980: 304). We may introduce it by way of considering sentences devised by Rizzi (1986: 503):

[4] a. This leads people to the following conclusion.
    b. This leads to the following conclusion.
    c. This leads people [PRO to conclude what follows].
    d. *This leads [PRO to conclude what follows].

[4a–c] are good, but [4d] is sharply ill formed. Bach's generalization, then, relates to the non-omissibility of a direct object that is the controller of a PRO. Rizzi (1986: 503) offers a particularly clear formulation of the generalization: "In object control structures the object NP must be structurally represented."

Bach's generalization is a powerful one. There do not seem to be convincing exceptions to it in the present pattern. To be sure, Bresnan (1982: 418) argues that the pattern of *signal* is a counterexample to Bach's generalization or, more precisely, that it is not explained by it. She points to such sentences as [5a, b]:

[5] a. Louise signaled Tom to follow her.
    b. Louise signaled to follow her.

In [5a] the NP *Tom* controls PRO. In Bresnan's (1982: 418) and Koster's (1984: 433) view, [5b] shows that the NP *Tom* of [5a] is omissible. These two scholars have then devised accounts of what they take to be the omissibility of the NP following *signal.* The accounts are not identical, but, if we ignore details and technicalities, we may say that both accounts relate what the two scholars take to be the omissibility of the NP *Tom* in [5a] to the admissibility of a *for to* clause, as in *Louise signaled Tom for him to follow her* (cf. Bresnan (1982: 418 ff.), Koster (1984: 433 ff.)). However, Rizzi (1986: 504) points out that what is omitted in sentences such as [5b] is not the NP *Tom* but rather the PP *to Tom.* Crucially, as Rizzi points out, sentences such as *Louise signaled to Tom to follow her* are good. (This latter sentence belongs to the pattern of Chapter 6 and we will return to it there.) For our purposes, Bach's generalization constitutes a syntactic method for differentiating the patterns of *promise* and *urge,* alongside Visser's generalization. The NP following *promise* in [3b] may be omitted, as witness the wellformedness of *I promised to leave at once.* By contrast, the NP following *urge* cannot be omitted, as witness the illformedness of **John urged to leave at once.* (On *help,* as in *I helped (to) solve the problem,* cf. Rizzi (1986: 504).)

Second, the subset of verbs relevant here should be distinguished from verbs such as *believe* and *expect,* as in [6a, b]:

[6] a. We believe these truths to be self-evident.
   b. I expect Jack to leave soon.

[6a, b] have the same sequence of constituents as [1], but verbs such as *believe* and *expect* should be sharply separated from Equi verbs such as *urge.* This separation is fairly uncontroversial in linguistic theory. However, the precise description of the *believe/expect* class is far from uncontroversial. In one framework, which is most comprehensively argued for in Postal (1974), these verbs are analyzed as Raising triggers. More precisely, in contradistinction to the type of Raising referred to in Chapters 2 and 3, which was A-type, or subject-to-subject Raising, these verbs trigger B-type, or subject-to-object Raising. Very roughly, in the derivation of [6b], subject-to-object Raising converts a structure of the form of [7] into one of the form of [7']:

[7] $[NP_1—Verb_1—[NP_2—Verb_2 \ldots]_{S_2}]_{S_1}$
      I   expect Jack leave soon

[7'] $[NP_1—Verb_1—NP_2—[to \ Verb_2 \ldots]_{S_2}]_{S_1}$
      I   expect Jack to leave soon

An influential school of linguists, including Chomsky, has consistently rejected the rule of subject-to-object Raising. Indeed, we may trace some important features of Chomsky's framework, at least indirectly, to his rejection of the rule of subject-to-object Raising, cf. the discussion of Chomsky (1973: especially p. 237 ff.) and Chomsky (1981: 66 ff.). In the present context, we note that Chomsky's (1981: 66 ff.) position incorporates a rule of S'-deletion for verbs of the *believe/expect* class, but that this rule is only one part of an elaborate system of rules and conditions. We will refrain from presenting Chomsky's system here, and from further discussing the controversy surrounding the description of the *believe/expect* class between Postal's and Chomsky's frameworks. The reason is that the difference between verbs of this class and Equi verbs such as *urge* is not in dispute in the controversy. We will refer to verbs of the *believe/expect* class as subject-to-object or B-type Raising verbs, but in the present context this is for the sake of presentational convenience only.

It is advisable very briefly to review evidence distinguishing such B-type Raising verbs as *expect* from the subset of Equi verbs under consideration in this chapter. First, consider such pairs of sentences as those in [8], with *urge* representing verbs governing object-controlled Equi, and [9], with *expect* representing B-type Raising verbs. (For the argument, cf. Chomsky (1965: 22 ff.), Rosenbaum (1967: 58 ff.), Quirk et al. (1974: 839 ff.), Akmajian and Heny (1975: 350).)

[8] a. John urged Dr. N to examine Jack.
   b. John urged Jack to be examined by Dr. N.

[9] a. John expected Dr. N to examine Jack.
   b. John expected Jack to be examined by Dr. N.

Even though all four sentences of [8] and [9] conform to the pattern of [1'], [8a, b] differ from [9a, b] in that the a and b sentences of the former are not synonymous, whereas those of the latter are. This difference is expressed in their derivations in that (object-controlled) Equi is relevant to [8a, b] and Raising to [9a, b].

Second, consider such NPs as *advantage, cognizance* and *heed*. As is well known, and as was noted in Chapter 2, they are very limited in their distribution (cf. [10a, b]) and typically occur in idiom chunks only, *advantage* in *take advantage of, cognizance* in *take cognizance of* and *heed* in *pay heed to* (cf. [10c–e]):

[10] a. *I like advantage/cognizance/heed.
   b. *Advantage/cognizance/heed is nice.
   c. They took advantage of our experience.
   d. They took cognizance of our plight.
   e. They paid heed to our warning.

Given the extra-NP analysis for verbs of the *urge* type and the Raising analysis for those like *expect,* the following contrasts are predicted:

[11] a. *I urged advantage to be taken of their inexperience.
   b. *I urged cognizance to be taken of their plight.
   c. *I urged heed to be paid to their warning.

[12] a. I expected advantage to be taken of their inexperience.
   b. I expected cognizance to be taken of their plight.
   c. I expected heed to be paid to their warning.

For instance, the contrast between [11c] and [12c] arises from the fact that while structures such as [11'] are inadmissible, those like [12'] are allowed, given the restriction on *heed:*

[11'] [I urged [heed]$_{NP}$ [[+Unspecified]$_{NP}$ [[pay]$_{Verb}$ [heed]$_{NP}$ to their warning]$_{VP}$]$_{S_2}$]$_{S_1}$

[12'] [I expect [[+Unspecified]$_{NP}$ [[pay]$_{Verb}$ [heed]$_{NP}$ to their warning]$_{VP}$]$_{S_2}$]$_{S_1}$

The argument can be widened to encompass such other distributionally restricted NPs as the weather *it* and existential *there* (cf. Milsark (1974; 1977)), as witness the contrast between the sentences of [13] and [14]:

[13] **a.** *I urged it to rain heavily.
  b. *I urged there to be a commotion.

[14] **a.** I expected it to rain heavily.
  b. I expected there to be a commotion.

In view of these arguments, the difference between verbs governing object-controlled Equi and those governing B-type Raising may be taken to be well established.

A third limitation on the scope of this inquiry is that only such structures of the form of [1'] will be dealt with where the lower sentence is a complement sentence. For instance, adverbials expressing purpose are therefore excluded. A relevant example is cited by Visser (1973: 2264): *I'll send the porter to show you the way* (from Waugh, *Brideshead Revisited*). The admissibility of an *in order to* paraphrase, applicable here, is a diagnostic for such adverbials of purpose. Adverbials of purpose, though they may involve object-controlled Equi, are not complement sentences and will not be considered here.

Fourth, sentences with the general form of [1'] may sporadically arise through extraposition. For instance, consider *it really would not corrupt me to listen to it for three-quarters of a minute* (quoted by Visser (1973: 2275), from B. Brophy, *Don't Never Forget*). That the *to* sentence here has been extraposed from sentence-initial position is shown by the presence of *it* in the sentence cited and the admissibility of the following without an *it: To listen to it for three-quarters of a minute really would not corrupt me.* Even though Visser includes cases of this sort among sentences such as [1], it seems that, because of the relevance of extraposition to the former, but not to the latter, it is plausible to separate the two.

Fifth, cases where a *to* sentence is a postmodifier of NP_2 of [1'], rather than a complement sentence governed by $Verb_1$, are also irrelevant for present purposes. An example of such a postmodifier construction, freely invented, is *He met the man to succeed him.* Here the *to* sentence can be viewed as an abbreviation of a relative clause: *the man who was to succeed him.*

4.2 VISSER'S CLASSIFICATION EXAMINED

In section 4.1 an attempt was made to delimit the class of verbs relevant here. The arguments that were adduced serve to provide a methodological and a presentational underpinning for distinguishing the class of verbs under discussion in this section.

Proceeding to actual verbs, Visser's (1973: 2250 ff.) classification of verbs occurring in the VOSI (Verb+Object/Subject+Infinitive) pattern can serve as a starting point because of its comprehensiveness. (All references to Visser in this section not otherwise attributed are to Visser (1973).) As a first step, Visser's classes will be examined. Their members will be considered both from the point of view of the class of verbs governing object-controlled Equi, as discussed in section 4.1, and also from the point of view of their currency in Modern English. Verbs that Visser implies are not current in Modern English are left out of consideration, unless issue is taken with a particular judgment. After going through Visser's classes, we will as a second step provide our own classification. Our classification will differ from Visser's and will seek to bring out interconnections between classes, which Visser's classification was apparently not designed to do.

Visser's (2250 ff.) first class of the VOSI pattern is that of verbs of physical perception. This class includes such verbs as *behold, descry, discern, feel, find, notice, observe, perceive, see* and some others. They are not Equi verbs, though. For instance, *I noticed Jack hitting Sue* and *I noticed Sue being hit by Jack* are synonymous and *I noticed there to have been a commotion* is possible, as is *I noticed cognizance to have been taken of their plight.* The argument that these verbs are not Equi verbs is underlined by data cited by Gee (1977: 468), including *We saw it rain* and *I've never seen there be so many complaints from students before.* The description of these verbs raises a number of issues in that these verbs apparently differ from ordinary Raising verbs in a number of ways (Akmajian (1977), Gee (1977)). Akmajian (1977) sets up a third analysis for them, where in *We saw it rain,* for instance, *it* and *rain* do not form an S at any point in the derivation. An *Aspects*-style (Chomsky (1965: 71), cf. also Chomsky (1981: 48)) definition of the notion of 'subject of' is then not possible to account for the fact that in the sentence *it* is the subject of *rain.* Akmajian (1977: 455) is aware of the problem and proposes a lexical redundancy rule, which, as he puts it, "must be subjected to a good deal of testing." In the meantime, the question of whether or not these verbs should be excluded from Raising verbs remains to be settled (cf. Gee (1977: 469, next-to-last paragraph). Regardless of how this question is resolved, it is clear that these predicates are not Equi predicates (cf. Gee (1977: 467 ff.)). Therefore, they are outside the scope of the present inquiry.

Visser's (2255 ff.) second class is that of verbs of causing:

bring	let	rouse
cause	make	set
draw	mund	take
dress	procure	turn
get	proke	win
give	put	work

The list requires comment. Here, as elsewhere, it is assumed that the currency or permissibility of a given verb in Modern English should be judged on the basis of the twin criteria, first, of recorded usage, preferably of recent origin, and, second, of introspection of native speakers. As in earlier chapters, these criteria can and should be balanced against each other: care should be taken to guard against idiosyncratic instances of both recorded usage and introspection. In general, it seems that the two criteria yield results that are not at all contradictory, for dearth of recorded usage of relatively recent origin tends to go together with rejection by native speakers and vice versa. Inevitably, though, there are marginal cases that need to be considered separately. Considerations analogous to those described in Chapter 2, including the notion of present-day English as outlined there, will be applied here as well. Similarly, Visser and the OED provide our main sources for recorded data.

Dress, mund, procure and *proke* from the present list are not current in Modern English (in the pattern of [1]: this proviso should be understood, here as elsewhere, unless indicated otherwise). *Dress, mund* and *proke*, the last two of which Visser (2262) terms rare, are clear cases. There is one relatively recent example of *procure*, from 1866, in *An ingenious lover procured his rival . . . to be arrested for lunacy*, (Visser 2262, from W. D. Howells, *Venetian Life* (from the OED, though there the example is more precisely *An ingenious lover procured his . . . rival to be arrested for lunacy*)), but it seems advisable to drop *procure*, because the instance does not seem to reflect current usage. *Draw*, as in *When he had drawn me to love him* (Visser 2258, from 1892, *Argosy*, May, through the OED) does not seem to be current today. The same goes for *win*, as in *The three at table talk heatedly in dumb show, Hopton playing the peacemaker, until at last he wins the disputants to shake hands* (Visser 2265, from c. 1912, B. M. Dix, *Allison's Lad*). *Work*, as in *He was constantly working the Squire to send him . . . to a public school* (Visser 2265, from 1857, Thomas Hughes, *Tom Brown's School Days*) seems obsolete as well. *Rouse* seems restricted to reflexive objects (cf. Visser's illustrations), as in *He roused himself to invite them*, modified from Visser, and we drop it as well.

Objection may also be taken to *take*. Visser (2264) does give one recent example of it (from 1956): *I must take her something to drink* (from 1946, M. Peake, *Titus Groan*), but the construction does not conform to the pattern of [1]. However, as David Robertson has pointed out to us, it is easy to form sentences with *take* that conform to the pattern of [1], as witness *I take her to swim every day*. We do not entirely understand the structure of this sentence and of sentences analogous to it. Perhaps the infinitive is an adverbial of purpose. (We thank Ian Gurney for this suggestion.) This interpretation becomes more plausible if the sentence is analyzed to contain an understood adverbial of place: *I took her (somewhere) (in order for her) to swim every day*. We then drop *take*. On the other hand, neither *give* nor *let* should be dropped from the list, even though they severely restrict the choice of Verb$_2$, the former to *understand, note, know* and *believe* (OED), the latter to *know* (Visser 2261). As for *make*, it drops *to* in the active voice in Modern English, as in *He made her go*. We can retain it if we stretch the pattern of [1'] slightly.

Cause is problematic from another point of view. Notably, *He caused advantage to be taken of their inexperience* is good, suggesting that *cause* is a

Raising verb. However, we differ from Quirk et al. (1974: 839) and suggest that *He caused Dr. N. to examine Jack* and *He caused Jack to be examined by Dr. N.* need not be synonymous, which, on the contrary, suggests that *cause* is an Equi verb. The solution to this apparent contradiction becomes apparent when it is noted that the active-passive pair may be synonymous in that both may mean that he brought about a state of affairs such that Dr. N. examined Jack (without coming into contact with either). Therefore, it seems plausible to argue that *cause* occurs both in an Equi and in a Raising structure. Only the former, where NP_1 acts on NP_2 (in terms of [1′]), is relevant here. (Cf. the treatment of *allow* below.)

Visser's (2265 ff.) third class consists of the verb *have,* generally described by grammarians under the heading of cause, permission, experience or assertion. For his part, Visser (2265 ff.) endorses the meanings of experience, as in *her husband wouldn't have her wear a soiled garment,* causing, as in *At the hotel he had Thami wait in the cab* (Visser 2266), and assertion or insistence (in a genre of critical prose) in combination with *will/would,* as in *Some interpreters will have the prophecy to be written after the event,* modified from the OED. It seems to us, first, that in the assertion reading *have* is a Raising and not an Equi verb, as witness the synonymy of *He would not have Dr. N. to have examined Jack* and *He would not have Jack to have been examined by Dr. N.* Second, although, as Visser (2269) implies, the meanings of cause and experience are at times difficult to keep apart, in the former reading *have* seems to be ambiguously either an Equi or a Raising verb (cf. *cause* above), and, in the latter, unambiguously a Raising verb. For instance, *I won't have Dr. N. to examine Jack* and *I won't have Jack examined by Dr. N.* seem potentially nonsynonymous under the cause reading, but synonymous under the experience reading. In conclusion, then, we drop the assertion and experience readings of *have* from further consideration, but retain the Equi causative reading of the verb.

Visser's (2270 ff.) fourth class is that of verbs of inducing, forcing, compelling, praying, and he suggests that the verbs of this class connote a more strenuous putting forth of power than the verbs of causation (class II):

abet	draw	move
adjure	drive	necessitate
admonish	egg	nudge
advise	embolden	oblige
allure	empower	occasion
ask	enable	ordain
assign	encourage	pain
beckon	enforce	persuade
beg	engage	pester
beseech	enharden	pray
bid	enjoin	press
bind	entice	procure

bribe	entreat	prompt
bully	excite	provoke
call	exhort	raise
caution	fire	recommend
challenge	fit	reduce
charm	force	request
coax	grete	require
coerce	haste	rouse
commission	impel	solicit
compel	implore	spur (up)
condition	import	stimulate
conjure	importune	stir (up)
constrain	incense	suggest
corrupt	incite	summon
counsel	induce	tease
cozen	influence	tempt
crave	inspire	thank
dare	instigate	torment
decoy	intend	torture
defy	invite	trouble
demand	invoke	urge (on)
determine	kindle	wheedle
direct	labor	wire
discipline	lead	woo
dispose	lure	worry
drag	motion	

Of the 113 verbs listed, quite a number should be dropped. *Cozen, enforce, enharden, grete, haste, import* and *ordain* can be dropped without further comment. *Draw* and *procure* are rather interesting, because both already occurred in Visser's class II. We dropped them there and we repeat our decision here. It is not very easy to see what the difference is between such instances as Visser adduces of *draw* when he assigns it to class II, instances such as the one cited above and those now adduced in support of class IV, such as *He began to draw the sobbing Ann to rest against his shoulder* (from 1962, I. Murdoch, *An Unofficial Rose*, Visser 2277). We also drop *crave, corrupt, decoy, importune, incense, labor, necessitate, occasion, pain, raise, reduce, torment, torture, wheedle* and *worry*. Here are some illustrations of some of these verbs, which all seem obsolete: *I crave the torment . . . To be measured by my faultless thought* (Visser 2275, from 1584, G. Peele, *Arraignment of Paris*); *. . . that poor girl, whom she has dragged or decoyed to assist her* (Visser (2276), from 1832, Lytton, *Eugene Aram*); *It occasioned them to make indignant remonstrance* (Visser 2283, from 1849, G. Grote, *A History of Greece*, IV, via OED); *Men still pain themselves to write Latin verses* (Visser 2284, from 1870, J. R. Lowell, *My*

Study Windows); *A word's enough to raise mankind to kill* (Visser 2286, from 1814, from Byron, *Lara*). We also drop *demand* and *suggest*, for they are not current in the pattern in the present-day English: **He demanded/suggested me to leave first.* Neither *allure* nor *lure* is very good in the pattern. Visser has one example of each. The two examples are from the sixteenth century. *Lure* is perhaps marginally better in the pattern than *allure*, as in ?*The sound lured him to visit us*, modified from Visser, as opposed to ??*The sound allured him to visit us.* Consequently, we drop *allure* and retain *lure*, but the decision is a marginal one. *Egg on* is a generally preferred variant of *egg* in Modern English, as in *He egged me on to buy another bottle.*

Additionally, *intend* and *require* should be viewed as Raising verbs, in view of the admissibility of such sentences as *I do not intend there to be any trouble* and *Rules require there to be two examiners present* and of the synonymy between *I intend/require Dr. N. to examine Jack* and *I intend/require Jack to be examined by Dr. N.*

On the analogy of *stimulate*, *motivate* may be added to the class, for both verbs are possible in *The new method may motivate/stimulate students to study more deeply.* (We thank Ian Gurney for the example and for drawing our attention to *motivate*.)

To sum up, Visser's class of 113 verbs is changed to one of 85.

Visser's (2290 ff.) fifth class is that of verbs of allowing, permitting, suffering and their opposites, e.g., *hinder, prevent.*

abide	endure	permit
admit	excuse	prevent
allow	incapacitate	scare
authorize	leave	suffer
bear	let	withhold
brook	license	

Of the seventeen verbs listed, seven should be dropped as being obsolete: *abide*, cf. **The Pope may not abide this word to be heard by people*, modified from Visser (2290); *brook*, cf. **He will die rather than brook his foe to usurp his seat*, modified from Visser (2291); *excuse*, cf. **I cannot excuse him to be late; prevent*, cf. **He did not prevent his children to be kept by the parish*, modified from Visser (2296); *incapacitate*, for an example such as *A reward which his evil qualities and defects incapacitated him to receive* (Visser 2293, from 1877, S. Cox, *Salvator Mundi*), does not reflect current usage; *scare*, cf. **He scared me to leave at once; withhold*, cf. **What withholds you to go*, as opposed to *What withholds you from going.*

Forbid may be added to the class, as witness *I forbade him to follow me.*

Several of the verbs of the class, such as *allow*, are compatible with both Raising and Equi structures. As Huddleston (1971: 157) notes (cf. also Postal (1974: 318 ff. and 368), whose suggestion concerning extra predicates must however be left for another treatment), *I allowed Bob to leave* may mean either 'I gave permission for Bob to leave', or 'I gave Bob permission to leave'. The former is the Raising reading, the latter the Equi reading. Predictably, idiom chunks are possible only under a Raising reading: *I allowed cognizance to be taken of their plight* leaves the addressee of the act of permitting unspecified. Only under the Equi reading are the verbs relevant to the discussion here.

Visser's (2298 ff.) sixth class is that of verbs of wishing, desiring, hoping, etc.:

choose	hope	want
desire	intend	will
expect	mean	wish

Above, it was mentioned that *intend* belonged to Visser's class IV. Interestingly, here it turns up in class VI as well. However, it is again a Raising verb, and as such irrelevant for the discussion.

All the other verbs in the list, except for *choose,* are Raising verbs as well, cf., for example, *I desired/*chose advantage to be taken of the offer.* Further, consider *I desired/chose Dr. N. to examine Jack* and *I desired/chose Jack to be examined by Dr. N.* The *desire* sentences here display synonymy, while the *choose* sentences do not.

Visser's (2300 ff.) seventh class is that of verbs of liking, loving, hating, abhorring, fearing, etc.:

dislike	fear	loathe
doubt	hate	love
elect	like	prefer

Of these *fear, hate, like, love* and *prefer* are Raising verbs, as are *dislike, doubt* and *loathe,* if the latter are accepted in the VOSI pattern at all (cf. ?*I dislike him to do it,* ?*I dislike it to rain on a Sunday*). Thus only *elect* remains as an Equi verb from this class. (Note that *We elected Dr. N. to examine Jack* and *We elected Jack to be examined by Dr. N.* are not synonymous.)

Visser's (2302 ff.) eighth class is that of verbs of ordering, commanding, forbidding, prohibiting:

appoint	direct	re-command
assess	forbid	sign
bid	motion	signal
bind	nudge	suborn
charge	order	tell
command	pledge	

Of these, we drop *assess* as being obsolete in the pattern: **He assessed me to do it.* *Re-command* ('to command once more') does occur in the pattern, but should not be cited, because *re* is a productive prefix (cf. Koziol (1972: 168 ff.),

Marchand (1969: 188 ff.)) and other possible forms beginning with it are not cited either. (Such possible forms include *recharge, redirect.*)

Regarding *direct* and *nudge,* it should be pointed out that they were members of Visser's class IV as well. Instances adduced to illustrate the two verbs of class IV and of class VIII are partially (*direct,* Visser 2276, 2305) or indeed totally (*nudge,* Visser 2283, 2306) identical.

Visser's (2307 ff.) ninth class is that of verbs of mental perception and affection:

account	doubt	mistrust
acknowledge	esteem	presume
allow (= acknowledge)	fancy	presuppose
apprehend	find	receive (= understand)
assume	foreknow	reckon
believe	foresee	recognize
conceive	guess	regard
conclude	hold	remember
conjecture	idealize	suppose
consider	imagine	surmise
construe	interpret	suspect
count	judge	take
devise	know	think
discover	learn	trust
distinguish	make (= consider)	understand
divine	mistake	

Several of the verbs cited are not current in the VOSI pattern in Modern English. *Devise,* as in **I devised him to leave, mistrust,* as in **I mistrusted them to lean to his side,* modified from Visser (2314), *receive,* as in **He received the scripture to be the word of God,* modified from Visser (2315), are clear cases and can be dropped. *Esteem* and *idealize* are somewhat marginal, as witness *They esteem him to be a man of honor,* as opposed to *They esteem him as a man of honor,* and *He idealized the Mother Country to be something great* (modified from Visser 2311), as opposed to *He idealized the Mother Country as something great.* In each case, the *as* construction seems preferable, and we are therefore inclined to drop *esteem* and *idealize,* but we make the decision with some hesitation. It is worth noting that the two verbs would have been Equi and not Raising verbs. (We thank David Robertson for pointing this out to us.) For instance, **They esteem there to have been a mistake* and **They idealize there to have been no problem* are completely impossible.

As for the rest of the verbs listed, all of them are Raising verbs. For instance, consider *imagine: I imagined there to have been a commotion* is good and *I imagined Dr. N. to have examined Jack* and *I imagined Jack to have been examined by Dr. N.* are synonymous. Thus the whole class is dropped.

Visser's (2318) tenth class is that of verbs of teaching, helping and showing:

aid	learn	teach
assist	lesson	train
help	school	tutor
instruct	show	

Of these we drop *show,* which is a Raising verb, cf. *His words show cognizance to have been taken of their warning.* **Lesson** is not current in the pattern in present-day English, as cf. **He lessoned me to ride horses.* **Learn** is perhaps too nonstandard to be retained. *Aid, assist* (cf. van Ek (1966: 31 ff.)) and *school* are somewhat strained. *Aid/assist someone in doing something* are preferred to *aid/assist someone to do something.* However, the three verbs may perhaps still be retained, with some hesitation.

Visser's (2323 ff.) eleventh class is that of verbs of saying and declaring:

accuse	deny	portend
affirm	describe	preach
agree	disclaim	prenote
allege	disclose	prescribe
announce	discourse	pretend
argue	explain	proclaim
argument	expone	profess
ascribe	expound	pronounce
assert	express	protest
assign	fable	prove
assure	feign	publish
attest	gainsay	recommend
authenticate	give out	record
aver	gloze	relate
avow	guarantee	report
bespeak	infame	represent
betray	interpret	repute
bewray	justify	reveal
boast	lie	sentence
brag	maintain	signify
claim	manifest	state
condemn	mention	swear
confess	nap	talk up
confirm	nominate	tell
construe	note	term
convict	notify	threaten
convince	observe	vote
declare	own	warn
decree	plead	warrant
deem	pledge	whisper
define	point	yield

Of the verbs cited, several may be dropped as being obsolete: *argument, bewray, expone, gloze, infame, prenote* can be left out without further comment. Additionally, we drop *accuse* (*He accused me to have done it,* as opposed to *He accused me of having done it*); *convict* (*The argument convicted him to do it/to have done it*); *fable* (*You fable them to have done it*); *gainsay* (*No man gainsaying them to be such,* modified from Visser (2328)); *justify* (*He justified the notion to be innocent,* from Bishop G. Berkeley, *Alciphron,* Visser 2329, no longer current); *publish* (termed very rare by Visser 2332); *lie* (*He lied the sum to be more than half his income,* modified from Visser 2329); *threaten* (*The clergy threatened everyone to accept the English King,* modified from Visser 2335); *whisper,* as in ??*He whispered her to go, but she hung back,* modified from Visser, and *yield* (*The judge yielded the sentence to be dreadful,* modified from Visser 2336). (Most of the verbs dropped would be Raising verbs, were they admitted.) The remaining verbs seem at least reasonably acceptable in the VOSI pattern. However, most of them are Raising verbs. It seems that only *assign, condemn* (*The judge condemned him to stay in a dark cell for a day*), *convince, nominate, notify* (if accepted at all, cf. *The Frier . . . notified . . . them . . . to go with them to Tordesillas,* from 1652, J. Wadsworth, *Sandoval's Civil Wars of Spain,* Visser 2330), *recommend* (again a double classification, recall class IV), *sentence, vote* (if acceptable, cf. *The Commons voted the prisoner to be sent to the Tower,* modified from Visser 2335), and *warn* are Equi verbs. Additionally, we may consider *nap,* 'to recommend (a horse as a certain winner)', OED, even though it is perhaps more common in British rather than in American English. (There are speakers even of British English who are not very familiar with it.) This sense of the verb is not found in Webster's Third. The usage, as in *I nap the mount to beat all his rivals,* modified from Visser, is an Equi construction, and relevant as such, for the following is not possible: *I nap there to be a dead heat in the next race.* The rest are Raising verbs. These include *tell,* which is quite correctly distinguished from the *tell* of class VIII. (An illustration of the *tell* of the present class is *Sextus Empiricus, the sceptic, whom Sudas plainly tells us to have been an African,* from 1683, Dryden, *Life of Plutarch,* Söderlind (1958: 38).)

4.3 AN ALTERNATIVE CLASSIFICATION

We now proceed to our own classification. Our most general claim is that all verbs occurring as $Verb_1$ in sentences of the form of [1'] that are derived from structures of the form of [1"] through object-controlled Equi mean that NP_1 influences NP_0 toward, or away from, realizing S_2. (As far as we can see, the only exceptions would have been *esteem* and *idealize,* if they had been retained; see above.) Since NP_0 and NP_2 are coreferential, NP_1, in effect, influences NP_2. The various subclasses of verbs specify the manner in which the influencing takes place. More specifically, we provide the following classification:

(1) $Verb_1$ means that NP_1 allows (forbids) NP_0 to realize S_2. Positive: *admit,*

allow, authorize, bear, empower, endure, leave, let, license, permit, suffer. Negative: *forbid.*

(2) Verb$_1$ means that NP$_1$ makes an effort for NP$_0$ to realize S$_2$.

(2.1) Verb$_1$ means that NP$_1$ chooses NP$_0$ to realize S$_2$: *appoint, assign, choose, elect, nap, nominate, select, vote.*

(2.2) Verb$_1$ means that NP$_1$ helps or instructs NP$_0$ to realize S$_2$: *abet, aid, assist, help, instruct, school, teach, train, tutor.*

(2.3) Verb$_1$ means that NP$_1$ moves NP$_0$ toward, or away from, realizing S$_2$.

(2.3.1) Verb$_1$ necessarily implies communication.

(2.3.1.1) Verb$_1$ necessarily implies verbal communication: *adjure, admonish, advise, ask, beg, beseech, bid, call, caution, challenge, charge, command, commission, condemn, conjure, counsel, dare, defy, direct, enjoin, entreat, exhort, implore, incite, invite, invoke, notify, order, pledge, pray, recommend, request, sentence, solicit, summon, tell, thank, urge (on), warn, wire, woo.*

(2.3.1.2) Verb$_1$ necessarily implies nonverbal communication: *beckon, motion, sign, signal.*

(2.3.2) Verb$_1$ does not necessarily imply communication: *bind, bribe, bring, bully, cause, charm, coax, coerce, compel, condition, constrain, convince, determine, discipline, dispose, drag, drive, egg on, embolden, enable, encourage, engage, entice, excite, fire, fit, force, get, give (understand), have, impel, induce, influence, inspire, instigate, kindle, lead, let (know), lure, make, motivate, move, nudge, oblige, persuade, pester, press, prompt, provoke, put, request, rouse, set, spur (up), stimulate, stir (up), suborn, tease, tempt, trouble, turn.*

In our classification a number of ways are distinguished in which NP$_1$ may influence NP$_0$ toward, or away from, realizing S$_2$. The verbs of class 1 express the mildest form of influencing and are defined by the element of allowing. Among them there are differences regarding selectional restrictions on NP$_1$: some verbs (*bear, endure, suffer*) limit the choice of NP$_1$ to a +human entity, cf. *Jack/*This letter cannot endure to be disobeyed.* Some others, including *empower,* allow NP$_1$ additionally to refer to an entity (a document, say) embodying a permission, as in *Jack/this letter empowered me to question orders.* When NP$_1$ is of neither type, as in *An open window allowed/permitted me to slip in unobserved,* Verb$_1$ means 'to make possible' and *allow* and *permit* are Raising verbs. Cf. *A new operating table allowed Dr. N. to examine Jack* and *A new operating table allowed Jack to be examined by Dr. N.,* which are synonymous.

The verbs of class 2 imply an actual effort on the part of NP$_1$ for NP$_0$ to realize S$_2$. The effort may be in the form of NP$_1$ choosing NP$_0$ to realize S$_2$ (2.1), of NP$_1$ helping or instructing NP$_0$ to realize S$_2$ (2.2), or of NP$_1$ moving NP$_0$ toward, or away from, realizing S$_2$ (2.3). 2.2 and 2.3 may be felt to be rather close, but it seems legitimate to distinguish them because one may help or instruct someone without moving that someone toward doing it. Within 2.3 there is a subclass of verbs that necessarily imply communication, either verbal (2.3.1.1) or nonverbal (2.3.1.2), while verbs of a second subclass (2.3.2) do not.

Choosing, helping, instructing, communicating, whether verbally or non-verbally, are obviously activities that only human beings can properly undertake. Consequently, the subjects of verbs of these classes are restricted to NPs that are +human. On the other hand, events, circumstances, etc. may move somebody, influencing him to realize, or not to realize, something. Thus, in general, the subjects of verbs of 2.3.2 are not restricted to +human NPs.

It bears stressing that the verbs of the various classes are not claimed to be synonymous, only that they share a common element. Among the verbs of each class there are generally some that most basically express the shared element: *allow, permit* for 1, *choose* for 2.1, *help* and *instruct* for 2.2, *ask* for 2.3.1.1, *signal* for 2.3.1.2, and *move* for 2.3.2. The other members of each class may express a variety of shades of meaning in addition to the basic element. Within the large class of 2.3.2 further subclasses can be distinguished on the basis of such extra meanings. For instance, some verbs, including *bribe, encourage* etc., imply that NP_1 moves NP_0 toward realizing S_2 by holding out the prospect of consequences pleasant for NP_0. Some other verbs, including *coerce* etc., imply that NP_1 moves NP_0 toward realizing S_2 by threatening consequences unpleasant for NP_0 if he fails to realize S_2. Some verbs of the class also carry such extra shades of meaning as exclude nonhuman subjects; for instance, cf. *coax*, which the OED defines 'to influence or persuade by caresses, flattery, or blandishment'.

Finally, two conclusions can be noted that emerge from our classification, provided that it is even approximately adequate. First, even though it was claimed above that the general force of $Verb_1$ of the pattern is 'to influence NP_0 toward, or away from, realizing S_2', it seems that in English at least there is an overwhelming tendency for $Verb_1$ to mean 'to influence NP_0 toward realizing S_2', rather than 'away from realizing S_2'. Only *forbid* seems to be a counterexample to this rule. Even *warn* observes the rule. Thus *He warned me to do it* means 'he asked me to do it' rather than 'he asked me not to do it'. (The latter would require *He warned me against doing it.*)

If it is true, then, that a $Verb_1$ of the pattern of [1'] characteristically means that NP_1 influences NP_0 toward realizing S_2, the question suggests itself as to why this should be so. A definitive answer to this question will not be attempted here, but it may be suggested, at least speculatively, that diachronic study of English may shed light on it. More specifically, we again suspect that at least part of the answer lies in the original meaning of *to,* which was that of 'toward' (cf., for example, Curme (1931: 256 ff.), Mustanoja (1960: 514)).

Second, the classification presented is of interest from the point of view of the division of verbs into implicative and nonimplicative, referred to in Chapter 2. With respect to the present classification, implicative verbs mean that the influencing that NP_1 exercises comes to fruition. A priori, on common sense grounds, we would expect the incidence of implicative verbs to be lower in class

1 than in class 2, because the verbs of the former express milder influencing. This prediction turns out to be correct, as we may ascertain if we consider the verbs in question:

CLASS NO.	VERBS	NO. OF IMPLI-CATIVE VERBS	IMPLICATIVE VERBS LISTED
1	12	0	
2.1	8	0	
2.2	9	0	
2.3.1.1	41	0	
2.3.1.2	4	0	
2.3.2	61	14	*bring, cause, coerce, compel, force, get, give (understand), have, induce, lead, let (know), make, persuade, turn*

The corroboration of the prediction made on commonsense grounds lends some credibility to the overall scheme of the present classification.

4.4 CASE GRAMMAR AND OBJECT-CONTROLLED INFINITIVAL EQUI

The object-controlled Equi pattern will be briefly discussed here from the point of view of case grammar. The version of case grammar assumed above will be used here as well, with the same caveats as in Chapter 2.

With verbs of class 1 NP_1 seems to be an Agent. This is quite clear with verbs that are unambiguous Equi verbs, such as *authorize*. It is slightly less clear with *allow* and other ambiguous verbs, but it seems that when the ambiguity is taken into account, the Equi reading of these verbs takes an Agent as NP_1:

Q. What did John do?
A. He allowed Sue to go home = He gave Sue permission to go home.

The pattern for NP_2 is in [15a–d]:

[15] a. John allowed/authorized Sue to make a speech.
   b. ??John allowed/authorized Sue to know the answer.
   c. John allowed/authorized Sue to get a letter in the mail.
   d. ??John allowed/authorized Sue to grow old/to be tall when grown up.

The markings in [15a–d] reflect the Equi reading of *allow*. For instance, [15b] can be paraphrased: 'John gave Sue permission to know the answer'. In the Raising reading of *allow,* most, or perhaps all, of the question marks of [15b] and [15d] should be erased. For instance, *Circumstances allowed Sue to know the answer,* with *allow* meaning 'to make possible' seems better than the Equi reading of [15b]. Such Raising readings should be recognized and kept separate from Equi readings. The Raising readings should not be allowed to obscure the Equi readings of [15a–d] and their restrictions.

It will be recalled that in the patterns of Chapter 2, PRO, that is, NP_2, is coreferential with NP_1 and there is no third NP, except if $Verb_1$ implies that there is an understood NP as in the case of *arrange*. In the *for to* pattern of Chapter 3, NP_2 is not PRO, but rather a full NP which is noncoreferential with NP_1. We noted in Chapter 3 how the presence of two noncoreferential NPs in the *for to* pattern of Chapter 3 makes external control readings more readily available in the *for to* pattern than in the *to* and *ing* patterns of Chapter 2. For instance, *John intended for Sue to get a letter in the mail* is good, while ?*John intended to get a letter in the mail* is slightly worse. The pattern of the present chapter again involves two noncoreferential NPs, NP_1 and NP_0, PRO being coreferential with the latter. As in Chapter 3, if NP_1 can be interpreted as controlling the realization of S_2, the resulting sentence is well formed (the external control reading). This seems possible when PRO is a Benefactive, as in [15c], but less so if PRO is an Experiencer or an Object, as in [15b] and [15d], respectively. The present pattern thus displays a close similarity to the *for to* pattern of Chapter 3. In both patterns, external control readings go together with predicates of Berman's (1970: 230) class [9c]-a, that is, with predicates that are controllable by someone other than their subjects.

Verbs of class 2.1 take agentive subjects. Sentences of the pattern are close to those of [15a–d]:

[16]   **a.** John chose Sue to make a speech.
    b. ??John chose Sue to know the answer.
    c. John chose Sue to get a letter in the mail.
    d. ??John chose Sue to get old/to be tall when grown up.

Again, the Agent is perfect as NP_2. The Benefactive as NP_2 is good as well, it being understood that NP_1 is capable of, and responsible for, realizing S_2 (the external control reading).

NP_1 of class 2.2 is an Agent. The pattern follows that of [15a–d] and [16a–d]:

[17]   **a.** John helped Sue to make a speech.
    b. ??John helped Sue to know the answer.
    c. John helped Sue to get a letter in the mail.
    d. ??John helped Sue to grow old/to be tall when grown up.

Verbs of class 2.3 imply a more strenuous effort on the part of NP_1 for the realization of S_2. They also express a more direct and immediate involvement of NP_1 with NP_0. Indeed, these verbs focus on the direct involvement, to the exclusion of NP_1 controlling the realization of S_2. Thus external control readings are less possible than above. The Agent as NP_2 is of course perfect, but the other case roles, including the Benefactive, not protected by external control readings, are somewhat strained:

[18] **a.** John challenged Sue to make a speech.
b. *John challenged Sue to know the answer.
c. ??John challenged Sue to get a letter in the mail.
d. ??John challenged Sue to grow old/to be tall when grown up.

[19] **a.** John forced Sue to make a speech.
b. *John forced Sue to know the answer.
c. *John forced Sue to get a letter in the mail.
d. ??John forced Sue to grow old/to be tall when grown up.

As in Chapter 2, provisos relating to the nature of predicates should be made here as well. For instance, we may consider *know*. The subject of *know* is an Experiencer and *know* itself is a verb of cognition. As argued in Chapter 2, Experiencers may also be governed by verbs of sensation, as in *John saw the explosion* and by verbs of emotion or feeling, as in *John felt elated*. Experiencers governed by verbs of sensation seem susceptible, in varying degrees, to agentive reinterpretations, perhaps more readily than verbs of cognition or emotion. For instance, *John chose Sue to see the explosion* is better than [16b] and ??*John chose to feel elated*. There is variation in the class of verbs of cognition as well. For instance, *believe*, as in *Sue believed the man's story*, is more readily susceptible to an agentive reinterpretation than *know*, for ?*John forced Sue to believe the man's story* seems better than [19b].

In conclusion, we note that in the object-controlled Equi pattern NP_1 is an Agent throughout. As regards NP_2, it may always be an Agent, without a trace of strain. Other roles for NP_2 are more doubtful, less compatible. In this book two considerations have been identified that mitigate the incompatibility of case roles of NP_1 and NP_2, making the selection of NP_2 less restricted. They are coreferential roles, with or without agentive reinterpretations, and external control readings. Of these, coreferential roles without agentive reinterpretations do not seem relevant to NPs of the present pattern. Agentive reinterpretations are relevant in a number of cases. So are external control readings, especially when NP_2 is a Benefactive. External control readings are less possible when $Verb_1$ focuses on the involvement of NP_1 with NP_0, to the exclusion of implying controllability with respect to the realization of S_2.

Chapter **5**

FLATTERING INTO AND *DISSUADING FROM:* PREPOSITIONAL OBJECT-CONTROLLED EQUI

5.1 INTRODUCTION

This chapter is an attempt to inquire into some properties of the pattern in contemporary English that is exemplified by sentences such as [1a–c]. ([1a] is taken, in a slightly modified form, from Visser (1973: 2369).)

[1] **a.** John flattered me into concealing my misgivings.
    b. John warned me against divulging my sources.
    c. John drove me to weeping.

In surface structure the sentences of [1a–c] exhibit the pattern of [1′]:

[1′] $[NP_1 \ Verb_1 \ NP_0 \ Prep \ Verb_2 ing \ . . .]_S$
John flattered me into concealing my misgivings.

Visser (1973: 2369) calls NP_0 the pivotal noun phrase and notes that NP_0 cannot be a possessive pronoun or a noun plus a sibilant. While the second part of the condition should more precisely refer to the inadmissibility of a noun phrase and a genitival sibilant, rather than to that of a noun and a sibilant, Visser's observation is basically correct, as witness the illformedness of *John flattered his best friend's into concealing his misgivings*.

     The purpose of this chapter is first to focus attention on some syntactic properties of the construction, and, second, partly interrelated with the first purpose, to attempt to provide some indication of what verbs may occur in the pattern. Beyond a list of verbs, an attempt will be made to look for such properties as may characterize verbs governing the pattern, that is, verbs occurring as $Verb_1$ in [1']. Case grammar will be employed as a tool in the analysis of the pattern.

When we endeavor to unravel the structure of [1a–c] in order to provide a more sophisticated structural representation for [1a–c], we note that the sentences of [1a–c] contain two predications. Consequently, it is reasonable to suppose that each of them contains two sentences, a main sentence and an embedded sentence, as well. Further, it seems clear that NP_0 of [1'] is a main clause constituent outside of the embedded clause. In Postal's (1974: 41) framework this is established by the fact that NP_0 can participate in Passivization of the main clause, as in [2]:

[2] I was flattered by John into concealing my misgivings.

However, Postal's assumption that Passivization is clause-internal is a controversial one. It is rejected outright by a school of leading linguists, including Chomsky (cf., for example, Chomsky (1981: 66 ff.)).

A second argument can be based on the preposition in the pattern. There is some evidence that the preposition in [1'] is not a complementizer and thus a constituent outside of the embedding clause. Rather, it seems to be part of the main clause only. We may consider the contrast between such pseudoclefts as [3a, b] and [4b, c], where [4a–c] contain an undoubted instance of the *for to* complementizer:

[3] **a.** What John flattered me into was concealing my misgivings.
   b. *What John flattered me was into concealing my misgivings.

[4] **a.** John preferred for me to conceal my misgivings.
   b. *What John preferred for was me to conceal my misgivings.
   c. What John preferred was for me to conceal my misgivings.

Further, the wellformedness of [3a] indicates that the embedded sentence of [1a–c] is a noun phrase (cf. Higgins (1973: 154 ff.)). This conclusion is confirmed by the fact that the embedded clause may be replaced by *it*, as in [5a], or be questioned by *what*, as in [5b]. (On the criterion of reduction to *it*, cf. Kajita (1967: 15 ff.))

[5] **a.** John flattered me into it.
   b. What did John flatter me into?

The discussion so far suggests that sentences such as [1a–c] may be represented by [1''], which is offered as a more sophisticated version of [1']:

[1''] $[NP_1 \ Verb_1 \ NP_0 \ Prep \ [[Verb_2ing \ . \ . \ .]_{S_2}]_{NP}]_{S_1}$

Presumably, in [1″] the preposition and the NP following it form a prepositional phrase. An even more crucial property of [1a–c] remains unexpressed in [1″]. There are two predications involved. NP_1 is the subject of the higher predication, but it is not the subject of the lower predication in [1a–c]. Rather, the subject of the lower predication is understood to be NP_0 of [1″]. NP_0, as was argued above, does not belong to the lower sentence. The understood subject of S_2 may then be represented by PRO, designated as NP_2. [1‴] is then offered as a still more sophisticated representation of the structure of [1a–c]:

[1‴] $[NP_1 \text{ Verb}_1 \text{ } NP_0 \text{ } [\text{Prep } [[[\text{PRO}]_{NP_2} \text{ Verb}_2\text{ing} \ldots]_{S_2}]_{NP}]_{PP}]_{S_1}$
John flattered me into concealing my misgivings.

5.2 DATA AND THEIR ANALYSIS

In the following we will attempt to provide lists of verbs occurring in the pattern of [1‴]. One purpose in so doing is the desire to guard against the danger of impressionism in the treatment of the pattern. As one source we will take account of Visser's classification. (In the following, all references to Visser are to Visser (1973: 2369 ff.) and all data that are documented come from the same source.) He groups relevant verbs on the basis of the preposition preceding the complement sentence. We will adopt the same practice here. A second source is Quirk et al. (1985: 1211). Their list under D2b is relevant, even though when offering it, the authors do not specifically discuss *ing* complements occurring in the prepositional phrase. Their discussion focuses on constructions where the constituent following the preposition is a nonsentential NP. However, it will turn out that some, though not all, of the verbs listed by Quirk et al. in their pattern take *ing* complement clauses of the pattern of [1‴] as well.

About. Visser's only verb is *warn*. The example is *you won't misunderstand me when I warn you about people talking* (1919, C. Mackenzie, *Poor Relations*). The instance must be dropped, though, because it does not exhibit the pattern of [1‴]. It can be made to conform to the sequence of constituents of [1‴] if the NP *people* is omitted. However, the result, . . . *when I warn you about talking,* will be more relevant from the point of view of the pattern of the present chapter if *about* is replaced with *against*. In the pattern of the present chapter PRO is necessarily controlled by NP_0. *Warn against* is then more relevant than *warn about* because of the following contrasts: ?*John warned Mary about perjuring herself at the trial, John warned Mary about perjuring oneself at the trial, John warned Mary against perjuring herself at the trial,* **John warned Mary against perjuring oneself at the trial.*

Against. Visser's only example is *warn*. An example would be *I warn you against talking,* to modify Visser's example cited in the paragraph above. *Caution,* a verb similar in meaning to *warn,* and *advise,* a verb with a potentially more general meaning, commonly occur in the pattern, though not attested by Visser. Each of them can replace *warn* in the example cited.

For. Visser cites *reproach,* as in *which he greatly reproached himself for not having done already* (1840, Dickens, *Master Humphrey's Clock*). It may be advisable to drop the instance, though. If we eliminate the relative clause construction, which is irrelevant in the present context, we may modify the instance to *He reproached John for not having done it.* The *for* clause expresses reason or cause and it is more felicitous to consider it an adverbial clause. Verbs similar in meaning to *reproach,* such as *reprimand,* or opposite in meaning, such as *commend, praise* and *thank* (for *thank* in the Quirk et al. pattern, see Quirk et al. (1985: 1211)), also take comparable *for* clauses. Even adjectives take them, as in *I am angry at John for having let me down.* Presumably, they are all most appropriately analyzed as adverbial clauses.

In. The most recent instance that Visser cites of a verb taking *in* in the pattern is one of the verb *set,* as in *He set the bodies above in working,* to modify Visser's instance. This usage is obsolete. However, Quirk et al. (1985: 1211) mention *interest* as taking their nonsentential pattern, and it seems relevant in the present context as well. Thus, *In spite of intense efforts, I could not interest John in taking part in the project* is possible.

Into. Quirk et al. (1985: 1211) do not mention any verbs in their nonsentential pattern governing *into.* Visser lists the following nine verbs: *argue, bluff, bully, coax, entrap, flatter, ginger, provoke, talk.* All of these clearly belong to the pattern. Two illustrations, chosen at random from Visser, will be sufficient: *Andrew . . . had coaxed her at last into buying a pretty and reasonably sized house in Dalkey* (1965, I. Murdoch, *The Red and the Green*); *You're trying to bluff Proctor-Gould into letting himself be blackmailed* (1966, M. Frayn, *Russian Interpreter*). As an aside, in the present context, it may be noted that several of the verbs listed can take nonsentential prepositional objects as well. These include *bluff, coax, entrap* and *provoke,* as in *He bullied/provoked his partner into a premature commitment.*

Of. Visser's instances are all obsolete, the most recent being from about 1475. Quirk et al. (1985: 1211) list quite a number of verbs in their nonsentential pattern: *accuse, convict, convince, deprive, inform, persuade, relieve, remind, rob, suspect, warn.* Of these, *accuse, convict, suspect* and *warn* occur in the sentential pattern as well, as in *The judge accused/convicted/warned/suspected the prisoner of ignoring the bounds of propriety.* The others clearly take nonsentential prepositional phrases, as in *John convinced Sue of the advantages of the project.* However, they do not take sentential prepositional objects, cf. **John convinced me of taking part in the project. Inform* does allow a sentential object of the preposition, as in *John informed me of having completed the job,* but the pattern is not relevant, because NP_2 is interpreted as NP_1, not as NP_0.

To. Visser cites *command, drive* and *set* in the pattern. All are relevant. One illustration may be sufficient, *that set me to dreaming of nannies in distress* (1967, J. Barth, *Giles Goat-Boy,* Visser 2370).

Quirk et al. (1985: 1211) list *confine, introduce, refer, sentence, subject* and *treat* in their nonsentential pattern. Most of these preferably co-occur with nonsentential objects of *to* only. For instance, consider *treat*, as in *The host treated his guest to a glass of port*, vs. **The host treated his guest to drinking a glass of port*. *Confine* seems to be the only verb of Quirk et al.'s list which takes sentential complements as well, as in *They confined the prisoner to eating dog food*.

Restrict may be added as a fifth verb relevant in the *to* pattern. (We thank Robert MacGilleon for pointing it out to us.) An example: *He restricted his guest to drinking juice*.

Upon. Visser cites *put* and *set*. Both are more marginal than *set* with *to*, as quoted above: *it puts both upon appearing in their most agreeable forms*, modified from Visser; *Set him upon guessing how it could come to pass* (1759–67, Sterne, *Tristram Shandy*). Both verbs sound archaic in the pattern and we drop both from further consideration.

With. Quirk et al. (1985: 1211) cite *charge* and *compare* in their nonsentential pattern. Of these the former is relevant in the sentential pattern as well, as in *The judge charged the prisoner with loitering with intent*.

From. Visser devotes a separate section to *from*. The pattern is clearly very common. Altogether, Visser lists and illustrates 61 verbs in the *from* pattern:

absent	fear	redeem
ban	fend	refrain
banish	forbear	reject
bind	forbid	repel
bless	forshut	restrain
catch	free	restrict
caution	frighten	save
check	help	secure
confine	hinder	shadow
contain	hold	shame
cover	incapacitate	stày
curb	inhibit	steer
defend	intimidate	stop
detain	keep	sustain
deter	let	terrify
disable	look	vindicate
discourage	preclude	wit
dissuade	preserve	withdraw
disturb	prevent	withhold
drive	prohibit	
excuse	put	

Of the 61 verbs cited above, 19 seem obsolete or abnormal in the pattern. They are *bind, bless, confine, fear, fend, forbear, forshut, help, let, look, put, redeem, refrain, reject, restrict, shame, vindicate, wit, withdraw*. For instance, to take an example of the type of data cited by Visser, consider *reject* as in *he*

hath also rejected thee from being king (the King James Bible, i Sam. 15, 23).
Virtually all the other 18 verbs are exemplified with only one sentence each,
most of which are even more archaic than this one from the 1611 Bible. We may
perhaps add an illustration of *refrain* and *withdraw*. Neither verb is possible in
the pattern in present-day English, as witness **I refrained/withdrew him from
making a premature commitment.*

Cover and *shadow* are peculiar in that S_2 must be in the passive, as in *He
covered his hair from being seen,* to modify Visser's example. Because of this
peculiarity, we drop them from further consideration. The same goes for *absent,*
which requires for NP_0 to be a reflexive, as in *Madeline . . . could scarcely
absent herself from sharing the lesson* (Lord Lytton, *Eugene Aram*). It does not
allow a nonreflexive as NP_0, cf. **She could not absent me from sharing the
lesson.*

We have omitted 22 verbs from Visser's class of 61. We may add *exclude,*
as in *The rule excluded John from joining the club.* (We thank Robert Mac-
Gilleon for drawing our attention to *exclude*.) Visser's class is then changed to
one of 40.

The description of a number of verbs in the list brings up an issue of some
theoretical significance. The surface structure of verbs of the pattern under
discussion was considered above. It was stated that the subject of the lower
sentence is understood to be NP_0, the object of the higher sentence. It was not
argued explicitly whether this relation was to be established by Subject to Object
Raising or by Equi, to use the traditional terminology of transformational grammar, which seems sufficient in the present context. It is advisable to briefly
consider these alternatives at this point.

Before a choice can be made, the alternatives should be made more precise.
For the purpose of illustration, we will consider the verb *prevent,* as in [6]:

[6] John prevented Sue from leaving.

If Raising is the rule relevant to [6], the underlying structure of [6] may be
presented schematically as in [6'] and the surface structure, after Raising, as in
[6"]. In [6'] and [6"] a number of such issues as are not immediately relevant in
the present context are glossed over, including the introduction, status and position of *from ing.* It will be recalled that Rosenbaum (1967: 89 ff.) proposed that
from ing form a complementizer, an assumption rejected by Postal (1974: 162).

[6'] $[[\text{John}]_{NP} [[\text{prevented}]_{Verb} [[\text{Sue}]_{NP} [\text{leave}]_{VP}]_{S_2}]_{VP}]_{S_1}$
[6"] $[[\text{John}]_{NP} [[\text{prevented}]_{Verb} [\text{Sue}]_{NP} [[\quad]_{NP} [\text{leaving}]_{VP}]_{S_2}]_{VP}]_{S_1}$

In a Raising analysis, the subject of S_2 is filled in deep structure. It is then
raised into S_1 and an empty node is left behind.

If Equi is the rule operative in [6] and if the rule is a rule of control, the
structure relevant to [6] is [6'''']:

[6'''] $[[\text{John}]_{NP} [[\text{prevented}]_{Verb} [\text{Sue}]_{NP_0} [[\text{from}]_{Prep} [[[\text{PRO}]_{NP_2}$
$[\text{leaving}]_{VP}]_{S_2}]_{NP}]_{PP}]_{VP}]_{S_1}$

In [6'''] NP_2 is PRO and PRO is controlled by NP_0.

There is an old and venerable tradition going back to Rosenbaum (1967: 89 ff.) according to which sentences such as [6] are derived by Raising and not by Equi. This tradition includes Postal (1974: 162 ff.) and Horiguchi (1978: 226 ff.). Even Bresnan (1976: 497), while casting doubt on a number of arguments that were put forward by Postal in support of Subject to Object Raising, regards the view that the rule is relevant to *prevent* as "quite plausible." Rosenbaum's presentation of the Subject to Object Raising analysis is recognized as a model, for example by Postal (1974: 162 ff.). Consequently, it is advisable to refer to it here.

Rosenbaum (1967: 89 ff.) presents four arguments in all in support of a Raising, as opposed to an Equi, derivation of sentential complements governed by *prevent*. The first is what is taken to be the synonymy of [7a, b]:

[7] a. I prevented the doctor from examining John.
 b. I prevented John from being examined by the doctor.

In an Equi analysis "the underlying structures, and hence the semantic interpretation, of the sentences . . . are different" (Rosenbaum (1967: 89)), while in a Raising analysis [7a, b] come from the same deep structure.

Second, an Equi analysis "predicts incorrectly the grammaticality of the pseudocleft sentences in [153]."

To make comparison easier, we will use Rosenbaum's numbering where appropriate:

[153] a. *What I prevented the doctor from was examining John.
 b. *What I prevented John from was being examined by the doctor.

[153a, b] are quoted from Rosenbaum (1967, 89), *what* capitalized.

Third, the Raising analysis "explains the introductory 'there' phenomenon in sentences like [155]":

[155] a. Wyatt Earp prevented there from being trouble on the range.
 b. Shelters will not prevent there from being great destruction.

(The quote and [155a, b], *shelters* capitalized, are from Rosenbaum (1967: 91.))

Fourth, according to Rosenbaum (1967: 91), the Raising analysis explains the synonymy of our [7a, b] and [8a, b]:

[8] a. I prevented the doctor's examining John.
 b. I prevented John's being examined by the doctor.

Rosenbaum's analysis has been influential for subsequent research. Even so, it can be called into question. In the present connection, we will largely disregard the fourth argument, because the pattern of [8a, b] is not under discussion here.

The second and third arguments are the most interesting in that they are syntactic. Neither is convincing, rather the opposite. To start with the second argument, it does not seem that there is any appreciable difference in wellform-edness between Rosenbaum's [153a, b] and our [3a], repeated here for ease of reference:

[3] **a.** What John flattered me into was concealing my misgivings.

[3a] was claimed above to be well formed. It seems to us that [153a, b] are good as well. To give some substance to this claim, we should compare [153a, b] and [3a], on the one hand, and true Subject to Object Raising constructions, on the other, with respect to relevant pseudocleft constructions. Rosenbaum does not do this.

Assume and *believe* are verbs governing Subject to Object Raising, as in [9a, b]:

[9] **a.** John believed Sue to be an authority on linguistics.
b. Everyone assumed Mort to be the culprit.

When we place the infinitival sentences of these genuine Raising construc-tions into the focus position of pseudocleft sentences corresponding to [153a, b] and [3a], the result is ill formed:

[10] **a.** *What John believed Sue was to be an authority on linguistics.
b. *What everyone assumed Mort was to be the culprit.

Both [3a] and [153a, b] are appreciably better than [10a, b]. There is a qualitative difference between the two sets. Consequently, they should have different derivations.

Rosenbaum's third argument is based on *there* constructions. [155a, b] are claimed to be good with *there,* analogously as in Raising constructions, while corresponding Equi constructions are ill formed. Again, we must call Rosen-baum's view into question.

Rosenbaum's underlying assumption, viz. that in Raising constructions *there* can occur in the position after the verb while in Equi constructions it cannot, is correct and unimpeachable. This may be independently illustrated by the contrast in [11a, b]:

[11] **a.** John believed there to have been a fresh development in the story.
b. *John induced there to be a fresh development in the story.

As is well known, the contrast in question is not limited to *there,* but carries over to idiom chunks that are restricted in their distribution, cf. [12a, b]:

[12] **a.** John believed tabs to have been kept on his movements.
b. *John induced tabs to be kept on his movements.

While the contrast between Raising and Equi constructions is clear in [11a, b] and [12a, b], we contest the claim that [155a, b] are well formed. They seem equivalent in acceptability to [11b] and to [12b], or at least they are closer in acceptability to [11b] and [12b] than to [11a] and [12a].

The judgments are confirmed when [11a, b] and [155a, b] are passivized:

[11]   **a.'** There was believed by John to have been a fresh development in the story.

     b.' *There was induced by John to be a fresh development in the story.

[155] **a.'** *There was prevented by Wyatt Earp from being trouble on the range.

     b.' *There will not be prevented by shelters from being great destruction.

Again, [155a', b'] are equivalent to [11b'] in acceptability, or rather lack of it, rather than to [11a']. In conclusion, the nonoccurrence of *there* in the postverbal position after *prevent* is evidence for an Equi, as opposed to a Raising derivation of the pattern. It is of some interest to note that by 1977, Postal too had some doubts about the acceptability of *there* in the pattern of *prevent,* cf. Postal (1977: 142).

Rosenbaum's arguments 1 and 4 are based on synonymy. They have the form that because sentences such as [7a, b] are synonymous, they should be derived from the same deep structure.

The claim that [7a, b] are synonymous may be called into question. [7a] may mean that I acted on the doctor with the result that he did not examine John and [7b] may mean that I acted on John with the result that he was not examined by the doctor.

The difference is confirmed if a *by* clause expressing manner is added to [7a, b]:

[7]   **a.'** I prevented the doctor from examining John by locking the front door.

    b.' I prevented John from being examined by the doctor by locking the front door.

By contrast, corresponding Raising structures do display synonymy, as witness [13a, b]:

[13] **a.** I believe the doctor to have examined John.

    b. I believe John to have been examined by the doctor.

In addition to nonsynonymous readings, [7a, b] may both have a reading to the effect that I brought about a state of affairs such that the doctor did not examine John. Even if this is so, it is difficult to use this as a basis for a syntactic description. This was more plausible in the *Aspects* framework, to which Rosenbaum (1967) belongs, where meaning was anchored in deep structure. It is less plausible in later frameworks where it is recognized that structures other than deep structures may contribute to semantic interpretation. Under such circumstances evidence based on synonymy becomes less forceful.

The Equi analysis is clearly the only possibility for a number of the verbs listed, including *dissuade, deter,* etc., for which synonymous readings for pairs of sentences analogous to [7a, b] are out of the question:

[14] **a.** I dissuaded the doctor from examining John.

    b. I dissuaded John from being examined by the doctor.

Given that even semantic evidence is in favor of *dissuade* governing object-controlled Equi, it is predicted, syntactically, that NPs such as *there, it, advantage*, etc. cannot be found in the position of NP_0. This is confirmed by [15a, b]:

[15] **a.** *I dissuaded there from being trouble on campus.
    b. *I dissuaded advantage from being taken of the offer.

Further, the sequence after *from* should be capable of occurring in the focus position of pseudoclefts, analogous to [3a], [153a, b], but contrasting with [10a, b]:

[16] **a.** What I dissuaded the doctor from was examining John.
    b. What I dissuaded John from was being examined by the doctor.

Semantic evidence is less clear for some other verbs, such as *keep, prevent* and *stop*. On account of syntactic evidence, it seems advisable not to exclude an Equi analysis for them. In this connection, also compare Chomsky (1981: 147 ff.).

Above, an attempt was made to collect a sample of verbs that appear as $Verb_1$ in the pattern of [1''']. The collecting of verbs is worthwhile and helps the investigator to allay the fear of impressionism. However, it can at best be only a first step.

When a semantic analysis is undertaken of verbs that occur as $Verb_1$ in the pattern of [1'''], it is clear that there is a reasonably close match between the meaning of the verb and of the choice of the preposition in the pattern. The main outlines of a description are not hard to discern. Before a classification is attempted, it is helpful to note that not all prepositions that occur in the pattern can be found even if Visser's and Quirk et al.'s (1985: 1211) treatments are combined. Neither source mentions *out of*. Alongside of [17a], we find [17b]:

[17] **a.** John talked Sue into accepting a bribe.
    b. John talked Sue out of accepting a bribe.

Talk, then, co-occurs with both *into* and *out of*. However, such symmetry of construction, where the meanings of the two constructions are symmetrically, or diametrically, opposed, is not observed with all verbs of the pattern, at least not with equal ease. *Argue, bluff, frighten* and *terrify* allow both *into* and *out of* without appreciable strain. *Intimidate* takes *into*, but *out of* is less good. Apparently, there are some speakers who accept *out of* with *coax* and *flatter*. However, the combination is strained and we mark them in [19b] with two question marks. *Out of* is quite impossible with *entrap* and *provoke*, as witness [20b]:

[18] **a.** John argued/bluffed/frightened Sue into making a commitment.
    b. John argued/bluffed/frightened Sue out of making a commitment.

[19] **a.** John intimidated/coaxed/flattered Sue into making a statement.
    b. John ?intimidated/??coaxed/??flattered Sue out of making a statement.

[20] **a.** John entrapped/provoked Sue into making a promise.
    b. *John entrapped/provoked Sue out of making a promise.

The lack of symmetry observed in [20a, b] is true of most verbs taking *from*, cf. [21a, b] and [22a, b].

[21] **a.** John restrained Sue from making a long statement.
b. ?John restrained Sue into making a short statement.

[22] **a.** John checked/dissuaded/prevented Sue from making a statement.
b. *John checked/dissuaded/prevented Sue into making a statement.

Talk, argue, bluff, frighten and *terrify,* and perhaps *restrain* and one or two other verbs are neutral in that they do not specify the direction of the movement in which NP_1 acts on NP_0 in the pattern of $[1''']$. To put it another way, these verbs allow two mutually incompatible prepositions and the meaning of the construction depends on the choice of the preposition. Other verbs of the pattern, by contrast, specify the direction, and this does not allow a reversal of the direction. To put it another way, they allow only one preposition.

From the discussion presented there emerges the following classification of verbs that occur as $Verb_1$ in the pattern of $[1''']$. The classification admittedly glosses over a number of distinctions of acceptability, some of which were pointed out above:

(1) $Verb_1$ expresses desideration, intention and endeavor. NP_1 acts on NP_0 endeavoring for NP_0 to realize S_2 or not to realize S_2.
(1.1) $Verb_1$ is positive. NP_1 acts on NP_0 endeavoring for NP_0 to realize S_2.
(1.1.1) The preposition is *in: interest, engage.*
(1.1.2) The preposition is *into: coax, entrap, flatter, ginger, provoke.*
(1.1.3) The preposition is *to: command, set.*
    $Verb_1$ has a restrictive meaning: *confine, restrict.*
(1.2) $Verb_1$ is negative. NP_1 acts on NP_0 endeavoring for NP_0 not to realize S_2.
(1.2.1) The preposition is *against: advise, caution, warn.*
(1.2.2) The preposition is *from: ban, banish, catch, caution, check, contain, curb, defend, detain, deter, disable, discourage, dissuade, disturb, exclude, excuse, forbid, free, hinder, hold, incapacitate, inhibit, keep, preclude, preserve, prevent, prohibit, repel, save, secure, stay, stop, sustain, withhold.*
(1.3) $Verb_1$ expresses desideration, intention and endeavor. Direction of volition may be either positive or negative.
(1.3.1) The preposition is either *into* or *out of: argue, bluff, bully, frighten, intimidate, talk, terrify.*
(1.3.2) The preposition is either *into* or *from: drive, restrain, steer.*
(2) $Verb_1$ does not express desideration, intention and endeavor. $Verb_1$ has a legal meaning. The preposition is *with: charge.* The preposition is *of: accuse, convict, suspect.*

It would be very rash to claim that the lists of verbs presented are comprehensive. While they are not, they do shed some light on verbs of the pattern of

[1$'''$]. Apart from verbs of class 2, which seem few in number, the core class of verbs taking the pattern mean that NP_1 acts, or exerts influence, on NP_0. The influence may be positive or negative. If it is positive, the preposition is either *in, to* or *into*. If it is negative, the preposition is either *against, from* or *out of*. Most verbs of the pattern are either positive or negative only, but a fair number are neutral. For neutral verbs the direction of the influence depends on the choice of the preposition.

It is of interest to examine $Verb_1$s of the present pattern in relation to Bach's generalization, which was introduced at the beginning of Chapter 4. Essentially, the generalization is that an object NP controlling a PRO cannot be omitted. As far as we know, Bach's generalization has not been considered with respect to the present pattern of complementation in previous research. The lists of verbs above afford us an opportunity to do so here. It is clear that the generalization is a powerful one in respect of the present pattern. Virtually all verbs listed obey it. We may take *prevent* as a case in point: *John prevented Mary from taking precipitate action* is good, but **John prevented from taking precipitate action* is not.

There are verbs in the present pattern that are ambiguous, in that they allow PRO to be controlled by NP_1. However, the number of such verbs is remarkably small. (This in itself may not be unrelated to Bach's generalization.) *Keep, withhold* and *engage* are verbs, perhaps the only verbs, that suggest themselves here. Of these, *engage* is less relevant. Sentences such as *I engaged him in working on the project* and *The candidate engaged in denigrating his opponent* are conceivable, although reactions to them are not always favorable. (We thank Ian Gurney for the second sentence.) More seriously, the sense of the verb does not remain constant in the sentences. *Keep* is more relevant, for both *I kept Sue from making a rash statement* and *I kept from making a rash statement* are possible and the sense of *keep* remains constant (apart from the difference relating to control). Analogous sentences seem possible for *withhold*. However, the existence of such verbs does not threaten Bach's generalization. These verbs allow, or, more precisely, require the object NP to be omitted when NP_1 is the controller of PRO, but when the object of $Verb_1$ is the controller of PRO, it cannot be omitted, as witness *John kept Mary from perjuring herself, *John kept from perjuring herself, *John kept Mary from perjuring himself,* and *John kept from perjuring himself.*

The verbs of the present pattern, then, observe Bach's generalization in quite a regular fashion. There seems to be just one class of verbs that constitutes an exception. The class is 1.2.1. In *John advised/cautioned/warned Mary against taking precipitate action*, the object may be omitted and the result is good: *John advised/cautioned/warned against taking precipitate action*. In the resulting sentence without the object PRO has no expressed controller. (The rule deleting the object may be a variety of Postal's (1970: 480) *one* deletion rule, for, while **John advised/cautioned/warned against perjuring myself/yourself/himself/herself* are bad, *John warned against perjuring oneself* is good.)

At present we are unable to provide a principled explanation for the exceptional behavior of *advise/caution/warn against*. It is notable that the class is semantically coherent, in terms of our classification. It is clear that we do not want to abandon Bach's generalization. We may speculate, then, that the coherence of class 1.2.1, when understood properly, may eventually offer a deeper insight into Bach's generalization.

When verbs of class 1 are considered with respect to their implicativeness or the lack of it, it is observed that they are in general implicative. More precisely, verbs of positive volition are in general implicative, those of negative volition are in general negative implicative:

[23] **a.** John coaxed/provoked Sue into making a rash statement.

    b. John dissuaded/prevented Sue from making a rash statement.

A valid inference from [23a] is that Sue in fact made a rash statement while [23b] implies that she did not. We recall from Chapter 2 that noncontrastive stress patterns should be taken for granted throughout the book when implicative and nonimplicative verbs are discussed. In [23a, b] the main stress then falls on *statement*.

The only notable exception to the implicativeness is class 1.2.1. Its verbs are nonimplicative. For instance, *He cautioned me against speaking out* leaves it open whether I did or did not speak out.

It is of interest to note that some verbs, including *coax,* of the present pattern also occur in the object-controlled infinitival Equi pattern, as noted in Chapter 4. [23a] may be contrasted with [23a']:

[23] **a.'** John coaxed Sue to make a rash statement.

One notable difference between [23a] and [23a'] is that in the infinitival pattern *coax* is not an implicative verb.

The verbs of class 2 are not implicative. For instance, *The police accused the prisoner of committing a crime* does not warrant the inference that the prisoner had committed a crime.

5.3 CASE GRAMMAR AND PREPOSITIONAL OBJECT-CONTROLLED EQUI

In Chapter 2 of the book a version of case grammar was proposed for the analysis of complementation. In Chapter 2 and in subsequent chapters, the version of case grammar adopted was argued to have predictive power. It is clearly of interest to consider the present pattern from the point of view of case grammar.

Taking class 2 of the classification first, we note that its verbs do not express volition. The case role of NP_1 is that of the Agent. Given the conclusions reached in Chapter 2, the prediction is then that the case roles of the Agent, Experiencer, Benefactive and Object are all possible for NP_2. This is confirmed by [24a–d]:

[24] **a.** The judge accused the prisoner of having assaulted a passerby.

    b. The judge accused the prisoner of having known of the conspiracy.

    c. The judge accused the prisoner of having received a letter from the gang leader.

    d. ??The coach accused the players of the team of growing old/of not being tall enough for the team.

Of course, the legal verbs of class 2 require that the proposition of S_2 is, or can be interpreted, as an offense. This makes [24d] slightly odd.

The verbs of class 1 express volition. For the most part, NP_1 is +Animate and unambiguously an Agent only. The classes of 1.1.2, 1.3.1, and a number of verbs of the large class 1.2.2 only allow this interpretation, cf. [25a, b]:

[25] **a.** John/*circumstances bullied/flattered Sue into accepting a bribe.

     b. John/*circumstances dissuaded Sue from competing.

Some verbs of 1.2.2 allow for NP_1 to be an inanimate NP as well, as witness [26]:

[26] John/circumstances kept/prevented/stopped Sue from competing.

Given the considerations of Chapter 2, *circumstances,* as an inanimate NP_1, cannot be an Agent. It is an Instrument. The Instrument, or Instrumental, to use Fillmore's (1968: 24) term, is "the case of the inanimate force or object causally involved in the action or state identified by the verb."

The discussion of Chapter 2 predicts that when $Verb_1$ is a verb of volition and NP_1 is an Agent only, NP_2 can be an Agent only, on account of the Agent Rule. The roles of the Experiencer, Benefactive and Object are excluded, cf. [27b–d] and [28b–d]:

[27] **a.** John bullied/flattered Sue into writing a letter to a friend.

     b. *John bullied/flattered Sue into being aware of the conspiracy.

     c. *John bullied/flattered Sue into getting a letter from a friend.

     d. *John bullied/flattered Sue into growing old/being tall enough for the basketball team.

[28] **a.** John dissuaded Sue from writing a letter to a friend.

     b. *John dissuaded Sue from being aware of the conspiracy.

     c. *John dissuaded Sue from getting a letter from a friend.

     d. *John dissuaded Sue from growing old/from being tall enough for the basketball team.

[27b–d] and [28b–d] are all bad, on account of the Agent Rule. Neither of the two mitigating factors—neither coreferential roles, with or without agentive reinterpretations nor external control readings—is relevant to [27b–d] or to [28b–d]. Predicates in [27] and [28] are such as do not display coreferential roles. It seems impossible for NP_1 to display them in the present pattern, but PRO may display them if a different $Verb_2$ is chosen. For instance, *John bullied/flattered Sue into seeing the explosion/into experiencing a new sensation/into believing the story/into sleeping on the floor* are all good, on account of the mitigating influence of coreferential roles. As for external control readings, *to get a letter* is a predicate that is under the control of someone other than its subject. Therefore, it is a candidate for an external control reading. However, verbs occurring as $Verb_1$ of the present pattern focus on the relation of NP_1 and NP_0 and neither NP is interpreted as controlling the realization of S_2. It seems difficult to interpret [27b–d] or [28b–d] as within the scope of external control readings.

When NP_1 is an Instrument, the constructions corresponding to [27b–d] and [28b–d] are appreciably better. The construction corresponding to [27a] and [28a] is good as well:

[29] a. Circumstances prevented Sue from writing a letter to a friend.
  b. Circumstances prevented Sue from being aware of the conspiracy.
  c. Circumstances prevented Sue from getting a letter from a friend.
  d. Circumstances prevented Sue from growing old/from being tall enough.

The Agent, as NP_2, cf. [29a], is perfect. So is an Experiencer as NP_2, as in [29b]. The same goes for a Benefactive as NP_2, as in [29c]. The Object case seems possible for NP_2 as well, as in [29d]. The sentence *Circumstances prevented Sue from being tall enough for the basketball team* is well formed and means something like 'due to circumstances, Sue was not tall enough for the basketball team'.

To sum up, there is no class of $Verb_1$s in the present pattern expressing desideration only. Consequently, there is no class of NP_1s that are Experiencers only. All NP_1s governed by verbs of volition in the present pattern are Agents and the sentences in question are subject to the Agent Rule. Regarding mitigating factors, coreferential roles are relevant, but external control readings are not. That is, in the present pattern the realization of S_2 is not viewed as within the control of an NP of the higher clause, for, as in the pattern of Chapter 4, $Verb_1$ focuses on the involvement of NP_1 with NP_0, rather than implying controllability.

Chapter 6

VERBS GOVERNING PREPOSITIONAL PHRASES AND INFINITIVAL COMPLEMENT CLAUSES

6.1 INTRODUCTORY OBSERVATIONS

The focus of attention in the present chapter is on the type of construction in Modern English that is initially exemplified by [1a, b]. ([1b] is from Visser (1973: 2241).)

[1] **a.** He could count on his father to express the opposing point of view.
b. I depended on him to come.

It will be argued below that *count on* and *depend on* are somewhat exceptional members of the class of verbs governing the pattern, but they may serve to highlight some features of it.

With minimal and uncontroversial assumptions about bracketing taken for granted, the sentences of [1a, b] exhibit the form of [2] in surface structure:

[2] $[NP_1 \text{ Verb}_1 \text{ Prep } NP_0 \text{ to Verb}_2 \ldots]_S$

Central properties of sentences such as [1a, b] are still a matter of investigation (cf. Seppänen (1984)). Under such circumstances, it is audacious to hazard presenting an account of sentences such as [1a, b]. It should be understood that the account to be offered has provisional status, and there is no doubt that it is partial at best.

Of central importance in the present context is the precise position of NP_0 in

[2]. A relevant point of departure is provided by Visser. When introducing the construction, he (1973: 2241) notes that "the verb is one of those that form a semantic unit with a following preposition. The (pro)noun that is the subject of the infinitive is consequently at the same time the prepositional object of the introductory verb."

The term NP, and NP_0, specifically, is used here instead of the term (pro)noun. Visser, then, visualizes NP_0 as being simultaneously the subject of the infinitive and the prepositional object of the higher verb. This solution possesses a certain appeal, but it is difficult to reconcile it with an explicit structural representation in that it is not clear how the double classification should, or could, be bracketed. For instance, it is hard to say whether, under such circumstances, NP_0 is a constituent of the lower sentence, that is, of S_2, in terms of the bracketing used in earlier chapters. Even though Visser's solution cannot therefore be accepted here in the precise form in which it was offered, the solution that will be adopted is perhaps only a variation of Visser's solution.

In order to tackle the problem of the constituent structure of [1a, b], it is helpful to provide and to consider representations of the alternatives available that are as explicit as possible. They are given in [3a, b]:

[3] **a.** $[NP_1 \; Verb_1 \; [Prep \; NP_0]_{PP} \; [[PRO]_{NP_2} \; to \; Verb_2 \ldots]_{S_2}]_{S_1}$
    b. $[NP_1 \; Verb_1 \; Prep \; [NP_2 \; to \; Verb_2 \ldots]_{S_2}]_{S_1}$

In [3a] NP_0 is not part of S_2, but rather forms a prepositional phrase with a preceding preposition. Since the subject of S_2 in [1a, b] is understood to be coreferential with NP_0, provision is made in [3a] for an empty NP, NP_2, representing the subject of S_2. NP_2 is designated as PRO. PRO is controlled by NP_0. As for [3b], in accordance with the usage adopted in this book, the subject of S_2 is designated as NP_2. In [3b] NP_2 is then to be identified as NP_0. There is no PRO in [3b].

The structures of [3a, b] are offered as potential approximations of structures close to surface structures. At a deeper level, provision should be made, at least in [3b], for two occurrences of a preposition, the second one being *for*. Or, conceivably, rather than a preposition, *for* should perhaps be considered the first part of the *for to* complementizer. Evidence for *for* is provided by pseudocleft sentences such as [4a, b]:

[4] **a.** What everyone could count on was for Father to express the opposing
      point of view.
    b. What I am depending on is for you to come to the party.

The structures of [4a, b] are of the form of [4′]:

[4′] $[[[\text{What everyone could count on/what I am depending on}]_{S_3}]_{NP} \; [[be]_{Verb}$
     $[[\text{for Father to express the opposing point of view/for you to come to the}$
     $\text{party}]_{S_2}]_{NP}]_{VP}]_{S_1}$

In [4'] NP_2, *Father* and *you*, belong to S_2 only. Presumably, then, the relevant underlying structure is of the form of [4"]:

[4"] $[[\text{Everyone/I}]_{NP}$ could $[[\text{count/rely}]_{Verb} [[\text{on}]_{Prep} [[\text{for Father to express the opposing point of view/for you to come to the party}]_{S_2}]_{NP}]_{PP}]_{VP}]_{S_1}$

As argued by Seppänen (1981: 399), the *for* of the underlying structure is then later deleted, before surface sentences of the form of [1a, b] are derived.

The consideration presented, then, favors structure [3b] for the present pattern. The conclusion receives additional support from the occurrence of existential *there* and the weather *it* in the pattern, as noted by Seppänen (1984: 249 ff.):

[5] **a.** John was counting on it to rain heavily.
    b. John was depending on there not to be any problems.

It is clear, then, that structure [3b] must be available for *count on, rely on* etc.

Support for [3a] is provided by the Question Formation and Relativization tests of constituent structure devised by Berman (1974: 235 ff.). Sentences such as [6a, b] and [7a, b] are relevant in the present context:

[6] **a.** Who did everyone count on to express the opposing point of view?
    b. Who did you rely on to come to the party?

[7] **a.** The person who(m) everyone was counting on to express the opposing point of view was my Father.
    b. John, on whom you had relied to come to the party, failed to turn up.

The wellformedness of sentences such as [6a, b] and [7a, b], presumably, shows that with *count on* and *rely on* NP_0 is a main clause constituent and not part of the subordinate clause. To give the argument some substance, it is helpful to contrast the patterns of [6a, b] and [7a, b] with the *for to* pattern of Chapter 3. This is all the more relevant because, for instance, *rely on* and *long for* were cited by Hornby (1966: 75) as belonging to the same pattern. In Chapter 3 it was taken for granted that the NP following *for* in the *for to* pattern of Chapter 3, of verbs such as *long for* and *hope for*, is a constituent of the subordinate clause. (Certain verbs of the *for to* pattern of Chapter 3 are not exactly identical with *long for* and *hope for* in their syntactic properties, but the differences are irrelevant in the present context, in that they do not affect the position of the NP following *for*. For some discussion, see Rudanko (to appear).) Consequently, if the Question Formation and Relative Clause Formation tests are relevant for distinguishing structures with respect to the position of NP_0, it is predicted that the pattern of Chapter 3 should not allow the NP following *for*, designated as NP_2 in Chapter 3, to be questioned or relativized. The sentences of [8a, b] confirm this prediction:

[8] **a.** Everyone longed for/hoped for Father to express the opposing point of view.

—*Who did everyone long for/hope for to express the opposing point of view?

—*For whom did everyone long/hope to express the opposing point of view?

b. *The person who(m) John longed for/hoped for to express the opposing point of view was his Father.

—*The person for whom John longed/hoped to express the opposing point of view was his Father.

There does seem to be an appreciable difference in wellformedness between the sentences with Question Formation or Relativization of [6a, b], [7a, b], on the one hand, and those of [8a, b], on the other, in favor of the former. The question and relative clause sentences of [8a, b] are not improved even if the *for* is deleted, as witness the illformedness of *Who did everyone long/hope to express the opposing point of view* and *The person who(m) John longed/hoped to express the opposing point of view was his Father.* The wellformedness of [6a, b] and [7a, b] serves to motivate structure [3a] for *count on* and *rely on*.

A further piece of evidence, though of limited relevance, is provided by Passivization. As noted by Hietaranta (1983: 230), passive sentences of the form of [9a, b] are good:

[9] a. His Father could be counted on to express the opposing point of view.
  b. You can be relied on to be discreet.

If Passivization is a sentence-internal operation, as is assumed by Postal (1974), [9a, b] lend support for postulating a structure of the form of [3a] for *count on*, etc.

The Passivization argument embodies a clear prediction with respect to the verbs of the *for to* pattern of Chapter 3, such as *long for, want for*. If Passivization is sentence internal, the NP following *for* of the *for to* pattern of Chapter 3 should not be capable of being moved by Passivization of the higher verb. The prediction is all the more interesting, because, as Seppänen (1984: 247), referring to Quirk et al. (1974: 832), points out, *long for* and *pray for* are verbs that allow Passivization. (*Pray for* was another verb listed alongside of *long for* in the *for to* pattern of Chapter 3.)

Not all verbs of the *for to* pattern of Chapter 3 belong to the list of Quirk et al. (1974: 832). For instance, *want* does not: *Everyone wanted for peace, *Peace was wanted for by everyone*. Even so, it is true that Passivization may be possible for *long for* and *pray for*, as in *After so many years of war, everyone longed for/prayed for peace.—After so many years of war, peace was longed for/prayed for by everyone.* (Passivization seems more natural with *pray for* than with *long for*, but let us accept Quirk et al.'s list.) It is noteworthy, though, that in the passivized sentences cited and in the pattern discussed by Quirk et al. (1974: 832), these verbs occur in a simple sentence and there is no embedded sentence, and no *for to* sentence, in particular, present. In the present context, it is important to consider *long for,* and *pray for* and other verbs of the *for to* pattern of Chapter 3 when they actually occur with an embedded *for to* sentence. When this is done, Passivization does not seem to be possible, cf. [10a, b]:

[10] **a.** After so many years of war, everyone longed for a peace treaty to be concluded.

—*After so many years of war, a peace treaty was longed for by everyone to be concluded.

b. The prisoner prayed for the King to release him.

—*The King was prayed for by the prisoner to release him.

The contrast in wellformedness between the passivized sentences of [9a, b] and [10a, b] in favor of the former lends additional support to postulating structures such as [3a] for *count on* and *rely on.* For further considerations that motivate [3a], though not explicitly presented in support of [3a], we may refer to Williams (1980: 214 ff.).

To sum up the discussion so far, it has been argued that at least two sets of data support structure [3b], where NP_0 is the subject of S_2. First, pseudocleft sentences such as [4a, b] are good. Second, such NPs as the weather *it* and existential *there* may occur as NP_0, as in [5a, b]. On the other hand, three sets of data support structure [3a], where NP_0 is part of a PP outside of S_2. Questioning and Relativization of NP_0 are possible, as in [6a, b] and [7a, b], respectively. Further, NP_0 may be moved by Passivization, as in [9a, b]. These findings may go some way toward explaining the initial appeal of Visser's statement quoted above.

One solution to the apparent dilemma is to regard *count on, rely on,* etc. as structurally ambiguous, as we argued in passing in Rudanko (to appear), and to allow them to occur in both [3a] and [3b]. Visser apparently meant for [3a] and [3b] to be relevant simultaneously. Here it is suggested that though they are both relevant, they are not relevant simultaneously, but rather individually. This is one respect in which the present treatment differs from Visser's.

Some indirect evidence for the proposal may perhaps be gathered from a general theoretical consideration. We have argued that verbs such as *count on,* etc. are structurally ambiguous, allowing both [3a] and [3b]. Further, we have argued that such verbs as *long for,* of the *for to* pattern of Chapter 3, are structurally unambiguous, allowing pattern [3b] only. With these two classes established, it should not come as a surprise that there is a class of verbs that are structurally unambiguous and allow pattern [3a] only. Apparently, quite a number of verbs that exhibit the form of [2] unambiguously take pattern [3a] only. [3a], then, is the basic type of this chapter and the extent of its preponderance will be indicated below. At this point, it is important to note that the postulation of one type of structure only, that is, [3a], for a large number of verbs that occur in [2], but not for all of them, is a second difference between the present treatment and that of Visser.

[3a] is an Equi pattern. In [3a], NP_0, the NP of the prepositional phrase, is

the controller. As noted in Chapter 2, there exist verbs such as *vow*, which allow the sequence of constituents of [2] of the present chapter, but where the controller is NP_1, the subject of the higher verb, as in *John vowed to me to come back and win*.

One syntactic property of *vow*, which may be a reflex of the controller assignment rule, is the omissibility of the prepositional phrase. With verbs of Chapter 2, where NP_1 is the controller, the PP is always omissible. With verbs of the present chapter, the PP is in general much less freely omissible. We may perhaps try to be a little more specific. In Chapter 4 we introduced Bach's generalization. Essentially, it is that an object controlling a PRO is not omissible. The generalization provides a description of the non-omissibility of objects of *induce, urge* and of other verbs of the pattern of Chapter 4. It has been suggested by Bresnan (1982: 398) that *rely on* of the present pattern is subject to a Verb Preposition Incorporation rule, which converts a structure of the form of $[[rely]_{Verb} [on]_{Prep} NP]_{VP}$ into one of the form of $[[rely on]_{Verb} NP]_{VP}$. Motivation for this restructuring is provided by cleft sentences and passives. *Rely on*, as in the sentence *Mary relies on John to dress himself*, allows the cleft sentence *It is John that Mary relies on to dress himself*, but, significantly, it does not allow **It is on John that Mary relies to dress himself*. This shows that restructuring has taken place. This conclusion is confirmed by the admissibility of the passive *John is relied on by Mary to dress himself*. (All these sentences with *rely on* are from Bresnan (1982: 398 ff.).) To account for sentences displaying control as these do, Bresnan (1982: 398) implies that the Verb Preposition Incorporation rule is obligatory in them. If this is so, Bach's generalization is presumably directly relevant to *rely on*, explaining the inadmissibility of **Mary relies to dress himself*. Bresnan (1982: 398 ff.) does not discuss the generality of the Verb Preposition Incorporation rule, apart from *rely on*, but we may note that it is not limited to *rely on*. It applies to numerous other verbs of the present pattern, including *call on, count on* and *prevail on*. For instance, *call on*, as in *Mary called on John not to perjure himself*, allows *It was John that Mary called on not to perjure himself*, but does not allow **It was on John that Mary called not to perjure himself*. The rule is then fairly general, but it does not seem to apply to all verbs of the present pattern. *Appeal to*, as in *Mary appealed to John not to perjure himself*, allows *It was John that Mary appealed to not to perjure himself*, but, significantly, it also allows *It was to John that Mary appealed not to perjure himself*. The applicability of the Verb Preposition Incorporation rule is of interest in its own right, but in the present context our main concern is to note that even though *appeal to* is unaffected by the rule in the control sentences given, it still does not omit the PP, as witness the inadmissibility of **Mary appealed not to perjure himself* and of **Mary appealed to take quick action*.

We may speculate that even when a $Verb_1$, such as *appeal to*, is not subject to the Verb Preposition Incorporation rule and when Bach's generalization is therefore not directly relevant, the general difficulty of omitting the NP_0, and the PP, of the present pattern is related to Bach's generalization if the generalization is broadened to exclude the omission of such prepositional objects governed by Verb$_1$s as control PRO. This speculation is intuitively appealing, but it may not be possible to maintain it. The reason is the behavior of a class of Verb$_1$s that includes *signal to*. We will call it the *signal* class. Bresnan (1982: 418) has pointed to sentences such as *Louise signaled to follow her.* (As we noted in Chapter 4, Bresnan (1982: 418) and Koster (1984: 433) regard the sentence as resulting from the omission of an NP, not of a PP, from *Louise signaled Tom to follow her*, but we follow Rizzi's (1986: 504) suggestion that what is omitted is a PP and that the reduced sentence results from *Louise signaled to Tom to follow her.*) In *Louise signaled to follow her*, NP$_2$ is not controlled by NP$_1$. It lacks an expressed controller in the sentence. Therefore, *signal to* appears to be problematic if the generalization is understood in a broader sense so as to block the omission of prepositional objects that control PRO. In spite of the evidence of verbs such as *appeal to*, this broader interpretation of the generalization may then not be possible. In any event, the issue will need more investigation. In the present context, it should be mentioned that there exist dialects of English in which the reduced sentence *Louise signaled to follow her* is unacceptable. This suggests that it may be difficult to base any strong claim on it.

A second class of Verb$_1$s of the present pattern may omit the PP, without appreciable idiolectal variation, but it does not constitute a problem for Bach's generalization, either. The class includes Verb$_1$s such as *beg of*, if admitted in the pattern (see below), and *plead to/with*. We will call it the *plead* class. For instance, if the PP is omitted in *Everyone begged of Father to come along*, the result is *Everyone begged to come along*. That is, in the resulting sentence lacking the PP, the controller of PRO is NP$_1$ and the pattern is the infinitival subject-controlled Equi pattern of Chapter 2. Verbs such as *beg of* and *plead to/with*, then, belong to both the infinitival subject-controlled Equi pattern of Chapter 2 and to the pattern of the present chapter. They belong to the pattern of Chapter 2 even when a PP is present, provided that S$_2$ is in the passive voice, as in *John begged of Father to be allowed to come along*. For these verbs belonging to both patterns, a PP must be present and S$_2$ must be in the active voice for them to belong to the pattern of the present chapter. From the point of view of Bach's generalization, the *plead* class comprises Verb$_1$s that are ambiguous. They are not a problem for Bach's generalization, for when NP$_0$ is the controller it is not omissible.

Apart from the omissibility of the PP, a version of the *Ought* Modal Constraint referred to in Chapter 2 may be helpful in distinguishing the two patterns. Consider [11a, b]:

[11] **a.** John begged of Father that he would come along.
    b. John vowed to Father that he would come along.

In [11a] the *he* of the subordinate clause can refer only to Father, not to John. These judgments are reversed in [11b]. The same controller assignment holds of the corresponding Equi structures. As argued, in *John begged of Father to come along* the subject of the complement sentence is understood to be Father, but in *John vowed to Father to come along* the subject of the complement sentence is understood to be John.

6.2 VISSER'S LIST AND A CLASSIFICATION

It is to Visser that we turn to obtain a representative sample of verbs occurring in the pattern of [3a]. Visser's (1973, 2241 ff.) list of verbs of his type *I depended on him to come* is relevant. He does not provide any analysis or characterization of the verbs of his list. Nor does he indicate that several of the verbs that he lists are obsolete. On the other hand, all the verbs of his list, with one possible exception, belong to the pattern. Consequently, when as a first step we go through his list, we will in general only winnow out obsolete verbs. (The references to Visser here are to Visser (1973: 2241 ff.).)

VERB	COMMENTS
appeal to	
beckon to	
beg of	Somewhat marginal in Modern English, but may perhaps be retained. The influence of the rival infinitival sentence pattern, of Chapter 4, *beg* NP_0 *to* $Verb_2$, may be supplanting *beg of* NP_0 *to* $Verb_2$ in present-day English intuitions and usage. However, instances are found from this century, as in *Sir I beg of you not to speak of dancing to the mourners' bench* (Visser, from 1927, S. Lewis, *Elmer Gantry*), and they do not seem impossible for most speakers. The usage may be on its way out, though.
beseech to	Obsolete.
bid to	Obsolete. A modernized version of one of Visser's instances would be *The religious men . . . bid to their underlings . . . to live chaste*.
brag of	Obsolete. The one citation that Visser has is from Shakespeare, *Romeo and Juliet* I, v, *Veronica brags of him . . . To be a virtuous . . . youth,* but this does not represent current usage of the verb any more.
call on	
call to	
command to	
commit to	Obsolete. Visser's most recent instance is from c. 1450 and does not represent current usage. (**To me you have committed to minister the sacrament,* to modernize Visser's citation a little.)
count on	
cry after	
cry (up)on	Obsolete, as in *??He was crying upon her to come back*.

desire of	Very marginal in the pattern in Modern English, as in *He desired of me to make a fire upstairs,* to simplify one of Visser's examples somewhat. On balance, we omit it.
depend on	
expect of	Seems obsolete in the pattern in Modern English. Visser has one example (from Shakespeare, *Much Ado,* I, i), *he hath indeed better bettered expectation than you must expect of me to tell,* but this does not seem to reflect current usage.
fond to	Obsolete.
forbid to	Obsolete. One of Visser's two citations is from c. 1449 and is no longer current, even if irrelevant features of spelling and diction are modernized *. . . they must forbid to the underlings . . . to be wedded.*
frain at	Obsolete.
frain to	Obsolete.
give to	Obsolete.
grant to	Obsolete.
hallo at	The one instance in Visser is *He halloed and waved at Yvonne to halt* (1947, M. Lowry, *Under the Volcano*). Since *and waved* may be omitted without an effect on the grammaticality of the sentence, the instance is genuine.
hear of	Visser's most recent instance is from Shakespeare, Henry VIII, I, iv, *having heard . . . Of this so noble . . . assembly This night to meet here* and does not represent current usage.
judge of	Visser's one instance, from 1569 Th. Preston, *Cambises, I judge of him to be a man right fit,* does not represent current usage.
make of	Obsolete. Visser's most recent citation is from Pepys's Diary (ed. Braybrooke) 1663, *we are going upon making of all ships . . . to perform their Quarantine.*
motion to	
object against	Obsolete.
ordain to	The usage is perhaps obsolete, cf. ??*We do not know what services you have ordained to us to do,* to modify Visser's most recent example.
plead to	
plead with	
pray to	
prevail on	
prevail with	
prophesy of	Obsolete. The one instance in Visser is from 1565, Th. Stapleton, *A Fortress of the Faith, Daniel . . . hauing expressely prophecyed of the coming of Christ, of his church to be dispersed through the whole world, . . . he concludeth . . .*

propose to	Very marginal, cf. ?*John proposed to Mary to go away for a time. On balance, we omit it.
rely on	
say of	The usage does not seem current. Visser's citation is from 1662, Pepys's Diary *all people say of her to be a very fine and handsome lady.*
say to	Obsolete.
shout at	
show to	Obsolete, cf. *Who shows to you to flee from the wrath to come?*, to paraphrase Visser's one example.
sign to	
signal to	
suggest to	
sue to	Sounds slightly archaic (cf. the OED) in the pattern, cf. *Divers other Nations have . . . sued to them . . . to come into Alliance with them,* OED, but may perhaps be retained.
take up(on)	Should presumably be *take (up)on.* Visser has only one illustration of the verb, from 1602, which may be modified to *Parliaments took upon them to define religion.* In current English a reflexive would be used and many speakers would prefer to have an *it* inserted, as in *He took it upon himself to define religion.* The *it* suggests that the *to* clause has been extraposed. (We recall the analysis of *find in one's heart* in Chapter 2.) We drop the verb, also because the choice of NP_0 is restricted to reflexive pronouns.
tell to	
trust to	
urge (up)on	
watch of	Visser's one citation, from 1922, Galsworthy, *The Forsyte Saga, She was spared the watching of the branches jut out,* is unconvincing as evidence for classifying the verb into the present pattern.
wave at	
write (un)to	

In all, there remain 24 verbs and among them there emerges what seems to be a fairly natural classification. On the most general level, all the 24 verbs listed imply positive volition on the part of NP_1, representing the subject of the higher sentence, for the realization of S_2. Within this overall class, the main division is into verbs of communication and those that do not express communication:

(1) Verb$_1$ expresses communication.
(1.1) Verb$_1$ expresses verbal communication: *appeal to, beg of, call on/to, command to, cry after, hallo at, plead to/with, pray to, shout at, sue to, suggest to, tell to, urge (up)on, write (un)to.*

(1.2) Verb$_1$ expresses nonverbal communication: *beckon to, motion to, sign to, signal to, wave at.*

(2) Verb$_1$ does not express communication, but desire or effort on the part of NP$_1$ for S$_2$ to be realized: *count on, depend on, prevail on/with, rely on, trust to.*

Given the classification of verbs, it is possible to venture a comment on the incidence of verbs that are syntactically ambiguous, allowing both [3a] and [3b], such as *count on.* If the admissibility of pseudoclefts such as [4a, b] and of *there* and *it* constructions, such as [5a, b], is used as a positive criterion for assigning verbs to pattern [3b], it seems that only three verbs qualify: *count on, depend on* and *rely on,* all from class 2. For instance, consider *beg of* and *call on,* chosen from 1.1. With respect to the pseudocleft criterion, cf. [12a, b]:

[12] **a.** Everyone begged of John to make a speech.
 b. John called on Mary to come to the party.

If the NP following the preposition in [12a, b] were part of the embedded sentence, as in [3b], pseudocleft sentences such as [13a, b] should be good, analogous to [4a, b]:

[13] **a.** *What everyone begged of was for John to make a speech.
 b. *What John called on was for Mary to come to the party.

One possibility for capturing the difference with respect to the pseudocleft pattern is to represent S$_2$ as a NP in [3b], but as a plain S in [3a]. This was in fact observed in [4'] and [4''] above and is in line with Higgins's (1973: 191) suggestion that "it is only sentences that are also noun phrases that can appear in the focus position in pseudo-cleft sentences." Higgins's suggestion is somewhat tentative and so is the proposal that [3a] and [3b] should be distinguished by the presence of an NP node above S$_2$ in the latter, but not in the former. While the proposal is tentative, the structural difference is real.

As predicted, neither the weather *it* nor existential *there* is possible with *beg of* or *plead with,* as witness [14a, b]:

[14] **a.** *Everyone begged of it to rain heavily.
 b. *John called on there to be no problems.

As noted, *beg of* is somewhat marginal in the pattern in Modern English. This may go some way toward explaining why it fails to satisfy such positive criteria of pattern [3a] as Questioning and Relativization of NP$_0$, as witness [15b] and [16]:

[15] **a.** The prisoner begged of the King to release him.
 b. *Who did the prisoner beg of to release him?
 —*Of whom did the prisoner beg to release him?

[16] *The person who(m) the prisoner begged of to release him was the King.

—??The person of whom the prisoner begged to release him was the King.

Apart from the three verbs *count on, depend on* and *rely on,* which are syntactically ambiguous, and *beg of,* the rest of the verbs listed seem to be syntactically unambiguous, occurring in pattern [3a], and satisfying its positive criteria in a reasonable way and failing to satisfy the positive criteria of [3b]. Some of these verbs are more current than others in the pattern of [3a]. The former generally meet the positive criteria of [3a] with more ease than do the latter. For example, consider *prevail on* and *trust to.* Of these, the former seems to be more current in the pattern:

[17] a. John prevailed on Mr. Smith, a lawyer, to draw up his will.
      b. John trusted to Mr. Smith, a lawyer, to draw up his will.

Questioning, Relativization and Passivization all seem more natural with *prevail on* than with *trust to.* Compare the sentences of [18a–c] with those of [19a–c]:

[18] a. Who did John prevail on to draw up his will?
      b. The person who(m) John prevailed on to draw up his will was Mr. Smith, a lawyer.
      c. Mr. Smith, a lawyer, was prevailed on by John to draw up his will.

[19] a. Who(m) did John trust to to draw up his will?
      b. The person who(m) John trusted to to draw up his will was Mr. Smith, a lawyer.
      c. Mr. Smith, a lawyer, was trusted to by John to draw up his will.

While a question mark or even two might be added to some of the sentences of [19a–c], it would be too harsh to star them. By contrast, the following must be starred, indicating that structure [3b] is not possible for these verbs:

[20] a. *What John prevailed on was for Mr. Smith, a lawyer, to draw up his will.
      b. *What John trusted to was for Mr. Smith, a lawyer, to draw up his will.
      c. *John trusted to there not to be any trouble.
      d. *John prevailed on it to rain heavily.

Overall, verbs of pattern [3a] predominate. This serves to motivate the choice of [3a] as the basic pattern of the present chapter.

Of the 24 verbs that were listed, the *plead* class, of Verb$_1$s that belong to the present pattern and to that of subject-controlled infinitival Equi of Chapter 2, comprises at least *beg of, plead with, pray to* and *shout at. Appeal to* also allows such sentences as *John appealed to Bill* PRO *to be allowed to leave* (Radford (1981: 381)), where the PRO immediately preceding *to be allowed* is controlled by NP$_1$, *John. Appeal to* differs from the other four verbs in that it is less ready to omit the PP, even when the NP of the PP is not the controller of PRO, as witness *John begged/pleaded/prayed/?shouted to be allowed to leave* vs. **John appealed to be allowed to leave.*

The *signal* class is defined by two properties. First, subject to idiolectal variation, the Verb$_1$ in question may omit its PP. Second, in the resulting sentence PRO is not controlled by NP$_1$, and lacks an expressed controller in the reduced sentence. The class seems limited to verbs of nonverbal communication taking the preposition *to: beckon, motion, sign,* and *signal.* Of these, *sign* seems to be the most marginal in the reduced, and in the full, pattern. Among the rest of these verbs, there is idiolectal variation in respect of the omissibility of the PP.

A comment may be ventured on the content of the subordinate clause on the basis of corresponding *that* clause constructions or paraphrases. As in Chapter 2, some of these *that* clause constructions are forced and not idiomatic in English, but their potential content is of interest. Given the presence of volition in the verbs of the pattern, the appearance of a modal or a modal equivalent in the paraphrase is not altogether surprising. For instance, *He appealed to me to show mercy* may be paraphrased as *??He appealed to me that I should show mercy.* (What was said in Chapter 3 about the greater definiteness of a *that* clause in surface structure still holds.) Also in the light of Chapter 3 it comes as no surprise that verbs of communication, especially those of verbal communication, are also compatible with *that* clauses. Those of nonverbal communication are compatible with them as well. For instance, consider *He signaled to me to follow him* and *He signaled to me that I should follow him.* Since *signal* expresses nonverbal communication, neither sentence implies a verbal act, but the *that* clause version still highlights the specific content of the act of communication. In the *that* clause version it is not immediately obvious whether the lower clause should be considered a complement clause, because the insertion of *in order that* in place of plain *that* is possible, cf. *He signaled to me in order that I should follow him.* The construction is perhaps systematically ambiguous between a complement interpretation, where the lower sentence expresses the contents or the message of the signalling, and an adverbial interpretation, which expresses the purpose of the communication. In point of fact, both types may co-occur, as in *He signaled to me with flares to blow up the bridge (in order) that I might notice his signals in the dark.*

No 'endeavor' component (cf. Chapters 2 and 3) is present in the verbs of the present pattern, with the exception of *prevail on/with.* It comes then as no great surprise that the same verb should be implicative. All the other verbs of the present pattern, including those of communication, are clearly nonimplicative.

6.3 CASE GRAMMAR AND THE PREPOSITIONAL EQUI PATTERN

A brief section will be sufficient to cover the prepositional Equi pattern from the point of view of case grammar.

Verbs of class 1 express communication and therefore take an Agent as NP_1. Since they are verbs of volition and since the NP_1 in question is an Agent, we expect on the basis of the Agent Rule that NP_2 can be an Agent, but that other case roles for NP_2 are worse, except if a mitigating factor is operative. Two such mitigating factors have been identified in this book: coreferential roles and external control readings. Coreferential roles with respect to NP_1 do not seem very relevant to verbs of 1.1, or indeed to other verb classes of the present pattern. NP_1 is an Agent only with verbs of class 1.1. External control readings are not very relevant either, for $Verb_1$ focuses on the involvement of NP_1 with NP_0, rather than implying controllability. Agentive reinterpretations of NP_2, on the other hand, are relevant to the same predicates as allowed them in earlier chapters. Predicates of Berman's (1970: 205) class [9b] provide good examples of agentive reinterpretations here as well:

[21] **a.** John appealed to Susan to make a speech.
   b. *John appealed to Susan to know the answer.
      —John appealed to Susan to win the race.
      —John appealed to Susan to experience a new sensation.
   c. *John appealed to Susan to get a letter in the mail.
   d. *John appealed to Susan to grow tall/to be tall when grown up.

The same judgments hold true of verbs of nonverbal communication.

Class 2 contains verbs that run the gamut from wanting/wishing to effort on the part of NP_1 for S_2 to be realized. Most of the verbs express wanting/wishing. These include *count on, rely on*. Effort is implied by *prevail upon*.

Case grammar makes significantly different predictions for the two classes. Verbs of wanting/wishing take Experiencers as subjects and this predicts, on the basis of the Equi patterns of Chapters 2 and 4, that all four case roles are allowed for NP_2. In the main, this prediction bears up well enough:

[22] **a.** John counted on/relied on Sue to make a speech.
   b. John counted on/relied on Sue to know the answer.
   c. John counted on/relied on Sue to get a letter in the mail.
   d. John counted on/relied on Sue to grow old/to be tall when grown up.

[22a–d] seem capable of having the structure of [3a]. For instance, *Sue* can be questioned and the sentence may be passivized, as in *Who did John count on to receive a letter in the mail* and *Sue was counted on by John to receive a letter in the mail.* These may be contrasted with *There was counted on to be no trouble at the football match* and *It was counted on not to rain tomorrow*, which have the structure of [3b] (cf. Rudanko (to appear)).

As for *prevail on*, its subject is an Agent. The prediction, then, is that NP_2 can only be an Agent, unless there is a mitigating factor. Again, agentive reinterpretations of NP_2, producing coreferential roles for NP_2, seem the only mitigating factor that is relevant in the present pattern:

[23] **a.** John prevailed on Sue to make a speech.
    b. *John prevailed on Sue to know the answer.
      —John prevailed on Sue to win the race.
      —John prevailed on Sue to experience a new sensation.
    c. *John prevailed on Sue to get a letter in the mail.
    d. *John prevailed on Sue to grow old/to be tall when grown up.

Chapter 7

CONCLUDING OBSERVATIONS

A work of art may be so finished and so perfect that a single stroke, or a single line, meant to improve it, may in fact detract from it. By contrast, a treatise with scientific or scholarly pretensions is never complete or perfect. As regards the present study, other patterns could have been included in it. Also, the patterns that were selected for consideration could have been discussed more thoroughly. No doubt, there exist factors that are relevant to the syntactic or semantic description of the patterns selected, but that were either overlooked or neglected in the present study. Even with such allowances made and taken for granted, the present study did yield a number of results. Also, the selection of patterns for consideration was not accidental. Rather, Equi was a common theme running through every chapter of the book. Of the seven patterns listed in the introduction, [2a, b] and [2e–g] involve Equi. [2c, d] and a subclass of [2g] do not, but they too were contrasted with Equi patterns.

In each chapter an effort was made to identify the pattern in question and to isolate it from constructions that appear to be similar but are not. After the pattern was isolated, an attempt was made to compile a list of verbs governing the pattern in present-day English. No such list can ever be considered comprehensive, but it does serve a purpose that should be neither disparaged nor called into question. Linguistic writings occasionally—perhaps rather too frequently—display an impressionistic air. It is as if the author were considering a few verbs that happen to have suggested themselves to him. To allay the fear of impressionism, it is advisable to compile lists of verbs, which, while neither complete nor even comprehensive, may be representative. We sought to compile such lists in the individual chapters. As we did so, we were fortunate in that we were able to draw on Visser's pioneering work as the indispensable source of data for the patterns selected.

Syntactic considerations provided the underpinning for the identification of the patterns of complementation that were considered. Previous work relating to the patterns was reviewed. It was argued that even Visser's collections of verbs needed to be subjected to syntactic analysis. In each chapter the pattern under consideration was isolated syntactically from constructions that looked similar at first sight, but turned out to be different when syntactic considerations were taken into account. Our classifications will hopefully serve to clarify the syntactic description of the verbs that were considered.

In three patterns the classifications that emerged are of syntactic interest from the point of view of Bach's generalization. In the patterns of [1e], [1f], and in a more limited way, of [1g], of Chapter 1, the controller of PRO is the object of $Verb_1$. It is then of interest to investigate the omissibility of such objects as control PRO. It was found that Bach's generalization is a very powerful one and that an object that controls a PRO is very rarely omissible. ($Verb_1$s that ambiguously take NP_1, the subject of $Verb_1$, as the controller of PRO are not counterexamples to Bach's generalization.) It was found that if we ignored the *signal* class of Chapter 6, then only one small class of verbs, of the pattern of [1f] of Chapter 1, comprising *advise, caution,* and *warn against,* did not observe Bach's generalization. It is notable that this class is semantically coherent, in terms of our classification. In future work the discovery of this class may lead to a deeper understanding of Bach's generalization.

Proceeding to our semantic findings, we note that in some patterns there was more regularity in the results of the analysis than in other patterns, but in every Equi pattern it was found that the largest number of verbs occurring as $Verb_1$ expressed some kind of volition on the part of NP_1. More specifically, in the overwhelming majority of cases the volition was for, and not against, the realization of S_2. In the case of pattern [2g] of the introduction (*count on, rely on,* etc.), covered in Chapter 6, not a single verb expressing negative volition against the realization of S_2 was found. This is perhaps among the more striking findings of the study. It is not being claimed that no such negative verb of pattern [2g] could ever be found. If a more comprehensive study were undertaken, such a verb, or even more than one, might come to light. Rather, the prediction, in light of the present study, is that such negative verbs would constitute a small minority even in a more comprehensive list.

The preponderance of verbs of positive volition may be connected with the old force of *to,* as an element expressing purpose. This suggestion receives some support from the *for to* pattern, which was also found to co-occur with verbs expressing volition.

Also, it is of interest to note that among verbs governing the gerundive pattern [1b], verbs expressing negative volition were found rather numerous, in point of fact, more numerous than verbs expressing positive volition. Since there is no *to* in the construction, it is in light of the present inquiry perhaps only natural that verbs of positive volition should not predominate. In other words, it is being suggested here that Equi is characteristically governed by verbs expressing volition, and, further, that infinitival Equi constructions typically co-occur with verbs of positive volition while the *ing* pattern, lacking *to* and the historical associations of *to,* displays a tendency to favor verbs expressing negative volition. The former tendency is more marked than the latter.

The concept of volition was analyzed on the basis of the concepts of desideration, intention and endeavor. The three concepts are related and it was argued that they make it possible to establish three classes of verbs: verbs of desideration, verbs of desideration and intention and verbs of desideration, intention and endeavor. These three classes seem to be relevant, in varying degrees, to virtually all the infinitival and *ing* patterns under consideration. Further, the three classes of verbs are hierarchically structured. The hierarchical structure is based on entailment relations that obtain among statements containing verbs of the three classes as matrix verbs. More specifically, if we set aside such additional components of meaning as, for instance, the pleasure component found in some verbs of class 1.1.1 of section 2.3, we may say that any statement whose $Verb_1$ is from a class of verbs of desideration and intention entails the corresponding statement whose $Verb_1$ is from the corresponding class of verbs of desideration. With the same proviso understood, any statement whose $Verb_1$ is from a class of verbs of desideration, intention and endeavor entails the corresponding statement whose $Verb_1$ is from the corresponding class of verbs of desideration, or from the corresponding class of verbs of desideration and intention. Overall, the classification is designed to provide a framework for the description of dominant senses of verbs occurring as $Verb_1$s in the patterns under consideration.

The entailment hierarchy was found to be of relevance to the incidence of implicative verbs among verbs that occur as matrix verbs in the patterns under consideration. Not a single implicative matrix verb in any of the patterns was found that expressed desideration only. The incidence of implicative verbs increases somewhat in the class of verbs of desideration and intention. Quite generally, the number of implicative verbs is at its highest in the class of verbs of desideration, intention and endeavor.

Overall, one of the main conclusions of the book is that the notion of volition and its three categories of desideration, intention and endeavor are central to the description of the infinitival and *ing* clause patterns of complementation under discussion.

Elements other than volition are less typical of verbs taking infinitival or *ing* clauses, but one or two such elements were isolated. These include verbal communication. This element was argued to be typical of $Verb_1$s taking *that* complement clauses, but it is also found in a number of verbs taking infinitival or *ing* clauses as well. It is characteristic of the latter classes, though, that apart from very few exceptions, such verbs taking infinitival or *ing* clauses as express verbal communication express desideration and intention on the part of NP_1 for, or, more rarely, against the realization of S_2 as well. By contrast, verbs of verbal communication taking *that* clauses do not in general necessarily imply desideration or intention on the part of NP_1 for, or against, the realization of S_2. Combined with such verbs, the *that* clause pattern rather emphasizes the verbal character of $Verb_1$. The *that* clause provides an approximation of what was actually said or communicated verbally.

Verbs of verbal communication that do not express desideration or intention on the part of NP_1 are an important class of verbs taking *that* clauses. Apart from this class, verbs taking *that* clauses typically mean 'believe', 'understand', 'come to believe', 'come to understand' or 'demonstrate'. A number of verbs of emotion take *that* clauses and this class partly overlaps with verbs of desideration taking infinitival or *ing* clauses.

In the patterns of [1e] and [1f] of Chapter 1, as in *John coaxed Mary to come along* and *John coaxed Mary into coming along*, respectively, PRO is controlled by the direct object of $Verb_1$. In the pattern of [1g] of Chapter 1, as in *John called on Mary to come along*, PRO is controlled by the NP following the preposition. Or, if Bresnan's reanalysis rule is correct, numerous $Verb_1$s of the pattern of [1g] incorporate the preposition, which makes the following NP the direct object of $Verb_1$. In each of these three patterns an overwhelming plurality of $Verb_1$s express volition on the part of NP_1 for, or against, the realization of S_2. In the pattern of [1e] there is a very marked tendency for $Verb_1$ to mean that NP_1 influences NP_0, and NP_2, by extension, toward realizing S_2. Over one hundred verbs were listed in the pattern. Our survey is not complete, and the class of $Verb_1$s of the pattern of [1e], like virtually all other larger classes, includes a number of verbs that are not very common in the relevant pattern in Modern English. Even so, it seems significant that all of the over one hundred verbs, with only one exception, mean that NP_1 influences NP_0 toward, not away from, realizing S_2. More specifically, most verbs of the pattern mean that NP_1 makes an effort in order for S_2 to be realized by moving NP_0 to realize S_2.

Meanings of $Verb_1$s of the pattern of [1f] are similar to those of $Verb_1$s of the pattern of [1e] in a major respect. Again, NP_1 acts on NP_0 endeavoring for NP_0 to realize, or not to realize, S_2. Because of the similarity, it is no surprise that there are verbs such as *coax*, which belong to both patterns. However, there are significant dissimilarities between the two classes. In terms of sheer numbers, more verbs belong to [1e] than to [1f]. Over one hundred verbs, all of them verbs of volition, were listed as belonging to the pattern of [1e], and only about sixty verbs of volition, plus a few verbs that are not verbs of volition, were listed as belonging to the pattern of [1f]. More significantly, of the about sixty verbs of volition of the pattern of [1f], only about a dozen are unambiguously verbs of positive volition. Approximately another ten are ambiguously verbs of positive or negative volition, depending on the preposition chosen. However, the clear majority of $Verb_1$s of the pattern can express negative volition only. Another major difference between the two classes is that $Verb_1$s of the pattern of [1e] tend to be nonimplicative, while those of the pattern of [1f] are generally implicative or negative implicative. *Coax,* as in the sentences above, illustrates this difference.

In view of the differences relating to the direction of volition and to the implicativeness, or the lack of it, of $Verb_1$, our discussion suggests that the patterns of [1e] and [1f] have their own, fairly well defined functions in English grammar.

As for the pattern of [1g], all $Verb_1$s belonging to it were found to express positive volition on the part of NP_1 for the realization of S_2. $Verb_1$s of the pattern are overwhelmingly nonimplicative. We may speculate that these factors may contribute to a feeling that the pattern of [1g] is a rival of the pattern of [1e]. Our study does not have a primarily historical orientation, but even in our description we could not help noticing the large number of $Verb_1$s that have belonged to the pattern of [1g], but have become obsolete. A number of common $Verb_1$s belong to the pattern of [1g] in present-day English, including *appeal to,* and verbs with the preposition *on,* such as *count on, depend on, rely on* and *prevail on.* On the other hand, the pattern of $Verb_1$ *of* NP_0 *to* $Verb_2$ seems to be in decline, possibly in view of its semantic proximity to the pattern of [1e]. Our study invites a follow-up inquiry comparing the incidence of $Verb_1$s of the two patterns at earlier points in the history of English. Such an inquiry would be corpus-based, and it would provide an indication of whether our feeling that some parts of the pattern of [1g] are in decline is justified.

Case grammar was used as a tool of analysis of the patterns isolated. A great deal of attention has been devoted to the study of complementation, especially since Rosenbaum's (1967) pioneering study. Similarly, a great deal of attention has been devoted to the study of case grammar since Gruber's early work and since Fillmore (1968). However, these two areas of research have not been systematically combined so far. That is, English complementation has not been systematically investigated with the tool of case grammar. In this book, a first attempt is made to do so. Under such circumstances, it is perhaps inevitable that the discussion presented and the conclusions arrived at are tentative and subject to further investigation. Also, it should be borne in mind that the version of case grammar that was adopted may not turn out to be the most appropriate possible.

Even with such caveats taken for granted, at least some of the conclusions that emerged from the application of case grammar to the analysis of the patterns are of interest, with the exception of the *that* pattern, in the analysis of which the applicability and usefulness of case grammar is more limited. The *that* pattern aside, the *to* infinitive patterns of [2a], [2e] and [2g] of Chapter 1, the *ing* patterns of [2b] and [2f] of Chapter 1 and the *for to* infinitive pattern of [2c] of Chapter 1 lend themselves to analysis in terms of case grammar. To put it another way, case grammar facilitates the isolating of distributional data that are not the result of random variation, and, further, makes it possible to formulate systematic generalizations to cover such distributional regularities.

In all of the Equi patterns, it was found that when NP_1, the subject of the embedding verb, is an Experiencer only, NP_2, the subject of the embedded verb, can be any one of the four cases of Agent, Experiencer, Benefactive or Object. On the other hand, if the embedding verb is a verb of desideration and intention or one of desideration, intention and endeavor and, consequently, NP_1 is an Agent, the four infinitive patterns and the *ing* pattern display remarkably similar restrictions and require for NP_2 to be agentive, to the exclusion of the other three case roles. The restriction was termed the Agent Rule. The Agent Rule was argued to be central in the case grammar description of the patterns of complementation discussed.

Two factors mitigating the Agent Rule were noted: coreferential roles and external control readings. Coreferential roles may relate to NP_1s or to NP_2s. Coreferential roles relating to NP_2s may or may not involve agentive reinterpretations. Agentive reinterpretations were argued to be possible when a $Verb_2$ was a verb that is partly under the control of its subject. External control readings were argued to arise when a $Verb_2$ was not under the control of its subject but was under the control of someone else. The "someone else" may be designated by an NP of the higher clause that is noncoreferential with NP_2. It is also possible for the matrix verb to imply a reference to an understood entity in the matrix clause.

The Agent Rule, the factors mitigating it and the question of degree are subject to further investigation. The need for further work is underlined by the fact that case roles express semantic relations and by the difficulty of delimiting semantics against pragmatics in the discussion of case grammar. Violations of the Agent Rule and the nonapplicability of the mitigating factors produce deviance that is semantic, or even pragmatic, in nature. While further work remains to be carried out, the broader relevance of case grammar in the present book is to function as a largely new avenue for investigating complementation in English.

REFERENCES

Abraham, W. (ed.) (1978) *Valence, Semantic Case and Grammatical Relations*. Amsterdam: John Benjamins.

Aijmer, K. (1972) *Some Aspects of Psychological Predicates in English*. Stockholm: P. A. Norstedt & Söner.

Akmajian, A. (1977) "The Complement Structure of Perception Verbs in an Autonomous Syntax Framework," in P. Culicover et al. (1977).

Akmajian, A. and F. Heny (1975) *An Introduction to the Principles of Transformational Syntax*. Cambridge, MA: MIT Press.

ALD = *Oxford Advanced Learner's Dictionary of Current English*, Third ed. (1979). A. S. Hornby, ed., with the assistance of A. P. Cowie and J. W. Lewis. Oxford: Oxford University Press.

Alexander, D. and W. Kunz (1964) *Some Classes of Verbs in English*. Linguistics Research Project, Indiana University. Bloomington: Indiana University Linguistics Club.

Anderson, J. (1976) (First published in 1971.) *The Grammar of Case*. Reprinted. Cambridge: Cambridge University Press.

Anderson, J. (1977) *On Case Grammar*. London: Croom Helm.

Anderson, S. and P. Kiparsky (eds.) (1973) *A Festschrift for Morris Halle*. New York: Holt, Rinehart and Winston.

Austin, J. (1962) *How to Do Things with Words*. Cambridge, MA: Harvard University Press.

Bach, E. (1979) "Control in Montague Grammar," *Linguistic Inquiry* 10: 515–531.

Bach, E. (1980) "In Defense of Passive," *Linguistics and Philosophy* 3: 297–341.

Bach, E. and R. Harms (eds.) (1968) *Universals in Linguistic Theory*. New York: Holt, Rinehart and Winston.

Baker, C. (1968) *Indirect Questions in English*. University of Illinois Doctoral Dissertation, Urbana, Illinois.

Bendix, E. (1966) *Componential Analysis of General Vocabulary: The Semantic Structure of a Set of Verbs in English, Hindi and Japanese*. Part 2 of *International Journal of American Linguistics*, vol. 32, no. 2. Bloomington: Indiana University and The Hague: Mouton.

Berman, A. (1970) "Agent, Experiencer and Controllability," in *Mathematical Linguistics and Automatic Translation*, Report NSF-24: 203–236. Cambridge, MA: Harvard University.

Berman, A. (1974) *Adjectives and Adjective Complement Constructions in English*. Report No. NSF-29. Cambridge, MA: Harvard University.

Bierwisch, M. and K. Heidolph (eds.) (1970) *Progress in Linguistics*. The Hague: Mouton.

Bolinger, D. (1978) "A Semantic View of Syntax: Some Verbs that Govern Infinitives," in M. Jazayery et al. (1978).

Bouchard, D. (1983) *On the Content of Empty Categories*. Dordrecht: Foris.

Bouchard, D. (1985) "PRO, Pronominal or Anaphor," *Linguistic Inquiry* 16: 471–477.

Brame, M. (1980) "hope," *Linguistic Analysis* 6: 247–260.

Bresnan, J. (1970) "On Complementizers: Toward a Syntactic Theory of Complement Types," *Foundations of Language* 6: 297–321.

Bresnan, J. (1972) *Theory of Complementation in English Syntax*. MIT Doctoral Dissertation, Cambridge, MA.

Bresnan, J. (1976) "Nonarguments for Raising," *Linguistic Inquiry* 7: 485–501.

Bresnan, J. (1982) "Control and Complementation," *Linguistic Inquiry* 13: 343–434.

Chafe, W. (1975) (First published in 1970.) *Meaning and the Structure of Language*. Chicago: University of Chicago Press.

Chomsky, N. (1965) *Aspects of the Theory of Syntax*. Cambridge, MA: MIT Press.

Chomsky, N. (1973) "Conditions on Transformations," in S. Anderson and P. Kiparsky (1973).

Chomsky, N. (1980) "On Binding," *Linguistic Inquiry* 11: 1–46.

Chomsky, N. (1981) *Lectures on Government and Binding*. Dordrecht: Foris.

Chomsky, N. and H. Lasnik (1977) "Filters and Control," *Linguistic Inquiry* 8: 425–504.

Cole, P. and J. Sadock (eds.) (1977) *Syntax and Semantics*, vol. 8, *Grammatical Relations*. New York: Academic Press.

Comrie, B. (1984) "Subject and Object Control: Syntax, Semantics, Pragmatics," in *Proceedings of the Tenth Annual Meeting of the Berkeley Linguistics Society*: 450–464. Berkeley: Berkeley Linguistics Society.

Cook, W. (1979) *Case Grammar: Development of the Matrix Model (1970–78)*. Washington, DC: Georgetown University Press.

Cruse, D. (1973) "Some thoughts on agentivity," *Journal of Linguistics* 9: 11–23.

Culicover, P., T. Wasow, and A. Akmajian (eds.) (1977) *Formal Syntax*. New York: Academic Press.

Curme, G. (1931) *Syntax*. Boston: D. C. Heath and Company.

Davidson, D. (1985) (First published in 1980.) *Essays on Actions and Events*. Reprinted with corrections. Oxford: Clarendon.

Davidson, D. and G. Harman (eds.) (1972) *Semantics of Natural Language*. Dordrecht: D. Reidel.

Ek, J. van (1966) *Four Complementary Structures of Predication in Contemporary British English*. Groningen: Wolters.

Ellegård, A. (1971) *Transformationell svensk-engelsk satslära*. CWK Gleerup.

Ellinger, J. (1910) "Gerundium, Infinitiv und *That*-Satz als adverbiale oder adnominale Erganzung," *Anglia* 33: 480–522.

Fillmore, C. (1968) "The Case for Case," in E. Bach and R. Harms (1968).

Fillmore, C. (1969) "Review of Bendix (1966)," *General Linguistics* 9: 41–65.

Fillmore, C. (1977) "The Case for Case Reopened," in P. Cole and J. Sadock (1977).

Fischer, S. and B. Marshall (1969) *The Examination and Abandonment of the Theory of Begin of D. M. Perlmutter*. Bloomington: Indiana University Linguistics Club.

Fodor, J. (1974) "Like Subject Verbs and Causal Clauses in English," *Journal of Linguistics* 10: 95–110.

Foley, W. and R. van Valin, Jr (1984) *Functional syntax and universal grammar*. Cambridge: Cambridge University Press.

Fraser, B. (1970) "Some Remarks on the Action Nominalization in English," in R. Jacobs and P. Rosenbaum (1970).

Fraser, B. (1974) "An Analysis of Vernacular Performative Verbs," in R. Shuy and C. Bailey (1974).

Gazdar, G. (1979) *Pragmatics: Implicature, Presupposition, and Logical Form*. New York: Academic Press.

Gee, J. (1977) "Comments on the Paper by Akmajian," in P. Culicover et al. (1977).

Grimshaw, J. (1977) "Complement Selection and the Lexicon," *Linguistic Inquiry* 10: 279–326.

Grossman, R., J. San, and T. Vance (eds.) (1975) *Papers from the Parasession on Functionalism*. Chicago: Chicago Linguistic Society.

Gruber, J. (1967) "Look and See," *Language* 43: 937–947.

Gruber, J. (1976) *Lexical Structures in Syntax and Semantics*. Amsterdam: North-Holland Publishing Company.

Hietaranta, P. (1983) "Which 'for' Is It?," *Neuphilologische Mitteilungen* 84: 228–232.

Higgins, F. (1973) "On J. Emonds's Analysis of Extraposition," in J. Kimball (1973).

Hintikka, J., J. Moravcsik, and P. Suppes (eds.) (1973) *Approaches to Natural Language. Proceedings of the 1970 Stanford Workshop on Grammar and Semantics*. Dordrecht: D. Reidel.

Horiguchi, I. (1978) *Complementation in English Syntax: A Generative Semantics Approach*. Georgetown University Doctoral Dissertation, Washington, DC.

Horn, L. (1985) "Metalinguistic negation and pragmatic ambiguity," *Language* 61: 121–174.

Horn, W. (1905) "I intended to have written," *Archiv* CXIV: 366–370.

Hornby, A. S. (1966) *A Guide to Patterns and Usage in English*. London: Oxford University Press.

Hornstein, N. and D. Lightfoot (1987) "Predication and PRO," *Language* 63: 23–52.

Huddleston, R. (1971) *The Sentence in Written English*. Cambridge: Cambridge University Press.

Jackendoff, R. (1972) *Semantic Interpretation in Generative Grammar*. Cambridge, MA: MIT Press.

Jackendoff, R. (1985) (First published in 1983.) *Semantics and Cognition*. Cambridge, MA: MIT Press.

Jacobs, R. and P. Rosenbaum (eds.) (1970) *Readings in English Transformational Grammar*. Waltham, MA: Ginn and Company.

Jacobsen, B. (1986) *Modern Transformational Grammar: with particular reference to the theory of government and binding*. Amsterdam: North-Holland.

Jakobson, R. and S. Kawamoto (eds.) (1970) *Studies in General and Oriental Linguistics Presented to Shero Hattori on the Occasion of His Sixtieth Birthday*. Tokyo: TEC.

Jazayery, M., E. Polome, and W. Winter (eds.) (1978) *Linguistic and Literary Studies in Honor of Archibald A. Hill* II: Descriptive Linguistics. The Hague: Mouton.

Jespersen, O. (1961) (First published in 1940.) *A Modern English Grammar on Historical Principles*. Part V. *Syntax*. Reprinted. London: Allen and Unwin.

Kajita, M. (1967) *A Generative-Transformational Study of Semi-Auxiliaries in Present-Day American English*. Tokyo.

Karttunen, L. (1970) "On the Semantics of Complement Sentences," in *Papers from the Sixth Regional Meeting of the Chicago Linguistic Society: 328–339*. Chicago: Chicago Linguistic Society.

Karttunen, L. (1971) "Implicative Verbs," *Language* 47: 340–358.

Karttunen, L. and S. Peters (1979) "Conventional Implicature," in C. Oh and D. Dinneen (1979).

Kempson, R. (1977) *Semantic Theory*. Cambridge: Cambridge University Press.

Kimball, J. (ed.) (1973) *Syntax and Semantics*, volume 2. New York and London: Seminar Press.

Kiparsky, P. and C. Kiparsky (1970) "Fact," in M. Bierwisch and K. Heidolph (1970).

Koster, J. (1984) "On Binding and Control," *Linguistic Inquiry* 15: 417–459.

Koziol, H. (1972) *Handbuch der englischen Wortbildungslehre*. Zweite, neu bearbeite Auflage. Heidelberg: Carl Winter.

Krüger, G. (1914) *Schwierigkeiten des Englischen. System der englischen Sprache*. II Teil, 4. Abteilung: *Zeitwort*. Zweite, neu bearbeite Auflage. Dresden und Leipzig: Kock's Verlagsbuchhandlung.

Kruisinga, E. (1925) (First published in 1911.) *A Handbook of Present-Day English*. Vol. II: *English Accidence and Syntax*. Utrecht: Kemink & Zoon.

Kuno, S. (1970) "Some Properties of Non-Referential Noun Phrases," in R. Jakobson and S. Kawamoto (1970).

Lakoff, G. (1966) "Stative Adjectives and Verbs in English," in Report No. NSF-17 to the National Science Foundation: 1.1.–1.16. Cambridge, MA: Harvard University.

Langacker, R. (1975) "Functional Stratigraphy," in R. Grossman et al. (1975).

Leech, G. (1968) "Some Assumptions in the Metatheory of Linguistics," *Linguistics* 39: 87–102.

Leech, G. (1983) *Principles of Pragmatics*. London: Longman.

Lees, R. (1963) *The Grammar of English Nominalizations*. Reissued. The Hague: Mouton.

Levinson, S. (1983) *Pragmatics*. Cambridge: Cambridge University Press.

Liberman, M. and I. Sag (1974) "Prosodic Form and Discourse Function," in *Papers from the Tenth Regional Meeting of the Chicago Linguistic Society: 416–427*. Chicago: Chicago Linguistic Society.

Lipka, L. (1972) *Semantic Structure and Word-Formation*. München: Wilhelm Fink.

Lyons, J. (1977) *Semantics*. Volume 1. Cambridge: Cambridge University Press.

Makkink, H. (1978) (First published in 1934.) *An English Grammar*. Fifteenth ed., revised by D. L. Hijmans, 's-Gravenhage: B. V. Uitgeverig & van Ditmar.

Manzini, M. (1983) "On Control and Control Theory," *Linguistic Inquiry* 14: 421–446.

Marchand, H. (1969) *The Categories and Types of Present-Day English Word-Formation*. Second revised and enlarged edition. Munich: C. H. Beck'sche Verlagsbuchhandlung.

Mätzner, E. (1885) *Englische Grammatik*. Dritter Theil. *Die Lehre von der Wort- und Satzfügung*. Zweite Hälfte, dritte Auflage. Berlin: Weidmannsche Buchhandlung.

Menzel, P. (1975) *Semantics and Syntax in Complementation*. The Hague: Mouton.

Meyer-Myklestad, J. (1968) *An Advanced English Grammar for Students and Teachers*. Second edition. Oslo: Universitetsforlaget.

Miller, G. and P. Johnson-Laird (1976) *Language and Perception*. Cambridge: Cambridge University Press.

Milsark, G. (1974) *Existential Sentences in English*. MIT Doctoral Dissertation, Cambridge, MA.

Milsark, G. (1977) "Toward an Explanation of Certain Peculiarities of the Existential Construction in English," *Linguistic Analysis* 3: 1–30.

Mustanoja, T. (1960) *A Middle English Syntax*. Part 1. Helsinki: Société Néophilologique.

Nanni, D. (1978) *The Easy Class of Adjectives in English*. University of Massachusetts Doctoral Dissertation, Amherst, MA.

Newmeyer, F. (1969) "The Underlying Structure of the Begin-Class Verbs," in *Papers from the Fifth Regional Meeting of the Chicago Linguistic Society:* 195–204. Chicago: Chicago Linguistic Society.

Newmeyer, F. (1970) "The Derivation of the English Action Nominalization," in *Papers from the Sixth Regional Meeting of the Chicago Linguistic Society:* 408–415. Chicago: Chicago Linguistic Society.

OED = *The Compact Edition of the Oxford English Dictionary*. (1971). Reprinted 1980. Oxford University Press: Oxford.

Oh, C. and D. Dinneen (1979) *Syntax and Semantics*, vol. II, *Presupposition*. New York: Academic Press.

Palmer, F. (1974) *The English Verb*. Second ed. (First edition published in 1965 as *A Linguistic Study of the English Verb*.) London: Longman.

Partee, B. (1973) "The Semantics of Belief-Sentences," in J. Hintikka, J. Moravcsik and P. Suppes (1973).

Perlmutter, D. (1970) "The Two Verbs *Begin*," in R. A. Jacobs and P. S. Rosenbaum (1970).

Postal, P. (1970) "On Coreferential Complement Subject Deletion," *Linguistic Inquiry* 1: 439–500.

Postal, P. (1971) *Cross-over Phenomena*. New York: Holt, Rinehart and Winston.

Postal, P. (1974) *On Raising: One Rule of English Grammar and Its Theoretical Implications*. Cambridge, MA: MIT Press.

Postal, P. (1977) "About a 'Nonargument' for Raising," *Linguistic Inquiry* 8: 141–154.

Poutsma, H. (1904) *A Grammar of Late Modern English*. Part I: *The Sentence*. Groningen: P. Noordhoff.

Quirk, R. et al. (1974) (First published in 1972.) *A Grammar of Contemporary English*. Fourth impression. London: Longman.

Quirk, R. et al. (1985) *A Comprehensive Grammar of the English Language.* London: Longman.

Radford, A. (1981) *Transformational Syntax. A Student's Guide to Chomsky's Extended Standard Theory.* Cambridge: Cambridge University Press.

The Random House Dictionary of the English Language. Unabridged Ed. (1981) (First published in 1966.) New York: Random House.

Riddle, E. (1975) "Some Pragmatic Conditions on Complementizer Choice," in *Papers from the Eleventh Regional Meeting of the Chicago Linguistic Society:* 467–474. Chicago: Chicago Linguistic Society.

Riemsdijk, H. van and E. Williams (1986) *Introduction to the Theory of Grammar.* Cambridge, MA: MIT Press.

Rizzi, L. (1986) "Null Objects in Italian and the Theory of *pro,*" *Linguistic Inquiry* 17: 501–558.

Rosenbaum, P. (1967) *The Grammar of English Predicate Complement Constructions.* Cambridge, MA: MIT Press.

Ross, J. (1967) *Constraints on Variables in Syntax.* MIT Doctoral Dissertation. Bloomington: Indiana University Linguistics Club.

Ross, J. (1972) "Act," in D. Davidson and G. Harman (eds.) 1972: 70–126.

Rudanko, J. (to appear) "On the Grammar of *For* Clauses," to appear in *English Studies* in 1988.

Růžička, R. (1983) "Remarks on Control," *Linguistic Inquiry* 14: 309–324.

Scheurweghs, G. (1959) *Present-Day English Syntax. A Survey of Sentence Patterns.* London: Longman.

Schibsbye, K. (1970) *A Modern English Grammar.* Second ed. London: Oxford University Press.

Searle, J. (1979) *Expression and Meaning.* Cambridge: Cambridge University Press.

Searle, J. (1983) *Intentionality.* Cambridge: Cambridge University Press.

Seppänen, A. (1981) "Two Points of English Verb Syntax," *Neuphilologische Mitteilungen* 82: 386–399.

Seppänen, A. (1984) "On an Analysis of the 'for-NP-to-V' Structure," *Neuphilologische Mitteilungen* 85: 242–253.

Shuy, R. and C. Bailey (eds.) (1974) *Towards Tomorrow's Linguistics.* Washington: Georgetown University Press.

Soames, S. and D. Perlmutter (1979) *Syntactic Argumentation and the Structure of English.* Berkeley: University of California Press.

Söderlind, J. (1958) *Verb Syntax in John Dryden's Prose.* Part II. Uppsala: A.-B. Lundequistska Bokhandeln.

Starosta, S. (1978) "The One Per Sent Solution," in W. Abraham (1978).

Vendler, Z. (1968) *Adjectives and Nominalizations.* The Hague: Mouton.

Visser, F. (1972) *An Historical Syntax of the English Language.* Part Two. *Syntactical Units with One Verb* (Continued). Reprinted (with corrections). Leiden: E. J. Brill.

Visser, F. (1973) *An Historical Syntax of the English Language.* Part Three. Second Half. *Syntactical Units with Two and with More Verbs.* Leiden: E. J. Brill.

Visser, F. (1978) (First published in 1969.) *An Historical Syntax of the English Language.* Part Three. First Half. *Syntactical Units with Two Verbs.* Reprinted. Leiden: E. J. Brill.

Wasow, T. (1977) "Transformations and the Lexicon," in P. Culicover et al. (1977).

Wasow, T. (1979) *Anaphora in Generative Grammar*. Ghent: E. Story-Scientia P.V.B.A.

Wasow, T. and T. Roeper (1972) "On the Subject of Gerunds," *Foundations of Language* 8: 44–61.

Webster's Third New International Dictionary of the English Language. Unabridged. (1976) Springfield: Merriam.

Williams, E. (1980) "Predication," *Linguistic Inquiry* 11: 203–238.

Wolfram, W. and R. Fasold (1974) *The Study of Social Dialects in American English*. Englewood Cliffs: Prentice-Hall.

Zandvoort, R. (1966) (First published in 1957.) *A Handbook of English Grammar*. Bristol: Longmans.

INDEX

INDEX OF VERBS